Global Ethics

Series Editor: **Christien van den Anker**, Reader, Department of Politics, University of the West of England, UK

Global Ethics as a field builds on longer traditions of ethical reflection about (global) society and discusses ethical approaches to global issues. These include but are not limited to issues highlighted by the process of globalization (in the widest sense) and increasing multiculturalism. They also engage with migration, the environment, poverty and inequality, peace and conflict, human rights, global citizenship, social movements, and global governance. Despite fluid boundaries between fields, global ethics can be clearly marked out by its multidisciplinary approach, its interest in a strong link between theory, policy, and practice and its inclusion of a range of work from strictly normative to more empirical.

Books in the series provide a specific normative approach, taxonomy, or ethical position on a specific issue in global ethics through empirical work. They explicitly engage with global ethics as a field and position themselves with regard to existing debates even when outlining more local approaches or issues. The *Global Ethics Series* has been designed to reach beyond a liberal cosmopolitan agenda and engage with contextualism as well as structural analyses of injustice in current global politics and its disciplining discourses.

Titles include:

Carlos R. Cordourier-Real
TRANSNATIONAL SOCIAL JUSTICE

Anna Grear
REDIRECTING HUMAN RIGHTS
Facing the Challenge of Corporate Legal Humanity

Shahram Khosravi
'ILLEGAL' TRAVELLER
An Auto-Ethnography of Borders

Ivan Manokha (*editor*)
THE POLITICAL ECONOMY OF HUMAN RIGHTS ENFORCEMENT

Mandisa Mbali
SOUTH AFRICAN AIDS ACTIVISM AND GLOBAL HEALTH POLITICS

Darrel Moellendorf
GLOBAL INEQUALITY MATTERS

Michal Nahman
EXTRACTIONS
Securing Borders, Trafficking Human Ova

Derrick M. Nault and Shawn L. England (*editors*)
GLOBALIZATION AND HUMAN RIGHTS IN THE DEVELOPING WORLD

Katherine Tonkiss
MIGRATION AND IDENTITY IN A POST-NATIONAL WORLD

AKM Ahsan Ullah
REFUGEE POLITICS IN THE MIDDLE EAST AND NORTH AFRICA
Human Rights, Safety, and Identity

Christien van den Anker and Ilse van Liempt (*editors*)
HUMAN RIGHTS AND MIGRATION
Trafficking for Forced Labour

Global Ethics Series
Series Standing Order ISBN 978–0–230–01958–4

You can receive future titles in this series as they are published by placing a standing order. Please contact your bookseller or, in case of difficulty, write to us at the address below with your name and address, the title of the series and the ISBN quoted above.

Customer Services Department, Macmillan Distribution Ltd, Houndmills, Basingstoke, Hampshire RG21 6XS, England

---

Global Rectificatory Justice

Göran Collste
Professor of Applied Ethics, Linköping University, Sweden

palgrave
macmillan

First published 2015 by
PALGRAVE MACMILLAN

Palgrave Macmillan in the UK is an imprint of Macmillan Publishers Limited, registered in England, company number 785998, of Houndmills, Basingstoke, Hampshire RG21 6XS.

Palgrave Macmillan in the US is a division of St Martin's Press LLC, 175 Fifth Avenue, New York, NY10010.

Palgrave Macmillan is the global academic imprint of the above companies and has companies and representatives throughout the world.

ISBN: 978–1–137–46611–2

This book is printed on paper suitable for recycling and made from fully managed and sustained forest sources. Logging, pulping and manufacturing processes are expected to conform to the environmental regulations of the country of origin.

A catalogue record for this book is available from the British Library.

A catalog record for this book is available from the Library of Congress.

To Kicki, my love and life companion

Contents

Preface and Acknowledgments

In my inquiries for this book I have used different sources. The book is primarily the result of ethical analyses of views and arguments, and is derived from so-called desk-top research, that is, the gathering of historical facts and background information found in literature on ethics, history, economics, and international relations. As part of the research, however, I also traveled. I visited South Africa, a nation that in some respects can be seen as a microcosm of the colonial legacy. During apartheid a small white elite, who owned most of the wealth, governed a majority of poor black people, who mostly lived in townships. I interviewed people involved in the Truth and Reconciliation Commission in order to find out how this system worked in practice. I visited the former Portuguese colony of Mozambique and had the privilege of interviewing men who had fought in the liberation movement 40 years before. I also travelled to Uganda, Malaysia, and China, where I constantly raised questions on the legacy of colonialism.

Museums are an important source of information. A visitor can learn from the stories of the past, and the artifacts on display fire the imagination. But museums are also informative for what they do not exhibit, suggesting a hidden history that has not been narrated. What did they reveal? The Tropen Museum in Amsterdam is a great source of knowledge about the Netherlands' colonial history. Its permanent exhibition tells the story of how the Dutch East India Company conquered East Asia. In order to remain in power, the Dutch had to face a number of upheavals. The Java war of 1825–1830 started when the Dutch colonists destroyed a holy tomb. Prince Diponegoro led the uprising. Peace negotiations took place and he was promised safe passage. The promise was broken and a drawing shows to the moment of his surrender. The museum also exhibits skulls of natives, illustrating anthropological inquiries of racial differences.

The Royal Museum of Central Africa in Tervuren outside Brussels was founded in 1898 by King Leopold II, who ruled Congo as his private domain. The museum's mission was – and seems still to be – "To promote Belgium's work of 'development and civilization' in Congo, and the latter's economic potential. Leopold II hoped to build some form of museum or 'showcase'". Livingstone and Stanley (the latter paving the way for Leopold's II atrocities in Congo) "have a place of honour among the great explorers," according to the *Guide Michelin*. The impression that remains after visiting this museum is that while the exhibits include great examples of traditional African art and handicrafts, the dark side of Belgian colonial history – including the murders, the forced labor, and the mutilations – is not revealed.

What stories do the museums in the global South tell? In Maputo in Mozambique there is nothing. The Museum of Colonial History is closed and has fallen into disrepair. However, I had the opportunity to visit the Slave Lodge in Cape Town in South Africa. In this building, now a museum, men, women, and children who were taken to Cape Town as slaves by the Dutch East India Company during the 17th and 18th centuries were confined. The museum depicts the horrors of slavery.

A Museum in Penang in northern Malaysia tells a story about ethnic and religious pluralism, but also about British colonizers who established law and order by keeping the fighting Chinese clans apart.

Finally, the National Museum of China in Beijing, near Tiananmen Square, provides a narrative of the struggle for an independent China. The visitor is informed about how Western powers occupied settlements and forced trading treaties upon China. More informative and less propagandistic, though, are the extensive ruins of the Old Summer Palace in the Imperial Gardens, where a sign proclaims: "They continue to stand here, reminding people of the national humiliation."

Victor Hugo commented in 1861 on the demolition of the Old Summer Palace:

> Two robbers breaking into a museum, devastating, looting and burning, leaving laughing, hand-in-hand, with their bags full of treasures; one of the robbers is called France and the other Britain ... We Europeans are the civilized ones, and for us the Chinese are the barbarians. This is what civilization has done to barbarism. (Hugo, 1985)

Global justice is a growing field in applied and political ethics and I have myself been doing research and teaching in it since the 1990s. Work on this book started in 2006 and I have had plenty of opportunities to discuss it with colleagues. I have the privilege of belonging to the teaching staff of the Centre for Applied Ethics at Linköping University. The Centre is a creative environment and offers plenty of opportunities to chat with colleagues, to teach and learn from students, and to get input from participants at seminars.

The first presentation of my ideas on global rectificatory justice took place at the Societas Ethica conference on Political Ethics and the

International Order in Oxford in 2006. Since then I have presented earlier versions of chapters at various conferences: Societas Ethica in Sibiu in 2012, the Swedish National Research School in Ethics in Uppsala in 2012, the XXIII World Conference of Philosophy in Athens in 2013, the Swedish National History Conference in Stockholm in 2014, and Societas Ethica in Maribor in 2014.

Academic departments in philosophy, ethics, and political science have opened their doors to me. I have discussed the project and presented chapters at seminars held in Stellenbosch University, South Africa; University of Science, Malaysia; Makerere University, Uganda; the Swedish National Defense College; Uppsala University; and the Centre for Applied Ethics, Linköping University. I am truly grateful for the comments I received from generous colleagues during these discussions.

Great feedback has also come from my master's students. The question of global rectificatory justice has for many years been included in my course Globalization and Global Justice and my international students have given me valuable input, in particular the Master's Class in autumn 2013, which commented on a number of book chapters.

I would like to thank Markus Agnafors, Martin Andersson, Rui Baltazar, Maren Behrensen, Solomon Benatar, Theresa Callewaert, Joao Paulo Borges Coelho, Kees Dekker, Fanie de Toit, Peter Gan, Carl Henric Grenholm, Ronnie Hjorth, Rui Honvana, Jonathan Josefsson, Henric Lerner, Dixon Kanakulya, Finlay Mackie, Elena Namli, Jasmina Nedevska, Anders Nordgren, Gaudence Nyirabikali, Elin Palm, Bo Petersson, David Sigurthorsson, Per Sundman, Anton Van Niekerk, Wilfred Wamala, and Yusuf Yuksekdag for valuable comments.

In particular, I am grateful to two of my colleagues who read most of the preliminary manuscript. At a crucial stage of the writing, Martin Andersson inspired me with many insights and challenging observations. Maren Behrensen, while improving the quality of my English, also gave me many thoughtful remarks on the manuscript, which I have incorporated in the final version. Thank you, Martin and Maren!

I am grateful to the Swedish Research Council, which provided a generous research grant, and to the Faculty of Arts and Sciences at Linköping University.

The editorial team has done a great job and a special thanks to Joseph Laredo for more than copy editing.

Earlier versions of some of the chapters have appeared in the following journals:

"...restoring the dignity of the victims." Is global rectificatory justice feasible? *Ethics and Global Politics* 2/2010;

Specifying rights. The case of TRIPS, *Public Health Ethics* 4:1/2011;

Betydelsen av historisk rättvisa efter kolonialismen, *Etikk i Praksis* 1/2012;

Is a generous immigration policy a way to rectify for colonial injustices, *Review of Ecumenical Studies*, 5:1/2013;

Colonialism, epistemic injustice and global justice, *Global Policy*, 5:3/2014.

1 Introduction

The discussion on global justice is vibrant and expanding. The discussion has mainly focused on one aspect of justice, namely distributive justice. But as Aristotle showed, there are also other "...species of the just...," among them rectificatory justice (Aristotle, 1980: 114). In this book I argue for global rectificatory justice. The present global order (the global economy as well as global governance) mirrors colonialism in many respects. Hence we live in a post-colonial era and our understanding of global justice should reflect the legacy of colonialism. As a point of departure I will show how this history still stamps our world.

1. With the publication of John Rawls's *A Theory of Justice* in 1971, justice was rekindled as a subject in political philosophy and ethics. The theory was intended to apply to justice within nations, but as early as 1979 Charles Beitz argued for a global application of Rawls's theory of distributive justice, and Thomas Pogge developed the argument in his book *Realizing Rawls* (Beitz, 1979; Pogge, 1989). When Rawls published his own contribution to the discussion about international justice in *The Law of Peoples*, the debate on global justice intensified (Rawls, 1999). Rawls limited his discussion to international *political* justice – excluding the so-called difference principle, thus barring considerations of redistribution of resources in favor of the least advantaged on a global level. This move has been questioned by many (Buchanan, 2000; Tan, 2004; Caney, 2005a; Brock, 2009). Given the global inequalities and widespread poverty which persist today, Rawls's limitation is indeed questionable. However, what is striking about the present discussion on global justice is that it is mostly concerned with political justice and global *distributive* justice (Moellendorf, 2009; Armstrong, 2012; Risse, 2012), but justice is a wider concept than that.

The present borders between rich and poor nations coincide roughly with the historical borders between former colonial powers and their colonies. Is this merely a coincidence or is there a connection between the history of colonialism and the present global inequalities? During colonial times the economies of the European colonies in Asia, Africa, and Latin America were adjusted to suit the interests of the colonial powers. As a consequence of the Spanish and Portuguese exploitation of Latin America, the British, Belgian, Portuguese, German, and French exploitation of Africa, and the British, French, Portuguese, and Dutch exploitation of Asia, Europe prospered while many colonies sank into despondency. What happened during this period in history is well captured in the title of Uruguayan author Eduardo Galeano's (1971) book *Las venas abiertas de América Latina* (Open veins of Latin America); a "blood transfusion" took place from the South to the North.

2. The legacy of colonialism was addressed in the United Nations conference on racism in Durban in 2001 and the follow-up Durban review conference in Geneva in 2009. Under "General Issues," the final declaration from the Durban conference states:

> We recognize that colonialism has led to racism, racial discrimination, xenophobia and related intolerance, and that Africans and people of African descent, and people of Asian descent and indigenous peoples were victims of colonialism and continue to be victims of its consequences. We acknowledge the suffering caused by colonialism and affirm that, wherever and whenever it occurred, it must be condemned and its reoccurrence prevented. We further regret that the effects and persistence of these structures and practices have been among the factors contributing to lasting social and economic inequalities in many parts of the world today...
>
> We recognize the negative economic, social and cultural consequences of racism, racial discrimination, xenophobia and related intolerance, which have contributed significantly to the underdevelopment of developing countries and, in particular, of Africa and resolve to free every man, woman and child from the abject and dehumanizing conditions of extreme poverty to which more than one billion of them are currently subjected, to make the right to development a reality for everyone and to free the entire human race from want...
>
> We acknowledge and profoundly regret the untold suffering and evils inflicted on millions of men, women and children as a result of slavery, the slave trade, the transatlantic slave trade, apartheid,

> genocide and past tragedies. We further note that some States have taken the initiative to apologize and have paid reparation, where appropriate, for grave and massive violations committed. (United Nations, 2001)

The final document from the follow-up conference on racism in April 2009 contains a call for reparations for sufferings inflicted during colonial rule. It reads: The Conference

> *Recalls* that slavery and the slave trade, including the transatlantic slave trade, apartheid, colonialism and genocide must never be forgotten and in this regard welcomes actions undertaken to honour the memory of victims...
>
> *Notes* actions of those countries that have, in the context of these past tragedies, expressed remorse, offered apologies, initiated institutionalized mechanisms such as truth and reconciliation commissions and/or restituted cultural artifacts since the adoption of the Durban Declaration and Programme of Action, and calls on those who have not yet contributed to restoring the dignity of the victims to find appropriate ways for do so. (United Nations, 2009)

Both declarations emphasized the enduring consequences of colonialism, and in particular of slavery and the slave trade, while the need for remembrance and restoration was highlighted, and claims for rectification including compensation for the victims were hotly debated at both conferences.

3. In September 2011 a delegation from the Herero and Nama peoples in Namibia, led by Chief Kuiama Riruako, arrived in Berlin. The purpose of the visit was to bring home 20 skulls that had been brought to Germany after the genocide against the Herero and Nama tribes in 1904. "For us it means the return of our relatives, grandmothers and great-grandfather," Ida Hoffman, a member of the committee, said to journalists (*The Telegraph*, 2011).

The visit of the delegation to Berlin put a spotlight on the massacres committed by German soldiers under the command of General Lothar von Trotha. Von Trotha who was appointed by Emperor Wilhelm II ordered the extermination of the Herero nation in retaliation for threats to Germans in South West Africa. Before the massacres, the Herero population was estimated at 80,000; in three years it went down to 16,000.

The visit of the Herero delegation to Berlin was not the first time that descendants of the Herero had paid attention to the genocide. When the German Chancellor Helmut Kohl visited Namibia in 1995, Herero soldiers had presented him with a petition demanding payment for war crimes against the Herero people (Gewald, 1999: 1). Then, in 2004, on the centenary of the genocide, the German minister for Economic Development and Cooperation Heidemarie Wieczorek-Zeul apologized on behalf of the German government, but she ruled out any economic compensation to Namibia or to the descendants of the victims (BBC News, 2004).

4. In April 2011 four elderly Kenyans traveled to London. They had been among the thousands of prisoners detained by the British during the war against the Mau Mau movement in Kenya between 1952 and 1960. The four had been subjected to castration, torture, and rape in British detention camps. In a court decision of October 2012 the Kenyans were given the right to sue the British government. *The Guardian* reported in May 2013:

> When the claimants gave evidence at the high court in London last year, Wambugu Wa Nyingi told how he was detained on Christmas Eve 1952 and held for nine years, much of the time in handcuffs. He was beaten unconscious during a ... massacre at a camp at Hola in which 11 men died. "I feel I was robbed of my youth and that I did not get to do the things I should have done as a young man," he said. "There is a saying in Kikuyu that old age lives off the years of youth, but I have nothing to live off because my youth was taken from me." (Cobain, 2013)

5. In my class of international master's students of applied ethics I raised the question of whether colonialism had left "morally relevant traces" in the present. A bright Pakistani female student spoke out, not without some anger in her voice:

> Yes, certainly! Everything Pakistani is today considered of less worth compared to the West: we consider our own history as shameful and we feel that we are still slaves under the British rulers. These feelings have also a cultural impact today; to be beautiful is to have blond hair, not black, to be civilized is to eat with knife and fork, not to eat in our traditional way, and our traditional languages are superseded by English.

Her outcry mirrors what Rajeev Bhargava calls "epistemic injustice," a kind of cultural injustice whereby "concepts and categories" providing self-understanding and orientation are replaced and marginalized by a dominant power, in this case the colonizer (Bhargava, 2013).

What do the above-mentioned examples have in common? The present global economic order, the Durban conference against racism, the Herero bringing back their forefathers' skulls, the Mau Mau who sued the British government, and the Pakistani student's sense of humiliation remind us of the legacy of colonialism. How should we relate to this legacy? The former colonial powers have tried to repress these memories but we should not forget them. There are still victims among us who bear witness and the unjust global order mirrors the history.

Colonialism was a global phenomenon. European nations ruled over almost all of the peoples of Latin America, Africa, and Asia. At the height of the Empire, the British governed one quarter of the world's population. As my cases above illustrate, although decolonization began over 70 years ago, the consequences of colonialism are still evident. Indeed, as I will argue in this book, since this historical era still shapes the global order, the legacy of colonialism provides a strong case for global rectificatory justice.

How, then, can the legacy of colonialism have implications for a theory of global justice today? What does rectificatory justice mean in the light of colonialism? What does global rectificatory justice require in practice? The aim of this book is to respond to these questions.

A case-based argument

The following story illustrates the idea of global rectificatory justice:

> Assume that I live a life in prosperity and welfare. My next door neighbor, on the other hand, lives in poverty and misery. Let us also assume that many years ago my grandparents stole the land on which my present neighbor lives from his grandparents, and our present difference in welfare is the result of this historical fact. Then, it seems that my neighbor could with good reason demand a part of my land or income in return, that is, that I have a moral obligation to compensate my neighbor. And this obligation has been generated by the acts of my forefathers.

Today we live in a "global village." My neighbors are peasants in Malawi, miners in Bolivia, and slum-dwellers in the Philippines. Although the story is indeed a rough mirror of real history, it helps us to generate some moral intuitions for further analysis.

The present global economic and political order is characterized by inequality: poverty in some parts – almost 1 billion people ("the bottom billion") live on less than one dollar a day – and affluence in other parts, and unequal power relations visible not least in the structures of global institutions like the IMF, the World Bank, and the WTO. This order was to a large extent shaped by colonialism. Most of the former colonies are still, many decades after their independence, suppliers of raw materials or of basic industrial products for markets dominated by the global elite. The past endures in the present.

Political philosophy

Justice is a key concept in political philosophy and can be approached from different viewpoints. In his discussion on justice, Aristotle distinguishes between *distributive* and *rectificatory* justice. Distributive justice deals with the distribution of scarce resources and goods. Rectificatory justice, on the other hand, is backward-looking and focuses on correction for past misdeeds. Aristotle writes:

> for in the case also in which one has received and the other has inflicted a wound, or one has slain and the other been slain, the suffering and the action have been unequally distributed: but the judge tries to equalize things by means of the penalty, taking away from the gain of the assailant… [T]herefore, corrective justice will be the intermediate between the loss and gain. (Aristotle, 1980: 115)

Given that the history of colonialism is a story of "inflicting wounds," there is a *prima facie* case for rectificatory justice. But what does rectificatory justice imply if the harm was done a long time ago? Is there a time limit on claims for rectification, and can the descendants of victims of colonialism demand rectification? I will come back to these questions later in the book.

A theory of rectificatory justice can also draw on more recent work in philosophy. Building on John Locke's theory of property, Robert Nozick's influential and controversial entitlement theory is an example of a historical, backward-looking theory of justice. According to Nozick, a person is entitled to his or her property provided that it has been acquired in a just way. Hence, property rights depend on justice in acquisition and justice in transfer (Nozick, 1974).

Nozick's theory is a philosophical justification of libertarianism but it can also be instrumental in justifying a demand for global rectificatory justice.

Given that the present concentration of property and wealth in the rich parts of the world is at least partly the result of unjust historical acquisitions and transfers, that is plunder and theft, one could, based on Nozick's entitlement theory, argue for a global "...rectification of injustice in holdings" (ibid.: 152). Historical injustices thus beg for rectifying actions.

The main contribution of Nozick's book *Anarchy, State and Utopia* was that it introduced a historical perspective to the present discussion on justice. As a libertarian, Nozick emphasized property rights. My emphasis is different. I will focus on injustices during colonialism and the social and economic reverberations of colonialism today.

Rectificatory justice in practice

Historical injustice raises the issue of redress. In recent times we have witnessed the emergence of a number of truth and reconciliation commissions, inquiring into human rights violations during dictatorships and oppressive regimes. These commissions have in some cases resulted in prosecutions and court trials and in others public acknowledgements and apologies.

Acknowledgements of historical obligations and demands for rectificatory justice are not new in politics. They have been made in relation to various historical instances of oppression and exploitation. In 1928, in relation to a dispute between Germany and Poland, the permanent Court of International Justice (predecessor of the International Court of Justice) defined reparatory justice in the following way:

> The essential principle contained in the actual notion of an illegal act is that reparation must, as far as possible, wipe out all the consequences of the illegal act and re-establish the situation which would, in all probability, have existed if that act had not been committed. (quoted in Beckles, 2013: 13)

One much noticed example of historical rectification is the compensation given by Germany to Jews after the Holocaust, and another is the policy of affirmative action in favor of black people and former slaves in the United States. The creation of the Truth and Reconciliation Commission in South Africa after the fall of the apartheid regime in 1994 is perhaps the most systematic recent process of reconciliation and rectification. Initiatives were also taken in Latin America, for example in Chile and Argentina, to restore justice when democracy was reestablished after the military dictatorships in the 1970s and 1980s.

In his book *The Guilt of Nations*, Elizir Barkan gives an account of a number of rectificatory processes that have been going on in the wake of World War II and some examples of rectification for colonialism and its aftermath (Barkan, 2000).

Although the colonial powers did their utmost to hide the dark side of the colonial period after their colonies had become independent, there are at least some examples of rectificatory processes after colonialism. The Kenyans' request for a court trial in Britain reminded the world of the hidden history of detention camps and torture, the Herero people have repeatedly demanded rectification from Germany, and when French president François Hollande visited Algeria in 2012 to take part in the celebration of the nation's 50th anniversary as an independent state, he acknowledged trespasses by the French army during colonial times, although he refused to apologize. In 2013, Caribbean heads of state decided to form a commission with the aim of preparing rectificatory claims against Britain and other slave-trading nations for harms done during colonial times. These examples illustrate that the legacy of colonialism has both a personal and a political side. Individuals were subjected to harm and oppression, but entire nations and peoples were also victims of injustice.

Rectificatory justice in theory

The above-mentioned rectificatory political processes have fueled the discussion on rectificatory justice in history and political theory. Historians have reported on various cases of rectificatory processes after periods of dictatorship and human rights violations, and there is an ongoing philosophical discussion on the meaning of rectificatory justice and on the justification for compensation to afflicted groups. For example:

- John Torpey (2003) is mapping reparation claims; one scale refers to violations – from theft of cultural artifacts (e.g., artworks) to human rights violations – and another scale refers to possible forms of reparation – from symbolic to economic.
- Alfred Brophy (2006) takes the black Americans' claims for reparations as a point of departure for discussing controversial premises that lie behind the concept of rectification.
- Richard Vernon (2012) discusses matters of principle; for example, whether rights survive death, who should be responsible for

compensating victims of past misdeeds, and how past deeds continue in the present in relation to a number of cases of historical injustice.
- Jeff Spinner-Halev (2012) argues that our emphasis should not be on compensation for injustices in the past but on the fact that some past injustices become enduring and are therefore felt today.
- Janna Thompson (2002) examines a number of reparative demands, in particular the cases of the Aborigines in Australia and the Maori in New Zealand, and develops a theory of reparation and reconciliation with a focus on broken treaties.
- Bernard Boxill (2003) argues for African Americans' reparations after colonialism and slavery.
- Stephan Winter (2006) discusses whether uncertainty over what would have happened if history had taken a different path should undermine the reparative demands of black Americans.
- Rhoda Howard-Hassmann (2008) discusses whether there are good reasons for reparations to Africa.
- Hilary Beckles (2013) argues for "Britain's black debt," that is, that Britain has a debt to pay to the Caribbean peoples for enslavement and exploitation during colonial times.

Theoretical accounts relating the legacy of colonialism to the ethical discussion on global justice today are rare. Kok-Chor Tan (2007) argues that ideas of reparation for colonial injustices can supplement egalitarian arguments for global justice, David Miller (2007) raises the question whether former colonial nations have inherited responsibilities for what was done to the colonies and lines up alternative scenarios for how rectification could be made, and Daniel Butt (2009) argues that colonial injustices undermine the legitimacy of present resource holdings. According to Thomas Pogge (2002: 203–204), a root cause of the present gap between the global "haves" and "have-nots" is colonial oppression and genocide. However, he does not elaborate on the implications of these actions on present-day claims for global justice.

Among voices critical of demands for rectification are the philosophers Jeremy Waldron (1992, 2007), who argues that historical redress involves problematic counterfactual calculations, and George Sher (1980, 2006), who questions that descendants of victims of oppression and injustice have the right to claim rectification.

In the discussion on climate change, the argument that due to their historical emissions of greenhouse gases, the industrial nations have a debt to pay to the present poor nations, many of them suffering the consequences without having contributed to the climate crises themselves, is raised (Caney, 2005a; Kenehan, 2014). This is clearly an argument related to the topic of historical justice but I will not delve into it in this book.

Rectificatory justice in the present context

The argument for rectificatory justice that I develop in this book is built on the following premises: (1) there is a moral obligation to compensate for the consequences of harmful acts; (2) colonialism was in various ways harmful to the colonies; (3) the present unjust global structure is a legacy of colonialism; and (4) the obligation to carry out rectification is trans-generational so long as there are identifiable beneficiaries and victims of past injustices in the present.

My argument is based on the "do not harm principle" – in other words, the "principle of non-maleficence" (Beauchamp and Childress, 2001). When harm is perpetrated, the victim can claim redress. This is the basic idea behind rectificatory justice.

During the era of colonialism, the colonies were harmed in different ways. They were subjected to invasion, war, and occupation, to slavery and forced labor, to genocide and massacres, to the extermination of domestic religions and cultures, to the forced resettlement of populations, to economic dominance, and to exploitation and various other kinds of human rights violations. Individuals and peoples who were victims of these harmful acts have a right to redress. Rectificatory justice is a way to "...restore the dignity of the victims," as the follow-up UN conference on racism in 2009 stated. In this respect, my argument for rectificatory justice is backward-looking; what happened in the past is the basis for present claims for justice.

The legacy of colonialism is enduring. Since the global structure is still shaped by colonialism, the argument developed in this book is also forward-looking. Relations of dominance and subjection, as well as inequalities inherited from colonialism, ought to be changed. In this way, global distributive justice and global rectificatory justice are complementary, or, in the words of Nigerian philosopher Peter Osimiri,

> while the rectificatory theory of justice provides a sound basis for repairing historic injustices, it also provides a strong normative platform for reforming the present global economic order into one that is fairer to the poor. (Osimiri, 2010)

But is it really fair to assign to people duties of rectification for the deeds of their forefathers? When God in the Old Testament punishes "the children for the sin of the fathers to the third and fourth generation" (Deuteronomy, 5: 9), one could question both the rationality and goodness of such a God. Why should a person who has done nothing wrong be punished? This questioning of inter-generational rectification will be discussed later in the book.

Method

This is a book on ethics, or, more precisely, applied ethics. My aim is to contribute to the global justice discussion by raising the question if rectification for past wrongs is morally justified. Ethical questions are raised concerning the implications of past wrongful acts and their enduring consequences for the present relations between the global rich and the global poor, that is, ethics is applied to both a historical period and the present global order.

A common feature of ethics is an analysis of concepts and arguments. In this book, the meaning of rectificatory justice and related concepts are analyzed and arguments for and against rectificatory justice are identified, interpreted and their relevance, implications and validity are assessed. But the book also has a constructive approach. I develop arguments for a normative thesis and discuss possible objections. Some arguments have the form of thought experiments, such as the one about the poor neighbor above. In a thought experiment one tells a story that is analogous to an actual historical event and investigates what moral intuitions the story generates. The moral intuitions generated by the thought experiments are related to ethical principles and ethical theory, in this case a theory of rectificatory justice.

Like all argumentation in applied ethics, my argument depends on factual accounts. I rely on reports and interpretations of the history of colonialism and its political and economic consequences, and on accounts of how the present global world order works. As a consequence, my argument can be challenged from two angles. A critical reader can question either the ethical reasoning, that is, the author's moral intuitions, principles and ethical theory, or the factual basis and sources referred to.

Is history relative?

It has become fashionable to argue that history is relative. In the discussion on historical reparations one sometimes encounters the view that different groups interpret history differently and that history is subjective. One group has one view of what happened in the past and another group has a different view. "History has become increasingly malleable," as Barkan writes (Barkan, 2000: x).

History is always a matter of interpretation, and critical historians remind us that official historical accounts are normally written by the victors. As a consequence, the voices of the victims are seldom heard. As Klaus Neumann writes, "In many cases, the vast majority of sources about a past injustice were generated by those responsible for it. Often, the voices of victims only survive in the accounts of their tormentors" (Neumann, 2014: 7). One aspect of this subjectivity of history is that social identities and national sentiments are normally shaped by an established interpretation of historical events.

A pertinent illustration of the need to reevaluate history is the recent findings of historians David Anderson and Caroline Elkins regarding the British combat against the Mau Mau movement in Kenya in the 1950s (Anderson 2005, Elkins 2005). As a consequence of their findings, the established view that British civilization was fighting superstitious and brutal African warriors has to be reconsidered from the ground (see Chapter 4).

Does this view of history force us to adopt a relativist stance? And does it imply that demands for rectification are always based on one group's point of view and that those demands are thus inherently questionable? It is true that history is a battlefield for different interpretations. It is also true that different actors usually recapitulate the past in different ways and that their reports are informed by their values and interests. However, this does not imply that we must surrender to relativism. The Holocaust is not just a narrative told by Jews and the slave trade is not just a narrative told by Africans. There are historical facts behind the narratives and these can be critically examined.

The scientific virtues of objectivity, impartiality, and fair assessment do not necessarily conflict with sympathy for the victims and efforts to highlight historical injustices, as long as there are good reasons for this ethical positioning. For those involved in an endeavor of rectificatory justice it is of utmost importance to get the historical facts right. There are good reasons for rectification only if the stories told by the victims, and the interpretations of the history behind the rectificatory claims, have a solid empirical underpinning.

Overview

As a point of departure, in Chapter 2 I show how the present discussion on global justice ignores an important premise. I argue that the current global order, including the distribution of wealth and power, in different ways mirrors the colonial structure. Further, I argue that what Thomas Pogge calls the "international resource privilege," an alliance between multinational corporations on the one hand and authoritarian leaders in developing countries on the other, has its roots in colonialism. John Rawls's *Law of Peoples* has greatly influenced the discussion on global justice. In Chapter 2 I also argue that a principle of rectification should be added to the principles of international justice that Rawls suggests. I draw the conclusion that a historical perspective will contribute to a more comprehensive notion of global justice.

A discussion of whether there are good reasons for rectification after colonialism must relate to the legacy of colonialism; was colonialism detrimental or beneficial to the colonized peoples' situation and what are its political and economic consequences today? Chapter 3 gives a broad introduction to colonialism and imperialism; how European hegemony was established, "the scramble for Africa" when Africa was divided between European colonial powers at the Berlin Conference 1884–1885, the colonization of Asia, the United States' dominance over Latin America, and so on.

After a general overview of colonial history in Chapter 3, Chapter 4 presents and discusses five examples of the practice of colonialism. The examples illustrate different aspects of this period of history: a rather peaceful but nevertheless in the long run destructive colonial period (Uganda); a vicious quest for raw materials which undermined a country's future (Congo); a genocide that had lasting consequences (South West Africa/Namibia); a war of liberation that was violently resisted by the colonial power (Kenya); and finally an example of how colonies and pseudo-colonies were integrated in the world market with problematic consequences for the countries' own economic development (India).

The point of departure of Chapter 5 is the question of how colonialism and imperialism shaped the present global structure. The primary question is: How were the present poor nations and former colonies affected by the fact that they were dominated by foreign powers for hundreds of years? The second question is: How did colonialism affect the development of today's wealthy nations? Both questions arouse considerable controversy and experts in the field are divided in their answers. The aim of the chapter is to relate my argument to some answers given by historians and economists and discuss the implications of the argument for rectificatory justice after colonialism.

The impact of colonialism was not restricted to the political and economic spheres. There was also a colonization of minds, traditions, and cultures. This form of enduring colonialism has been revealed by post-colonial theory. In Chapter 6 the "epistemic injustice" of colonialism is discussed, with the help of the Indian social theorist Rajeev Bhargava's theory of the colonization of "epistemic frameworks."

In the Durban Declaration of the United Nations conference on racism in 2001, slavery and the slave trade were in focus. The delegates expressed their sorrow about this dark period in history and demanded that it should be commemorated. The question of rectification was hotly discussed. Is there a moral reason to compensate African nations for the harmful impact of the slave trade? This question is discussed in Chapter 7.

To what extent did former colonies demand rectification when they achieved independence? Chapter 8 gives an overview of rectificatory claims after colonialism. Examples of claims are the Herero claims against Germany, the claims of former Mau Mau adherents against Great Britain, those of the Aborigines in Australia, and the Caribbean states' claims for rectification for slavery and the slave trade.

What is the *meaning* of rectificatory justice? In Chapter 9 I analyze the concept of rectificatory justice. I start by giving an account of some philosophical views of rectificatory justice. The main part of the chapter contains an analysis of the concept and theory of rectificatory justice. In order to structure the discussion, a model of rectificatory justice is developed and the model is then applied to historical rectification after colonialism. I develop a theory of rectificatory justice and address the questions of who can rightly claim rectification and who owes rectification, whether there are temporal limitations to rectification, and what is owed in the name of rectification after colonialism. Finally, I discuss the question of whether it is unfair or even anachronistic to claim rectification for past wrongs.

The idea of rectificatory justice is controversial and a number of philosophical arguments have been raised against it. The arguments that claims for rectificatory justice are in conflict with ethical presentism and ethical individualism, that they presuppose problematic counterfactual premises, that they are insensitive to changing circumstances and that descendants have no right to claim rectification because they would not have existed if the previous harm had not taken place (the non-identity problem) are discussed in Chapter 10. It is concluded that none of these objections undermines the argument for rectificatory justice after colonialism.

Do demands for rectification merely reopen wounds that have been healed? Are forgiveness and reconciliation perhaps better alternatives than rectification? The relation between rectification on the one hand and forgiveness and reconciliation on the other is discussed in Chapter 11. Although rectificatory justice, forgiveness, and reconciliation cover similar conceptual spaces and in some ways overlap, there are also crucial differences between them, and neither forgiveness nor reconciliation can replace rectification.

What are the practical implications of historical rectification and how should the relations between former colonies and former colonial powers be shaped in the future? In the remaining part of the book these questions are addressed.

Migration from former colonies to former colonial powers is an important feature of international migration flows during the latter part of the 20th century. The question discussed in Chapter 12 is if a generous immigration policy on behalf of persons from former colonies is an appropriate measure for former colonial powers to compensate for colonial injustices. I conclude that since migration from the global south to the global north on the whole is detrimental to the long-term interests of the south it is not a fitting way to rectify.

Colonialism shaped the global order and had enduring consequences for the relations between the former colonial powers and the former colonies. How can these relations of dominance and submission be changed? Critics of TRIPS (Agreement on Trade-Related Intellectual Property Rights, 1994), which regulated patents and intellectual property rights on a global level, argued that the interests of the global poor in terms of access to pharmaceutical products were in conflict with the pharmaceutical companies' interests in terms of global intellectual property rights. Surprisingly, the resistance from developing nations and many NGOs to the agreement were at least partly successful in shaping revised regulations that were more favorable to the global poor. In Chapter 13 the TRIPS controversy is analyzed from the point of view of rectificatory justice. I argue that the way in which the global poor and former colonies managed to influence the regulations could be seen as a model for how more equal relations between the global rich and the global poor might be realized in the wake of rectificatory justice.

The conclusions of the argument are drawn in Chapter 14. First, it is argued that rectification is a way of realizing justice and restoring a moral equilibrium and respect for the victims of past wrongs. Through rectification, former perpetrators of harmful acts will enhance their own international reputation at the same time as restoring the self-respect of the citizens of a nation that is guilty of historical wrongs.

How then is global rectificatory justice related to global distributive justice? According to theories of global distributive justice, there is a need for global redistribution in favor of the poor in the developing countries. A theory of global rectificatory justice has similar implications. However, even to the extent that the social and economic implications are similar, the motives behind the two ideals are different. Hence, a theory of global rectificatory justice is complementary to a theory of global distributive justice and it will enable us to develop a more comprehensive understanding of the meaning of global justice.

How can former colonial powers compensate for past and present injustices? This question has been raised by the heads of the Caribbean states, who claim rectification for the slave trade, and they are still awaiting a response. The British apology and compensation to former adherents of the Mau Mau movement could be seen as an example to other former colonial powers of how this question should be answered.

2
The Discussion on Global Justice: A Missing Premise

During the last few decades we have witnessed a significant increase in the literature on global justice. Scholars in philosophy, political science, international relations, and other disciplines are turning their attention to global relations and in particular the implications of globalization on ethics and international politics.

Globalization implies global interdependence. Decisions taken in one place reverberate in another place far away and thus the scope of our responsibility is widening. People from different parts of the world come closer and we learn about the lifestyles and living conditions of peoples far away. Widespread poverty and the gaps between the global "haves" and the global "have-nots" challenge our sense of justice. These global injustices have been enduring since colonial times. Yet, strangely enough, ethicists involved in the discussion on global justice have almost entirely focused on one aspect of justice, namely distributive justice, and neglected the history behind the global injustices we encounter today. As I argue in this chapter, there is a missing premise in much of the argumentation. Obviously, questions of distributive justice are crucial for the normative discussion of global justice but, as I argue throughout this book, the discussion on global justice should also be informed by a historical perspective. In this chapter I show that the legacy of colonialism provides an important background to the main issues in the present discussion on global justice.

In the first part of the chapter I raise the question of whether some key issues in the global justice discussion – global poverty, global inequality, and global migration – are related to the legacy of colonialism. Then, in the next section, I introduce Thomas Pogge's theoretical notion of an "international resource privilege" and argue that this privilege has its origin in colonialism.

Some authors have argued that there exists a "global basic structure," that is, a set of economic and political global institutions that affect the distribution of burdens and benefits among peoples and individuals. This structure, I argue, is basically a continuation of the colonial world order. Finally, I relate my argument to Rawls's "realistic utopia" of "a Society of Peoples," a concept which has significantly influenced the global justice discussion. Rawls sketches eight principles for a Law of Peoples that all "decent" peoples should observe (Rawls, 1999). I argue that a principle of historical redress should be added to Rawls's principles for international justice.

Global poverty

Global poverty is one of the points of departure for the ethical discussion on global justice. It is a dire moral challenge that a large part of the world's population lives in utmost despair alongside the affluent part of the world. Not surprisingly, many authors of books on global justice begin with facts relating to global poverty. For example, according to Thomas Pogge, the World Bank estimated that 1214 out of 5820 million human beings lived below the poverty line in 1998 and the UNDP (United Nations Development Programme) reported that 14% of world's population was undernourished and 15% lacked access to health services (Pogge, 2002: 97). Kok-Chor Tan refers to UNDP reports in saying that about half of the world's population lives on US$2 per day or less, that the infant mortality rate in Sub-Saharan Africa is 15 times that of developed countries (Tan, 2004: 20), and Gillian Brocks cites UNDP figures that 3,900 children die every day from diseases transmitted through water or human waste and 800 million adults are illiterate (Brock, 2009: 120). Although the latest UNDP reports (UNDP, 2013) show – gratifyingly – that there have been improvements regarding human development, these figures on global poverty illustrate the scale of the problem.

The UNDP reports on the HDI (Human Development Index) of the nations of the world as a measure of development. The HDI integrates measures of income, health, and education. When one takes the HDI as a measure of poverty, one finds that of the world's 45 poorest countries, 44 are former colonies. In fact, all official poverty measures indicate that the countries that are lowest on the lists are former colonies and most of the ones at the top are former colonial powers (UNDP, 2013; World Bank, 2013).

Is there a connection between the fact that the world's poorest nations are former colonies and some of the world's richest nations are former colonial powers? The issue will be further explored in Chapters 4 and 5.

Global inequality

Besides poverty, equality is a crucial aspect of justice; hence global inequality of global injustice (Cohen, 2008; Brock, 2009; Tan, 2004).

Global inequalities were emphasized by the UNDP in the World Development Report 1992 (UNDP, 1992). Since then the gaps have widened further. In 2007 the richest 20% of the world's population earned 82.8%, the second fifth 9.9%, the third fifth 4.2%, the fourth fifth 2.1%, and the poorest 20% earned 1% of total income (see Figure 2.1).

Due to the economic growth in some developing countries, especially the population giants China and India, global inequality between nations has actually decreased in the last decade. Nevertheless, the gaps are wide. 92% of the world's population controls half of the world's income and only 8% controls the other half. The global Gini coefficient[1] is around 0.70 (in comparison to Sweden's 0.26 and South Africa, the world's most unequal country, 0.63), which means that the gap between the global rich and poor is larger than between the rich and poor in the world's most unequal country, South Africa (Milanovic, 2012).

Global access to productive resources also mirrors global inequality. For example, 97% of all patents belong to the industrialized West and 90% of them are in the hands of transnational companies (UNDP, 2000). The wealthy, industrialized nations dominate research and development and the OECD countries accounted for 91% of the 347,000 new patents issued in 1998. Only 0.6% of the resources spent on health research were

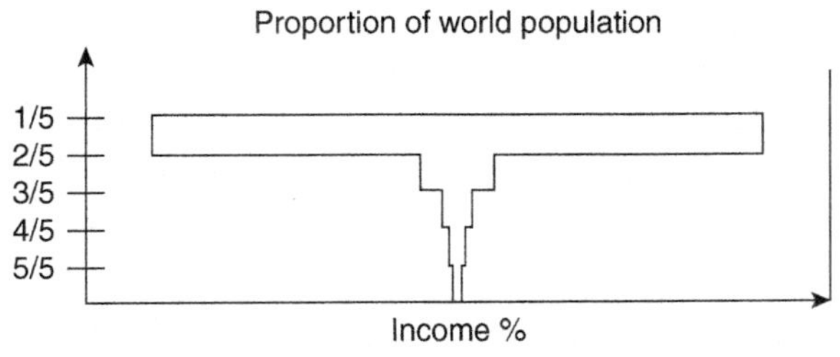

Figure 2.1 The ten nations at the bottom of the global income pyramid are all former colonies

Source: Ortiz and Cummins (2011: 19).

dedicated to vaccines for HIV/AIDS and malaria, that is illnesses that primarily threaten the global poor (UNDP, 2001).

The same is true of global inequality as for global poverty; the fact that former colonies are at the bottom of the global income pyramid and former colonial powers at the top does not necessarily imply that there is a connection between the colonial past and present income gaps but there are clearly reasons to explore the issue further (see Chapters 4 and 5).

Migration and global justice

The number of international migrants has risen continuously over the last 20 years, from 155 million in 1990 to over 210 million in 2011. This means that around 3% of the world's population are international migrants. In 2009, 16 million refugees crossed international borders and the number of internally displaced people (IDP) was double that number. The source countries are usually global and regional conflict zones; major source countries of refugees today are Syria, Afghanistan, Somalia, Iraq, Congo, and Burma, and most refugees go to other poor (neighboring) countries. Pakistan and Iran are currently the countries with the largest number of refugees. The burdens of refugee migration are unequally shared (United Nations Population Division, 2008; International Organization for Migration, 2013; UNHCR, 2012).

Amnesty International and other NGOs continually report on the maltreatment of refugees and immigrants. For example, in European border countries like Greece and Italy, migrants are often treated like criminals and detained in sub-human conditions, furthermore the EU agreed in 2010 with the former Libyan dictator Moammar Khadafy on measures to stop African migrants entering Europe.

What then are the rights of migrants and refugees? Several articles of the Universal Declaration of Human Rights (UDHR) relate to questions of refugee status and migration. Article 13 deals with freedom of movement: to migrate – both within a country and across national borders – is a human right. Article 14 deals specifically with the questions of refugee status and asylum. According to 14:1, "Everyone has the right to seek and to enjoy in other countries asylum from persecution."

Someone's right presupposes someone else's obligation. The UDHR signatories are nation states. Hence, the nation states are both the guarantor *of* and the primary agents *for* the enforcement of human rights within their borders. States have obligations, moral and legal, to respect human rights. However, Article 14 contains an asymmetry; refugee rights do not correspond to particular obligations of states. Refugees leave their home country due to persecution and suppression, that is, due to the fact that their human rights are violated. Who then has the obligation to secure their rights as refugees? The first country to receive a refugee has the legal duty to try his or her refugee status, which has led to strict border control both at the borders to the European Union and to the USA.

There are divergent views in the global justice debate on the ethics of migration and the rights of migrants. Some influential views leave refugees and immigrants without enduring protection. According to nationalism, the receiving countries have the right to decide admission criteria. Michael Walzer argues that nations are like clubs and the citizens/club members have the right to distribute membership to others according to their will (Walzer, 1983: 40). Walzer's argument supporting this claim is that the integrity of a community should be protected. David Miller argues that liberal states are entitled to close their borders to immigrants to protect their culture and control their populations (Miller, 2005: 199f.). Refugees belong to a different category from citizens. Although they have basic rights and deserve protection, no particular state has an obligation to admit any specific refugees. Miller hopes that states will informally agree on a fair distribution of responsibilities (Ibid.: 203).

Although international migration can have some positive consequences for global justice, Gillian Brock is on the whole critical of a policy of open borders, but for other reasons than Walzer and Miller. According to Brock, migration from poor nations to rich nations is not in the interest of the poor nations and comes into conflict with the aim of global justice. The reason is that it is mainly the well educated who leave and this "brain drain" is hurting economic development in the poor countries (Brock, 2009: 198–204).

Seila Benhabib argues that a human right to membership needs to be anchored in institutions that go beyond the nation state. Citizenship is no longer the ultimate ground for rights. The disaggregation of citizenship is, as she writes, "an inescapable aspect of contemporary globalization" (Benhabib, 2005: 173).

In his contribution to the global justice discussion Mathias Risse argues from a Lockean view that the earth is collectively owned. According to Risse, a territory is relatively *overused* if the per-capita use rate of commonly owned resources is above the global average and relatively *underused* if the value is below the average, that is, if fewer people than the average populate the territory. A nation has a *prima facie* duty to allow immigration if its territory is underused (Risse, 2012).

Increased migration is one aspect of globalization and the rights of migrants are one important aspect of global justice. Yet the colonial legacy as a driving force of present-day migration has so far been a neglected topic in the discussion.

Migration and colonialism

The European nations divided Africa and Asia at the end of the 19th century (see Chapter 3). The division into interest spheres and the subsequent occupation of territories were done in ways that neglected the interests of the native populations and without taking demography or ethnical differences into consideration. As a consequence, when the colonies became independent, many new nations acquired artificial borders with little natural correspondence between territory and ethnic groups or tribes.

The legacy of colonialism has various implications for present global migration. Much of today's migration is caused by borders that were drawn by colonial powers, either during the establishment of the colonial system or as the result of the independence of the colonies. As a consequence of these imposed and often arbitrary borders, a large proportion of today's forced migrants[2] come from former colonies.

In South East Asia there was a long pre-colonial history of travel and migration within Nusantara (the Malay world). It was due to European colonialism that borders divided Nusantara and that, later, different independent states were created. As a consequence, migration within the region became a political issue. Present regional conflicts, like the Patani conflict in Southern Thailand and the conflict in Mindanao, as well as conflicts over migration and the rights of migrants should be seen in this historical light. Many present borders are artificial legacies of colonialism, and internal and external conflicts and waves of migration are consequences of these historical policies.

Palestine is an example of how the colonial policy of divide and rule resulted in huge refugee problems. As the mandated power, Britain promised the creation of an Arab state in return for support against the Ottoman Empire in the First World War, and Britain also agreed with France in the Sykes-Picot Agreement (1916) on how to divide Palestine, mainly inhabited by Arabs. But parallel to theses promises to the Arabs, in the Balfour Declaration (1917), Britain declared Palestine as a national home for Jews. Not least due to the British policy at the time, conflicts arose between Palestinians and Jews over land, which resulted in millions of Palestinian refugees when they were forced from their homes as the result of the foundation of the state of Israel in 1948 (Laquer, 1969). The conflict between Israelis and Palestinians is enduring and there is still no solution in sight.

This is not to say that all of today's problems of international migration are the result of colonialism. My point so far is just that the background to present-day migration, and thus to one of the issues relevant to global justice, cannot be fully understood if it is not related to the legacy of colonialism.

We noted above that major source countries for refugees are Syria, Afghanistan, Somalia, Congo, and Burma. They have in common that they are all former colonies (in the case of Afghanistan, a semi-colony). Is there a connection here? Did colonialism determine the conditions of the future development of these countries that later led to internal wars, oppression, and so on; in other words, did it cause people to try to leave their countries? I will not attempt to answer that question here. I will only hint at a possible connection between their former colonial status and the present turmoil that has led to refugee problems.

The questions of forced migration and refugees has become a major topic for ethical discussions on global justice. Views presented range from restricted duties on behalf of the receiving nations to more radical views arguing for generous migration policies. When we look at forced migration and refugees from a justice perspective, it seems that the pertinent questions have to do not only with distributive justice, namely which countries should receive what number of migrants, but also with rectificatory justice: what is the historical background to a turmoil leading to forced migration and refugees and who is ultimately responsible for this turmoil? And, one may add, what responsibility does this history amount to today? So far, this is a missing question in the global justice discussion on migration.

The international resource privilege

We noted earlier that a large part of the global population live in misery and that the present global order is characterized by a huge gap between rich and poor. According to Thomas Pogge, these facts can be linked to what he calls a "global institutional order" that is sustained by powerful governments in the North and global organizations like the WTO and the IMF (Pogge, 2002: 172). This order is responsible for the current global resource distribution as it generates wealth in one part of the world and poverty in another part. Pogge writes:

> Our present global economic order produces a stable pattern of widespread malnutrition and starvation among the poor, with some

> 18 million persons dying each year from poverty-related causes. (Ibid.: 176)

Pogge criticizes "the existing global economic order" because it helps to maintain a double standard, namely the acceptance of injustices on the global level that would never be accepted within a nation. As a consequence of globalization we are all participants in a single, global institutional order, Pogge argues. The Western nations uphold the global economic order, partly through the WTO agreements, and as a consequence these nations are responsible for the poverty and deaths caused by this order. Pogge writes:

> By continuing to support the current global order and the national policies that shape and sustain it without taking compensation action toward institutional reform or shielding its victims, we share a negative responsibility for the undue harms they foreseeably produce. (Ibid.: 144)

This order is also maintained by what Pogge calls the "international resource privilege," an alliance between multinational corporations on the one hand and corrupt and authoritarian leaders in developing nations on the other. In many developing nations natural resources are controlled by dictators and corrupt leaders. Pogge takes Nigeria as an example. The country has been ruled by military dictators or authoritarian leaders for decades. In parallel, oil exports have amounted to US$6–10 billion annually but the vast majority of the population remains poor. Pogge writes: "Corruption in Nigeria is ... encouraged and sustained by the international resource privilege" (Ibid.). The multinational corporations that purchase resources from autocratic rulers are therefore preserving the unjust order.

The structure of the international resource privilege was established during colonialism but is enduring, with some new players added. I will give some current examples.

A recent feature of the international resource privilege is what has become known as "land-grabbing." Land-grabbing means that land in poor nations is taken over by international companies – Western, Malaysian, Arabic, Chinese, and others – often with the support of multinational banks and financial institutions like the World Bank and the European Investment Bank. In many poor countries land is communally owned but cultivated for private use by poor peasants. When governments are invited to sell the communal land to big corporations, they do so and the profit goes to the domestic elite, while poor peasants are expelled from the land they have cultivated for generations. The land is then used for commodity crops that are sold overseas. In this way food crops, mining products, and agro fuel are produced for the benefit of the global rich but at the expense of the peasants (Borras, Jr. and Franco, 2012; Friends of the Earth, 2010; Friends of the Earth International, 2012; Voget-Kleschin and Ott, 2013; Action Aid, 2014; Provost, Ford, and Tran, 2014).

A recent example of the international resource privilege relates to oil extraction in Sudan. Since the 1980s, Sudan has been torn apart by civil war. Government troops tried to curb upheavals in the southern part of the country, which ultimately got its independence in 2011. At the same time, foreign oil companies, including the Swedish company Lundin Petroleum in cooperation with Malaysian Petronas and Austrian OMV AG, continued to exploit oil resources situated in war-torn areas. The companies signed contracts with the government and used government troops to "clear" the areas for exploitation. In an investigation by ECOS (European Coalition on Oil in Sudan), a coalition of organizations working for peace and justice in Sudan and funded by the European Commission, the authors concluded:

> [B]etween 1997 and 2003, international crimes were committed on a large scale in what was essentially a military campaign by the Government of Sudan to secure and take control of the oil fields in Block 5A... [T]hey included indiscriminate attacks and intentional targeting of civilians, burning of shelters, pillage, destruction of objects necessary for survival, unlawful killing of civilians, rape of women, abduction of children, torture, and forced displacement. Thousands of people died and almost two hundred thousand were violently displaced. (ECOS, 2010)

Sudan oil extraction is a perfect example of "the international resource privilege" in practice.

Thomas Pogge is aware of the history behind the present unjust global economic order. He criticizes what he calls "explanatory nationalism," which explains present poverty by blaming it on bad domestic policies (Pogge, 2002: 142). He writes further:

> [M]ost of the existing international inequality in standards of living was built up in the colonial period when today's affluent countries ruled today's poor regions of the world: trading their people like

> cattle, destroying their political institutions and cultures, and taking their natural resources. (Pogge, 2005)

Pogge does not himself further develop the historical explanations of present global injustices. However, since they have their roots in the history of colonialism, the discussion on global justice should be more historically sensitive. Let me illustrate this argument with some examples. Many of the multinational companies that today exploit resources in developing countries in collaboration with corrupt regimes were established during the colonial era. For example, British Petroleum's (BP) interests in Iraq's oil date back to the 1920s, when Iraq was under British mandate. Despite nominal independence, British influence remained under King Faisal, as did the interest of British Petroleum, at that time under the name Iraq Petroleum Company. In 1972 Saddam Hussein nationalized the oil industry (Kwarteng, 2011). The American and British joint invasion of Iraq in 2003 paved BP's way back to Iraq and the company currently has an agreement with the Iraqi government to have concessions in the Rumaila oil field, which, according to *The Guardian*, took a "stranglehold" on Iraq's economy due to its favorable conditions for BP (Macalister, 2011).

Another example is the legacy of oil exploitation in Nigeria. In 1956, when Nigeria was still under British rule, the petroleum companies Shell and BP got concessions in the Niger delta. Since then the oil has been in the hands of the companies and the oil extraction has led to enormous environmental destruction (UNEP, 2011).

Similarly, much of current exploitation of raw materials like oil, gold, silver, copper, tin, and rubber by multinational companies in developing countries was initiated during the colonial period (Barrat-Brown, 1963: 234–238; Who Controls Africa's Minerals? 1997; Minerals and Mining in Africa, 2005).

The international resource privilege represents an enduring structure of power and property relations that was established during colonial times. Thus, we live in the shadow of colonialism. Although there are new players on the global arena, for example China as a growing world economic power, the main features of the present global injustices and power structures are inherited from colonialism.

A global basic structure

According to John Rawls in *A Theory of Justice*, the basic structure of society (i.e., society's social and economic institutions) is the "subject of justice" (Rawls, 1971: 3). As has been pointed out in some contributions to the ethical discussion on global justice, the emerging global basic structure requires principles of justice as much as the basic structures of nations. For example, in his review of Rawls's book *The Law of Peoples* (Rawls, 1999), Allen Buchanan argues that there is a global basic structure which is the subject of global justice. Buchanan writes:

> There is a global basic structure. Its existence and major features are documented in a vast and growing interdisciplinary literature that goes under various headings: globalization, structural dependency, and theory of underdevelopment. Among the elements of the global basic structure are the following: regional and international economic agreements (including General Agreement on Tariffs and Trade, North American Free Trade Agreement, and various European Union treaties), international financial regimes (including the International Monetary Fund, the World Bank, and various treaties governing currency exchange mechanisms), an increasingly global system of private property rights, including intellectual property rights that are of growing importance as technology spreads across the globe, and a set of international and regional legal institutions and agencies that play an important role in determining the character of all of the preceding elements of the global basic structure. (Buchanan, 2000: 705–706)

Kok-Chor Tan agrees with Buchanan, and claims that "the global basic structure" is crucial for any theory of justice with an institutional focus. A theory of global justice needs "principles to regulate these pervasive inequalities in the global basic structure," Tan writes (Tan, 2004: 28).

Developing a right-based approach to global justice, Simon Caney argues for a reform of the UN Security Council, the World Bank, and the International Monetary Fund in order for them to be more democratically accountable (Caney, 2005a: 161–162).

According to Buchanan, Tan, and Caney, the global basic structure, that is, organizations and institutions that distribute primary goods, including power, on a global level, should be included in the discussion of global justice. However, when we look closely at the structure of these global organizations, we see that they also in various ways mirror the global power structure installed through colonialism.

The first and in a way most obvious example is the United Nations. The United Nations was created after World War II, and in the post-war era decolonization became one of its aims. In 1960 the General Assembly adopted the Declaration on the Granting of Independence to Colonial Countries and Peoples.

The five permanent members of the Security Council, which ultimately is the most powerful UN organ, are China, France, Great Britain, Russia, and the United States. The composition mirrors the outcome of WWII, the rivalry between the Soviet Bloc and the West, and colonialism. Among the permanent members are the victors of WWII and the two most powerful former colonial empires. There are good reasons to question why France and Great Britain, but not the former colonies India, with a population 20 times larger, or Indonesia, with a population five times larger, are permanent members of the Security Council.

The International Monetary Fund (IMF) was conceived in 1944 and has today 188 member states. The mandate of the IMF is to promote worldwide financial cooperation, assist member countries in financial difficulties, and promote economic growth and financial stability. Voting power in the IMF is proportional to invested capital. As a consequence, the United States has 16% of the votes and, together with Germany, France, and Great Britain, 30%. The ca. 40 African member states south of the Sahara, all but one former colonies, have together less than 5% of the voting power (IMF, 2014).

The World Bank was, like the IMF, founded in 1944. The aim of the World Bank is to assist poor countries with development projects and financial loans. As in the IMF, the voting power in the World Bank is proportionate to payments to the Bank, and thus voting power disparities are similar to those of the IMF (World Bank, 2014).

The World Trade Organization (WTO) was founded in 1995 following negotiation in GATT and the Uruguay Round. It is a forum for nations to negotiate trade agreements, to settle trade disputes, and to open markets for trade. The WTO today has 159 member states and each member has one vote in the highest decision-making body, which is the ministerial conference (WTO, 2014). Even though the WTO member states formally have equal representation, many poor member states are in practice understaffed and have as a consequence less bargaining power than the richer members. As Mathias Risse states, the "WTO procedures favor the powerful" (Risse, 2012: 352).

So we can conclude that the set-up of many global institutions still mirrors the colonial power structure, which was, with some exceptions, formally abandoned in the 1950s and 1960s. This fact is visible not only in the formal decision-making structures of the institutions but also in their actual policy-making. As former World Bank Chief economist Joseph Stiglitz remarked, the IMF is "…dominated not just by the wealthiest industrial countries but by commercial and financial interests in these countries...", and the IMF and WTO are represented by the business communities in the rich and the poor countries. Who then speaks for the poor? According to Stiglitz, those who are mostly affected by the policies of the global organizations are "voiceless," and he continues: "All too often, the [International Monetary] Fund's approach to developing countries has had the feel of [that of] a colonial ruler" (Stiglitz, 2002: 18–22, 40).

A global Society of Peoples

In his above-mentioned contribution to the discussion on international justice, John Rawls constructs what he calls a Law of Peoples: "a particular political conception of right and justice that applies to the principles and norms of international law and practice" (Rawls, 1999: 3). Rawls's aim is not to formulate an international *law*, but rather principles of rights, justice, and the common good for the global order. The Law of Peoples provides the moral basis for a Society of Peoples.

Rawls's book on international justice has had a great influence on the discussion on global justice, but many contributors to the discussion are critical of Rawls's ideas (Buchanan, 2000; Pogge, 2002; Tan, 2004; Caney, 2005a; Brock, 2009). Here I will take up two things that Rawls in my view neglects. First, he does not consider that there is a history of dependency and exploitation behind poverty and underdevelopment (which he captures in the concept "burdened peoples"), and second, he fails to include a principle of rectification among his principles of a Law of Peoples.

In *A Theory of Justice* (1971) Rawls sketches a contract situation, "the original position," where people in a nation under a "veil of ignorance," that is, without knowing their position in a society, chose principles of justice. Rawls's aim in *The Law of Peoples* is to construct a moral foundation for a Society of Peoples. His ideal theory sketches a blueprint for harmonious and peaceful international relations. Analogous to the original position within a domestic, liberal society, Rawls constructs a second original position where representatives of liberal peoples and what he calls "decent societies" agree on the basic principles for the Society of Peoples. The great evils of the Holocaust and religious wars in European history notwithstanding, this ideal is possible to realize; it is a "realistic utopia," according to Rawls. He writes: "[W]e must support and strengthen our hope by developing a reasonable and workable conception of political rights and justice applying to the relations between peoples" (Rawls, 1999: 22).

According to Rawls's device of a hypothetical contract, representatives of peoples decide on what principles that should govern a Society of Peoples. Under the veil of ignorance, they do not know which peoples they represent but they choose principles that are "related to the fundamental interests of citizens as reasonable and rational" (Ibid.: 31). Among the principles included in *The Law of Peoples* are the principles that peoples "are to observe treaties," "are to observe a duty of non-intervention," "have the right of self-defense," and "are to honor human rights" (Ibid.: 37). When these principles are respected, Rawls assumes that we have achieved a Society of Peoples. The law implying "equality and due respect for all peoples" will ground a stable peace and it is a "stability for the right reasons," implying that all contracting parties have reasons to comply. Peace and harmony will result.

History is almost absent from Rawls's theory. In response to the critique that he takes established, but historically arbitrary, borders between nations for granted, Rawls merely states that there "*must* be borders of some kind" (Ibid.: 39). He also argues that the possible injustices following from arbitrary borders should be corrected by a Duty of Assistance.

Rawls makes reference to history when he discusses why some societies are not living up to the standards of liberal or decent societies. He writes that what he calls "burdened societies" are not well ordered due to "historical, social and economic circumstances" (Ibid.: 90). However, the historical circumstances Rawls has in mind are not previous dependencies on colonial powers or something of that kind, but instead domestic traditions and political cultures that have been obstacles to development (Ibid.: 108). Rawls's "internalism," that is, his view that present poverty and underdevelopment is largely dependent on internal factors, is indeed questionable. Rawls's view presupposes that global injustices have nothing to do with the historical legacy of colonialism and imperialism. Given that present global relations are a legacy of the colonial world system, Rawls's assumption is unhistorical and groundless.

Rawls admits that his list of principles for a Law of Peoples might be incomplete, and I argue for one additional principle that is actually coherent with Rawls's desiderata. Rawls's principles are for good reasons forward-looking. However, a Law of Peoples must also be historically sensitive. Imagine that a period of repressive colonialism or any other kind of unjust dominance has come to an end. It is perhaps in this situation that it is most challenging for a formerly oppressed people to become full-fledged members of the same Society of Peoples as its former oppressor. Although membership according to Rawls is limited to liberal and decent peoples and "out-law" states are excluded, one cannot rule out the possibility that a people that recently oppressed another people is, after a political turn, eligible for membership of the Society of Peoples. Nonetheless, the history is perhaps not forgotten and harmonious relations and stability require that the former oppressor offers rectification to the victimized people. In the original position, under a veil of ignorance, the representatives of the participating peoples do not know if their people is one that was recently oppressed and hence, it is reasonable for them to include a principle that says something like "Peoples are to rectify for injustices inflicted on other peoples." Such a principle is of course superfluous for peoples with a peaceful history but would play an important role for peoples that have a history characterized by exploitation, domination, and war.

Similarly, David Miller argues for an option to build historical redress into a Law of Peoples by supplementing the principle of a Duty of Assistance with "obligations on peoples whose ancestors exploited or oppressed their vulnerable contemporaries" (Miller, 2006: 201). The difference between Miller's and my view is that I propose an additional principle, while Miller wants to include a duty of rectification in the Duty of Assistance. Miller's principle would limit rectification to compensation, while a separate principle of rectification would include other possible rectificatory duties, like duties of recognition and apology (see Chapter 9).

It is a flaw of Rawls's theory of international relations that it does not take historical injustices into account. With an additional principle of the kind I have proposed, the Law of Peoples would be more historically sensitive.

Conclusion

In this chapter I have argued that the legacy of colonialism is of relevance to several global justice issues. I have not directly argued that present global poverty and global inequality are caused by colonialism but instead drawn attention to the fact that the poorest nations today were once colonies. Later in this book I will assess whether this is a coincidence or not.

I have also showed that the historical legacy of colonialism forms the background to many recent conflicts between nations and ethnic groups that generate refugee problems. Borders were often drawn arbitrarily and have since then been reasons for conflicts and triggered migration flows.

Reports on "land-grabbing" and other forms of resource acquisition in developing countries have revealed that there often is a collaboration between multinational corporations and corrupt domestic political leaders behind the exploitation of natural resources. Furthermore, the present global basic structure mirrors the historical colonial power structure. An additional player is the United States, a former colony but today the most powerful actor on the side of the former colonial powers. Former colonies have a weak representation in all the global institutions that exercise a vast influence on their destiny.

One of the most influential, but also most criticized, philosophical books on international relations and global justice is Rawls's *The Law of Peoples*. I have argued that in neglecting the historical background of present-day international relations Rawls omits an important premise from his Law of Peoples. All in all, there are good reasons to complement the ethical analyses of global relations with a historical perspective. Therefore, I proposed that the principle "Peoples are to rectify for injustices they have inflicted on other peoples" should be included in a Law of Peoples.

So far I have argued that colonialism in some respects shaped the present global order and that the discussion on global justice must take this historical legacy seriously. But what happened during this historical period and what were the consequences for the colonized nations? In the next chapter I will give an overview of the history of colonialism.

3
Colonialism

A discussion on rectification after colonialism must be based on an account of what happened during this period of history and of its long-term effects. This chapter gives a general introduction to colonialism and imperialism: How European hegemony was established, "the Scramble for Africa," when Africa was divided between European colonial powers at the Berlin West Africa Conference 1884–1885, the colonization of Asia, and the United States' dominance over Latin America from the middle of 19th century onwards. This general overview is based on historical accounts of colonialism. Obviously, history is not an exact science and I run the risk of uncritically accepting controversial claims. I have tried to mitigate this risk by choosing authors with different outlooks, like for example, neoconservative British historian Niall Ferguson and Adu Boahen, writing colonial history from an African perspective.[1]

The next chapter sketches five different historical cases that have generated demands for rectification: The British conquest of Uganda, the Belgian king Leopold II's personal ownership of Congo, the German genocide of the Herero people in South West Africa, the British detention camps in Kenya during the struggle against the Mau Mau movement, and the colonization of India. These cases illustrate different aspects of colonial rule that have given rise to demands for rectification.

In Chapter 5, I discuss the legacy of colonialism. My primary question is: How were the present poor nations and former colonies affected by the fact that they were dominated by foreign powers for hundreds of years? I further sketch the economic implications of colonialism and imperialism and outline the question whether there is a need for rectification.

Neither the term colonialism nor the term imperialism is used in a univocal way in the literature. Both terms refer to historical periods of foreign control and domination, for example the Roman Empire, the Ottoman Empire, and the Soviet Empire. In this book I will use colonialism for the period of European worldwide domination starting at the end of the 15th century and – with some exceptions – ending in the 1970s. Imperialism refers to a period of European and American economic and military dominance and indirect rule of distant territories from around 1870 (for further definitions, see Porter, 1994; Kohn, 2014).

Colonialism – the first centuries

European colonialism goes back to the 15th century, when Portuguese, Spanish, and Italian explorers crossed the oceans. They were driven by a curiosity to discover the world, by eagerness to find new trade routes, and by a duty to spread the Gospel. The journeys were made possible by new sailing techniques and new insights into navigation with the help of the compass. The primary challenge was to find a sea route from Europe to India. Asia, and in particular India, had for a long time provided Europe with highly esteemed products like cotton, porcelain, and spices, but the transport of these goods was dangerous and slow.

At the beginning of the colonial era, the royal families of Portugal and Spain competed in exploring the world. In 1484 the Genovese Christopher Columbus appealed to King John of Portugal to finance an expedition with the aim of finding a new trade route to Japan. The king rejected the offer and Columbus turned instead to the rulers of Castile and Aragon, who responded favorably to Columbus's request. In 1492 Columbus's expedition reached a new continent. It was not India, as was believed by the crew, but a continent so-far unknown to Europeans.

The Portuguese were also involved in the exploration of new continents. In 1483 Diego Cam reached Congo, in 1488 Bartolomeo Diaz rounded the Cape of Good Hope, and in 1498 Vasco da Gama reached the Indian coast. In 1502 he returned to India with an armed convoy and started a war against Arab merchants. Towns were burned, merchants and soldiers massacred, and prisoners tortured. This was, as historian R. R. Palmer writes, "unfortunately India's first encounter with the West" (Palmer, 1966: 82, my transl.). The Portuguese established trading posts in Goa, Aden, Ormuz, and Malacca and a trading empire was born. In their wake came Jesuit missionaries.

Another Portuguese, Ferdinand Magellan, explored new seaways on the other side of the globe. In 1519 he led the first expedition from the

Atlantic Ocean into the Pacific Ocean and he was then the first to cross the Pacific.

The race between Portugal and Spain threatened to lead to conflicts over territories and control of trade routes. To prevent war between the two competitors, Pope Alexander I took the initiative and decided that the Spanish emperors should gain control over the new territories. This was, of course, not acceptable to King James II of Portugal. A compromise was achieved and in the Treaty of Tordesillas in 1494 Spain and Portugal agreed to divide the world between them. Portugal got control over Africa and Asia and the eastern part of America, while Spain got control over the rest of America.

After the discovery of new continents came exploitation. While the Portuguese concentrated on trade, the Spaniards explored the newly discovered territories. Conquistadors, that is, groups of men with different social backgrounds – merchants, artisans, freed slaves, and so on – went into the interior of America to find gold and silver. The aim was not only wealth but also conquest. In the first decades of the 16th century the Spanish Marquis Hernan Cortéz conquered the wealthy Aztec Empire. In 1521 the capital Tenochtitlan was defeated and Cortéz established a new Spanish city called *Ciudad de México*, Mexico City.

Shortly after Cortés, Francisco Pizarro started his voyages southward to explore the interior of South America. The Spanish king Charles I funded Pizzaro's expedition. Pizarro and his men also confronted established empires. The Inca Empire with its capital Cuzco was the most advanced of the Indian empires. In 1533 the Indian empires were defeated and the rich natural resources of the area came under the control of the invaders. Of particular importance was the silver mine in Potosí in present-day Bolivia, which was opened in 1545.

Large reserves of manpower were needed for the exploitation of mines and plantations. The institution of *encomienda* was introduced by the colonizers. It implied that Spanish owners of mines and plantations should protect the Indians and instruct them in Christianity and in return they could demand labor from the natives. It was commonplace for Indians to be used as forced labor and slave labor. However, they were unaccustomed to this kind of work and many died. To fill the need for labor, slaves were imported from Africa. From the beginning of the century to 1560 as many as 100,000 African slaves were shipped to America.

The history of the colonization of America illustrates that exploration and trade were not sufficient for the Europeans. Their aims were power, control, and exploitation of human and natural resources. Often oppressive and brutal Indian empires were substituted by even more brutal European colonial rule (Ferro, 1997; Burns, 1982).

In the Americas, colonialism had devastating consequences for the native populations. Due to diseases, starvation, violence, and inhuman working conditions a "demographic catastrophe" followed in the footsteps of colonialism. There are somewhat different estimations of the numbers of Indians at the time of the conquest (Bethell, 1984; Mörner, 1969). In any case, a large proportion of the native population died in a very short time. It is estimated that the number of Indians in Mexico decreased from 25 million in 1519 to 1.9 million in 1580 (Wachtell, 1984). In the territory of the modern United States there were around 2 million Indians in 1500. In 1820 only 320,000 remained (Ferguson, 2004: 65f.). Similarly, during the 17th and 18th centuries, the native population of the Caribbean, the Kalinagos, was almost wiped out by the British in what Beckles calls the "genocide in the Windwards" (Beckles, 2013: 24–36).

The colonization of Latin America resulted in the death of vast majority of Indians. Historian Nathan Wachtell comments: "Even if it is accepted that these epidemics were the main cause of the demographic decline, it cannot be denied [that] the Spanish conquest was itself a period of murderous oppressions" (Wachtell, 1984: 213).

The Catholic priest Bartolomé de Las Casas was a witness of the terror against the Indians. He describes vividly how the Spanish invaders killed, tortured, burned, and terrorized the natives. When the Spanish took over New Spain (Mexico):

> the heinous outrages and acts of barbarity have been so vile, the violence so intense, the murders so frequent, other acts of despotism so extreme, and the havoc and devastation so widespread throughout the kingdoms of the Mainland that what we have so far set down in this account is as nothing compared to what went on in New Spain, and the scale and nature of the atrocities committed without a break from 1518 right up to this day beggars description.... (de Las Casas, 1992: 42)

De Las Casas, who himself later became Bishop of Chiapas, tried to influence the pope and the Spanish monarchs Ferdinand and his successor Charles to intervene in defense of the natives, but without success.

As a consequence of colonization, Latin American economies were adjusted to the needs of the colonial powers. The economic history of Brazil since the 16th century is a history of dependence. Gold was not found in Brazil until around 1700. As an alternative to mining, the Portuguese started large-scale plantations, *haciendas*, in the 16th century to grow sugar and other crops. As the Indians could not adjust to the plantation work, slaves from Portuguese colonies in West Africa were imported to Brazil. The work was hard and the slaves had an average useful life of seven years; then they were worn out (Frank, 1967).

In the 19th century, sugar plantations were replaced by cotton and coffee, now primarily in the hands of British landowners. However, neither product gave lasting economic stability to the region. When the markets declined, so did the northeastern part of Brazil. Economic historian Celso Furtado writes:

> The formation of the North-eastern population and its precarious subsistence economy – basic elements of the Brazilian economic problems in later epochs – are thus linked to this slow process of decadence of the large sugar enterprise.... (Furtado, 1959: 80)

This economic history of dependence created one of the most poverty-stricken regions of the world (Frank, 1967).

The exploration of North America was mainly pushed by the British (Henry Cabot) and the French (Jacques Cartier). North America was not as rich in metals as South America. Instead, the main purpose of exploration in the 16th century was to find a link to an oceanic Northwest Passage for trade with Asia.

The discovery of the so-called New World also gave an impetus to trade between Europe and America. Horses, cattle, and sheep were exported from Europe; tobacco, potatoes, maize, sugar, cotton, gold, and silver were transported the other way. Soon, the so-called triangular trade, involving Europe, Africa, and America, was developed, including the trading of slaves from Africa to America. British exports to Africa in exchange for slaves, who were sent to America, grew tenfold between 1713 and 1792 and imports to Great Britain from western India amounted to one fourth of Britain's total imports.

Hilary Beckles argues that a considerable part of the Industrial Revolution in Britain and the phenomenal British economic growth in the 18th century was based on the slave trade and the slave economy, and not least on the Caribbean sugar economy, which was controlled by the British (Beckles, 2013). However, the economy based on slavery was coming to an end and more and more people in Europe, and in Great Britain in particular, were opposed to the slave trade. In 1807 it was prohibited by Britain, and other European nations committed themselves to the same position in 1815 (Chamberlain, 2010).

It is a matter of contention how many slaves had been shipped from Africa to America since the slave trade started in the 16th century. Paul Lovejoy estimates the number of slaves that reached America at around 12 million. However, many died after being captured and on the boats to America (Lovejoy, 2000). (See Chapter 7 for a discussion of the long-term impact of the slave trade.)

The Treaty of Tordesillas (1494) between Portugal and Spain was for obvious reasons not accepted by other European nations. When the Protestant nations Netherlands and Great Britain acquired the economic and social capabilities to engage in exploration and trade, they immediately did so. Both the Dutch East India Company and the British East India Company were founded at the beginning of the 17th century. They were so-called chartered companies, that is, associations formed by shareholders with the purpose of trading, exploration, and colonization.

To be able to exert power behind their trading demands, the companies also had both naval and military force. For example, in order to control India the British East India Company had 100,000 men under arms. These men were used when the Company conquered Indian states. "What had started as an informal security force to protect the company's trade had now become the company's *raison d'être*: fighting new battles, conquering new territory, to pay for the previous battles," writes Niall Ferguson (2004: 44). Other European nations also wished to benefit from trade, which led to the formation of similar companies in Denmark, Sweden, and Scotland. As a consequence of the new companies, trade between Europe and Asia grew fast during the 17th century.

The British East India Company practiced "double government" with many Indian rulers. The agreements stipulated that the native rulers retained their positions and received an annual income from the Company, while the Company administered government and collected revenues. A mutually beneficial system developed, lasting well into the 19th century. The traditional Indian power structure was preserved. Local customs, including slavery, and religions were respected by the British. The power of local landowners over tenants and landless laborers endured, while the Company regained monopoly over very profitable trading (Stein, 2010).

Imperialism

Around 1870 European colonialism changed its character. At that time one-tenth of Africa was under European control. Forty-four years later – in 1914 – that figure had risen to nine-tenths. European nations had total control of Africa. This new version of colonialism is often labeled imperialism (Porter, 1994: 2).

European involvement in the colonies grew. Europeans invested in mining, plantations, ports, and railroads and they sought to protect these investments. Thus the colonies were more controlled by the colonial powers' military forces than before, although the demand for soldiers from Europe was low and most soldiers were natives. For example, the British needed only three administrators to control the 340,000 inhabitants of the Lango District in Uganda (Thompson, 2003).

Other motives for the European expansion were a need for markets for the increasing number of European products resulting from industrialization, lower production costs in the colonies, and missionary efforts by the European Churches. The British Prime minister, the Marques of Salisbury, stated the motives for British colonial policy in 1897 in the following words: "[T]he objects we have in our view are strictly business objects. We wish to extend the commerce, the trade, the industry and the civilization of mankind" (cited in Kwarteng, 2011: 278). The aim was shared by the other European powers – and by the upcoming imperial power, the former colony United States of America – which resulted in increased international tensions.

Trade between Europe and Africa and Asia was better facilitated when the Suez Canal linking Europe to Asia was completed in 1869. It had tremendous strategic and commercial importance and was protected by all means, including military. As a consequence, after anti-European demonstrations in Egypt, Suez was occupied by British troops in 1882.

Africa

Although Africa was already integrated in world trade and provided America with slave labor from the 16th to the 19th century, the interior of the continent was, in contrast to America, yet to be explored. In fact, European nations showed little interest in inland Africa until the 1870s (Chamberlain, 2010).

European exploration of the African continent started in the middle of the 19th century. The most famous were David Livingstone's expeditions to southeast Africa. Livingstone's aims were peaceful and humanitarian. He wanted to spread Christianity and commerce, or as he himself declared: "I go back to Africa to try to make an open path for commerce and Christianity; do you carry out the work which I have begun" (quoted in Ferguson, 2004: 155). In contrast, his successor, the reporter Henry

M. Stanley, initiated, with the support of the Belgian King Leopold II, the often violent exploitation of the inner parts of Africa, in particular Congo (see Chapter 4). In parallel with Stanley's expeditions, the French explorer Savorgnan de Brazza concluded a number of treaties with African chiefs on behalf of the French government (Ferro, 1997).

Was then Africa on the eve of imperialism a virgin, sleeping continent without culture and political life? No, argues the African historian A. Adu Boahen. On the contrary, different social and commercial processes had begun. He writes:

> [O]n the very eve of the colonial conquest and occupation, Africa was far from being primitive, static and asleep or in a Hobbesian state of nature. On all fronts – economic, political, social, and even intellectual – Africa was in a mood of change and revolution.... (Boahen, 2011: 23)

How then should the ambitions of different European colonial powers be balanced? And how should open conflicts between the colonial powers be avoided? There was an obvious risk of military confrontation. Many European nations had an interest in Africa and in order to create international regulations for the African situation, the German chancellor Bismarck called for a conference in Berlin in 1884. The specific topic in Berlin was how to regulate the European nations' interests in Congo and Niger. The Congo was administered by King Leopold II of Belgium and Niger by the British. However, Germany, France, and Portugal were also interested in increasing their influence over West Africa.

One important result of the Berlin West Africa Conference was the doctrine of "effective occupation." So far, European influence had been mainly built on trading rights. For example, the British Royal Niger Company had signed treaties with local African chiefs, giving them trading rights along the Niger River. But the doctrine of effective occupation stated that a European nation claiming territory in Africa must show an "effective" presence on the ground. The intention was to limit the claims of "historical rights" to territory, for example those asserted by Portugal. In effect the consequence of the doctrine of "effective presence" was that European states intervened in Africa in order to realize "effective occupation" (Chamberlain, 2010: 54). This led the British, for example, to transform its trading agreements with Niger into the establishment of a British protectorate in the region. Germany occupied southwest Africa and Cameroon in order to establish its territorial claims, while France waged wars in west Africa "and repression was conducted with harsh and often indiscriminate brutality" (Davidson, 1991: 288). As a consequence of imperial occupation, the peoples and nations of Africa – the Zulus, the Matabele, the Mahonas, the kingdom of Niger, the Islamic principalities of Kano, the Dinkas, the Msai, the Sudanese Muslims, Benin, and Bechuana – were forced to surrender to the Europeans (Ferguson, 2004: 239).

In parallel with the enforcement of political control over Africa, the African colonies became part of an international economic network controlled by the European powers and, as a consequence, "the trading operation was now carried on within a single political economy rather than between two political economies" (Wallerstein, 1970: 405). In 1889 the European nations agreed to end the slave trade in Africa. However, due to the need for African labor in the construction of railways and roads, in the mines, and on plantations, forced labor and different kinds of taxes aimed at forcing the Africans to work for Europeans were introduced. Large parts of the male population had to move to labor camps to earn their money. As a consequence, the traditional social structure broke down without being replaced by any alternative. Even where slavery was abolished, human exploitation continued in different forms (Palmer, 1966, 2: 161).

In spite of the agreements made at the Berlin West Africa Conference, the competition between European nations for colonies continued. Portugal took control of Angola and Mozambique, Germany, which had entered the race for colonies rather late, control of Cameroon, Togo, and South West Africa (see Chapter 4), and France of the major part of West Africa, from Algeria to the coast of Guinea. However, the supreme colonial power, Britain, could not accept French expansionism and as part of its effort to keep a belt of nations from the Cape to Cairo, the British explorer, businessman and politician Cecil Rhodes went northward from the Cape of Good Hope. French troops were confronted by British forces in Fashoda in present-day Sudan in 1898 and were forced to withdraw.

How was European imperialism viewed by the natives? According to Boahen, African attitudes towards imperialism were mixed. The majority of native Christians welcomed the Europeans and in some cases African kings even took initiatives and invited Europeans to take over. In many cases, however, the Europeans took advantage of the innocence of the natives. Negotiations between Europeans and Africans led to the exchange of land for liquor and other goods. Lord Lugard, who was one of the most influential British administrators at the time, wrote after a treaty between the British East African Company and King Kabaka

Mwanga of Buganda was concluded in 1892: "No man if he understood would sign it" (Boahen, 2011: 38).

Foreign occupation also led to resistance, for example in South Africa, South West Africa, Sudan, and Nigeria. But the only successful case of resistance was Ethiopia's victory over Italy in 1893. As a consequence, Ethiopia remained independent and became a symbol of African independence vis-à-vis Europe (Ibid.: 50ff.).

In order to establish and maintain their power in southern Africa the British had to suppress both native tribes and the Boers. In the battle against Chief Lobengula of Matabele land in 1893 half of the Matabele warriors, 1,500 men, were wiped out by Cecil Rhodes's troops, not least thanks to the new Maxim gun, which had the capacity to fire 500 rounds a minute (Ferguson, 2004: 224).

The British had also to subjugate the Boers. The Boers were white farmers who had emigrated from the Netherlands in the 18th century. A ruthless war broke out 1899. Boer settlements were erased and 30,000 men, women, and children were herded into concentration camps. It took three years for the British troops to defeat the Boers (Ferguson, 2004).

The Maxim gun was also decisive when the British enforced their control of northeastern Africa. The gun was used when the British suppressed the Mahdi in the battle of Omdurban in Sudan in 1898. Eleven thousand Sudanese were killed, but only 22 British soldiers died. In spite of these figures, suggesting a slaughter – 500 Sudanese killed for each British soldier – the British newspapers saw it as a struggle between "barbarism" (the Sudanese) and "civilization," represented by the British (Kwarteng, 2011: 228–229).

By the beginning of the 20th century, almost all of Africa and Asia had been divided into colonies, protectorates, and spheres of interest by the colonial powers. As the power of the European nations increased, the non-European empires, in particular the Ottoman Empire and China, were disintegrating. Therefore, European power was rarely disputed and when that occasionally happened, resistance was brutally crushed. However, conflicts between European nations over influence in Africa persisted and were one of the factors behind the outbreak of World War I in 1914.

Latin America

In the Western hemisphere the former colony USA became the most powerful player by the end of the 19th century. Backed by the Monroe

Doctrine (1823), proclaiming that European interference in North and South America would be considered an act of aggression, the United States forced Napoleon III of France, who aspired to control Mexico, to withdraw and the British to retire in a conflict over Venezuela. The United States also went to war against Spain in support of a liberation movement in Cuba in 1894. As a result, Spain had to depart from their colony, and the United States took charge of Cuba. Subsequently, the United States took control of political development in Latin America and this control was maintained through numerous military interventions in the following decades. During a crisis in Santo Domingo in 1904, President Theodore Roosevelt declared that the United States could intervene in Latin America whenever they deemed it necessary (Morray, 1968: 100). To protect their political and economic interests in Latin America, the United States intervened between 1898 and 1934 in Cuba, Mexico, Guatemala, Honduras, Nicaragua, Panama, Colombia, Haiti, and the Dominican Republic, and the marines remained in those nations for shorter or longer periods (Burns, 1982). In practice, the United States established a control over Latin America that mirrored the European control of Africa.

Asia

At the beginning of the 19th century, great parts of Asia were dominated by Great Britain and the Netherlands. Both India and Indonesia were easily administered and the interests of the colonial powers were served in different ways. Europe imported various natural resources, such as cotton, tea, palm oil, and wheat, from the Asian colonies, and the colonies provided for a growing market of industrial products from Europe. Textile production in India was hampered by the cheaper imports from Britain and British agencies took over banking and insurance (Stein, 2010; see also Chapter 4). In Indonesia, the Dutch used forced labor, so-called coolies, to ensure a steady production of coffee and cotton.

European rule in Asia was not unchallenged. During the 19th century a number of insurrections, the most serious being the Indian Sepoy insurrection against British rule in 1857, were suppressed. Following the suppression of the Sepoy uprising, the British crown took over more responsibility from the East India Company; this "visibly confirmed the fact, which had remained symbolically obscure, that India was actually ruled from Britain," Burton Stein writes (2010: 227).

Dissatisfaction with colonial rule grew among the educated native elites, and nationalistic movements were established at the end of the century. The tensions between the native Indian elite and the British colonizers focused in the 1880s around the dispute over whether Indian lawyers should be allowed to try British colonizers in court. The so-called "White Mutiny," when the British colonizers violently protested against giving the Indian lawyers this power and the authorities gave in to the protesters, intensified the conflict. This dispute convinced many educated Indians that the British were not sincere in their expressed efforts to equalize Englishmen and Indians (Ferguson, 2004: 200–204). In spite of these conflicts, the British managed to create an Indian elite. For example, in the 1870s, 6,000 Indian students were in higher education and under British rule the number of Indians in primary and secondary education grew steadily, from 0.6% in 167 to almost 4% in 1941 (Ibid.: 191).

The Manchu or Qing dynasty ruled China in the 19th century. It was a foreign rule that lacked legitimacy and stability. This helped Britain, France, the United States, and later Japan in their efforts to strengthen their influence on China.

British traders sold opium to China. This import resulted in both drug-related social problems and financial deficit. When the Chinese government tried to stop the import of opium, China was attacked by British gunships. Britain aimed to maintain the profitable trade and to open China for trade. Through the first Opium War 1839–1842, and a second attack by British and French troops in 1857, China was forced to surrender and to open its markets to European and American traders (Fairbank, 1992). The Europeans also exploited a disintegrating China by occupying countries and regions at its margin. For example, Britain annexed Hong Kong in 1842 and Burma in 1886 and France annexed parts of Indo-China around the same time.

British and French troops attacked the heart of China when they destroyed the emperor's palaces in Beijing. The Old Summer Palace had been built in the European style in 1747–1759. It was situated in a huge garden covering 350 million square meters and comprised of numerous palaces. In 1860 the palace was destroyed by British and French troops. The same happened to the New Summer Palace.

When walking around the site today, in front of each and every palace one reads the information: "The palace was burnt down by British troops in 1860." The ruins of the Old Summer Palace have not been restored. A sign says: "They continue to stand here, reminding people of the national humiliation."

The European nations humiliated China by forcing them to submit to European conditions of trade, to accept foreign control of their borders, to give up parts of their territory, and to accept that foreigners could reside in their country without having to obey Chinese laws.

Decolonization

At the height of its might, in 1909, the British Empire covered around 25% of the earth's surface and controlled the same proportion of the earth's population. It was at the time three times the size of the French Empire and ten times the size of the German Empire. The British Empire was the largest empire the world had ever known (Ferguson, 2004: 240). Altogether, in 1900, 90% of Africa, 56% of Asia, 98% of the South Pacific, and 27% of the Americas were under colonial rule (Macqueen, 2007).

Different colonial powers established different kinds of relations with their colonies. The British followed a pragmatic path, establishing indirect rule and maintaining their power while minimizing anti-colonial resentment. The French followed a policy characterized by assimilation and association, and the Portuguese saw colonialism as a national vocation, aiming to build a single nation with overseas provinces (Ibid.: 74ff.).

After World War I the era of decolonization began. Many colonies became independent around 1960; only the Portuguese colonies Mozambique, Angola, and Guinea-Bissau remained under external control until the middle of 1970s, when Portugal had to give up after years of liberation wars. However, despite the formal independence of the colonies, colonialism continued to map out the global order. As historian Corrie Macqueen summarizes: "The world of the 21st century is inescapably a product of colonialism ... Colonialism and its aftermath have determined the whole character of contemporary international relations" (Ibid.: 156).

After colonialism came post- or neo-colonialism. As historian Marc Ferro shows, the economic links between former colonies and colonial powers remained intact. He writes:

> Such was the first form taken by neo-colonialism, perpetuating the privileged links between Europe and its former colonies. The second form consists of the institutionalization of the connivance between the new leaders of the colonies and the political or financial circles in the colonial countries. (Ferro, 1997: 347)

The ground was laid for what Thomas Pogge calls "the international resource privilege," that is, the alliance between elites in former colonies who control the natural resources and Western institutions and multinational corporations that have acquired the rights to exploit these resources (Pogge, 2002: 113).

Balance sheet

So, on balance was colonialism and imperialism good or bad? Did it provide a net benefit to the colonies or not? These are in a sense pointless questions and simply asking them in this way amounts to an implausible generalization based on speculation. However, the legacy of colonialism is crucial for my argument and I will at least hint at some tentative answers to the question of the positive and negative aspects of colonialism by comparing the views of historians with very different backgrounds. The Ghanaian historian Adu Boahen examines colonial history from an African perspective in his book *African Perspectives on European Colonialism* (2011), while the British historian Niall Ferguson, in his book *Empire. How Britain made the Modern World* (2004), gives an overview of the history of the British Empire. They have in common that they both try to create a balance sheet of colonialism: Adu Boahen of colonialism's effects in Africa and Ferguson of British colonialism.[2]

Boahen argues that Africa before imperialism was going through a process of transformation. Boahen summarizes:

> It should be obvious from the above that on the very eve of the colonial conquest and occupation, Africa was far from being primitive, static, and asleep or in a Hobbesian state of nature. On all fronts – economic, political, social, and even intellectual – Africa was in a mood of change and revolution, accepting new challenges, showing ability at adaption and modification, fighting back against racist doctrines, and above all changing its economy and politics to suit the socioeconomic realities of the day. It is also clear from the writings of the scholars that the African never thought of himself as being in any way inferior to the European.... (Boahen, 2011: 23)

How then was Africa influenced by the period of imperialism? Boahen divides the implications into political, social, and economic. According to Boahen, the period of imperialism constituted a comparatively long period of peace and stability for Africa, although with some exceptions, for example the atrocities in Belgian Congo and the German genocide of Herero at the beginning of the 20th century. Further, Boahen sees the creation of African *states*, including new bureaucracy and juridical systems and a sense of nationalism, as consequences of imperialism. Although this was essentially a positive development according to Boahen, the fact that the borders between the states were arbitrarily drawn and the new states were unequal in size and resources has had lasting negative consequences.

The colonial powers provided Africa with infrastructure (roads, railways, etc.), although the aim of that infrastructure was to serve the needs of colonial exploitation, according to Boahen. Furthermore, with colonialism came education (with the exception of the Portuguese and Belgian colonies) and a common language. The fact that African states lost their sovereignty Boahen sees as a negative consequence of imperialism. This also had detrimental effects for long-term political development in Africa, Boahen argues.

New land was cultivated during the period of imperialism, Boahen shows. However, imperialism delayed the industrial and technological development of Africa and the continent became dependent on a few crops for export. This also meant that production for internal consumption was neglected. African countries became importers of basic foodstuffs.

While the colonial powers controlled the economic and monetary policies, foreign exchange earning was channeled to Europe and the surplus earned was transferred abroad and not used for internal African development.

In Africa, social status was traditionally related to birth. This implied little social mobility. Through colonialism, social mobility became increasingly related to individual merit in contrast to birth.

The colonial powers neglected Africans' need for social services and education, Boahen argues. He mentions the fact that there were 12 modern hospitals for 4,000 Europeans and 52 for 40 million Africans in Nigeria in 1930. As a consequence of the neglect of education, illiteracy remained high. Imperialism also implied a "downgrading of the status of women in Africa," Boahen argues, but without comparing with the status of women in pre-colonial Africa (Ibid.: 107). There was, according to Boahen, hardly any women appointed to upper-level positions in the colonial hierarchy.

Colonialism also had negative effects on African culture and African self-respect. Boahen argues that colonialism implied a disregard of African culture and that African elites developed flamboyant consumer lifestyles; and at the same time Africans in general internalized feelings of inferiority and loss of a sense of human dignity (Boahen, 2011: 94–108).

Boahen summarizes his assessment of the implications of European imperialism for Africa in the following words:

> [M]y charge against colonialism is not that it did not do anything for Africa, but that it did so little and that little so accidentally and indirectly... In short, given the opportunities, the resources and the power and influence of the colonial rulers, they could and should have done far more than they did for Africa. (Ibid.: 108–109)

In a comment on Boahen's balance sheet, in the introduction to the new edition of Boahen's book, historian John Lonsdale argues that later development shows that Boahen underestimated some of the negative aspects of what he deemed to be positive consequences. For example, the drawing of "artificial state boundaries" has made nation-building very difficult, leading to "the absence of the interpersonal trust which, elsewhere, one associates with nationhood, that community of the moral and political imagination" (Lonsdale, 2011: vi). According to Lonsdale, neither did Boahen see the fatal implications of Africa's forced "isolation from the modernizing and industrializing currents that flowed elsewhere in the world" (Ibid.: v) and perhaps even more importantly the "cultural alienation among the educated and a more general sense of African inferiority" (Ibid.).

As Boahen mentions, during the era of imperialism Africa witnessed a great increase in agricultural productivity and as a consequence a rise in population. Most African countries doubled or tripled their population between 1901 and 1961 (Boahen, 2011). Production of export crops like cotton, sisal, cocoa, and palm oil increased enormously and food production followed population growth (Duignan and Gann, 1975).

Niall Ferguson concludes his book *Empire. How Britain made the Modern World* with an account of the pros and cons of the British Empire. Ferguson's general view is that the British Empire contributed to the development of the colonies in various ways. First, according to Ferguson, the present worldwide expansion of liberal capitalism, that is, the present global economy, would be unthinkable without the British Empire. Second, the global expansion of parliamentary democracy is an achievement of the British Empire, according to him. He cites political scientist Seymour Lipset, who argues that former British colonies had a better chance of being democratic than former colonies ruled by other empires (Ferguson, 2004: 370–371).

Other valuable phenomena with roots in the British Empire are, according to Ferguson, the worldwide prevalence of the English language, modern communications, and the rule of law. He also argues that the empire, like the Roman Empire 2,000 years earlier, maintained global peace in a unique way. Finally, British overseas investments encouraged foreign investors to put their money into developing countries (Ibid.: 366–371).

When assessing Ferguson's arguments it is important to bear in mind that he refers to the legacy of the *British* Empire. It is possible that these beneficial consequences did not occur in other colonial empires. For example, British rule of Uganda was more peaceful than, for example, German rule of South West Africa or Belgian rule in Congo, and British rule of Malaysia stood in positive contrast to the ruthless Japanese occupation of Malacca during World War II. On the other hand, Ferguson seems to disregard some less beneficial implications of British rule. In a number of colonies, internal strife and domestic tyranny followed after the British left. Uganda is one telling example, but Kenya and Zimbabwe also fall into the same category. Thus, it seems that the British did not succeed in establishing enduringly peaceful and harmonious political institutions.

Second, most former colonies faced enduring poverty after their liberation. This is true of most British colonies in Africa, except the white-ruled South Africa, as well as of India, Pakistan, and Burma in Asia. Hence, it seems that the British failed to establish cultural, social, and economic institutions that could ensure lasting social and economic development. Instead, in India the British sustained traditional feudal systems. As Kwarteng notes:

> The family of that rich man ruled Kashmir for a hundred of years because it was convenient for the British that the family should do so. It is ironic that revisionist historians have pointed to Indian democracy as the British Empire's greatest legacy. (Kwarteng, 2011: 140)

Ferguson himself discusses the fact that former colonies have remained underdeveloped. He argues that it is a mistake to blame poverty in former colonies on the British Empire. He takes Zambia as an example. It is true, Ferguson argues, that British GDP today, about 50 years after independence, is something like 28 times higher than Zambian GDP. However, when the British left Zambia, British GDP was only seven times higher than Zambian GDP. Hence, the gap has increased substantially after independence. The same is true, Ferguson argues, of other Sub-Saharan former colonies (Ibid.: 368).

However, one must ask *why* the gap between Britain and its African colonies has widened after their independence. Is it fully explained by the corruption and incompetence of African leaders? Or is it at least partially also explained by the fact that the former colonial powers failed to establish sustainable institutions? The colonial infrastructure was adjusted to the colonists' commercial interests and the colonial powers failed to educate the population.

Also, Ferguson's view that the British Empire blessed its colonies with democracy and the rule of law is only partly true. After independence many new states were more often characterized by corrupt and authoritarian leadership than by democracy and the rule of law. Even if Britain aimed at instituting democracy in the colonies, this often failed in practice. In order to be stable, democracy requires popular mobilization from below and a decent social standard.

When historians L. H. Gann and Peter Duignan try to make a balance sheet of British imperialism 1870–1914, they mention on the negative side the use of forced labor, the disruption of traditional life, and other devastating effects of colonial occupation and wars. On the other hand, the British established law and order, assured periods of peace, abolished old-fashioned servitudes, and put an end to the practices of bondage and mutilation. A market economy was introduced but at the expense of traditional crafts (Gann and Duignan, 1978: 342–365). Further, as a general consequence of colonialism they argue that "local despotism," "intellectual narrowness," and "rigid social stratification" were replaced by rule of law and education (Ibid.: 360–382) and they summarize the economic consequences of colonialism in Africa in the following way:

> Taking colonial development as a whole, it is nonsense to say that the imperialists joined in plundering Africa. The dramatic increases in production in most colonies benefitted all concerned, the peasant producers and the workers as well as expatriate interest. (Ibid.: 369)

Historian Basil Davidson draws a somewhat different balance sheet of the consequences of colonialism in Africa. In his assessment of whether colonialism implied gains or losses for Africa, he first states that at the end of the 19th century there was a need for Africa to reconstruct its institutions. Africa could not resist the influence of industrialism. But did colonialism provide a constructive response to modernity, Davidson asks. His answer is negative. Davidson opines that European conquest did not provide a constructive response. On the contrary, the African crisis was unresolved at the time of independence, with devastating results for the new nations (Davidson, 1991: 317).

It is indeed difficult, and perhaps even impossible, to draw up a balance sheet for such a long and disparate historical period as colonialism. As Gann and Duignan write:

> [H]istorical balance sheets are always hard to draw up. They involve their accountants in problems of extreme complexity, of differing standards of comparison, and of making value judgments. (Gann and Duignan, 1967: 382)

After this general overview of the history of colonialism and some different evaluations of this historical period, I will in the next chapter focus more closely on some problematic aspects of colonialism.

4
Five Cases of Colonialism

After the general overview of colonial history in Chapter 3, I will in this chapter introduce and discuss five examples of the practice of colonialism. The examples illustrate different aspects of this period of history: Uganda of a rather peaceful but nevertheless in the long run destructive colonial reign, Congo of a vicious quest for minerals and other raw materials which undermined the future of the subjected peoples, Namibia of a genocide that left enduring traces, Kenya of a war of liberation that was violently suppressed, and finally India of how colonies and pseudo-colonies were integrated in the world market with problematic consequences for the countries' own economic development. After giving a brief account of the five cases I will in the final part of this chapter demonstrate how they represent different problematic aspects of the legacy of colonialism.

Case 1: Uganda

We saw in the previous chapter that Africa was divided between the European nations at the end of the 19th century. After having conquered the kingdom of Buganda to the northwest of Lake Victoria in 1890, British colonizers aimed to also conquer the kingdom of Bunyoro, situated in the northern part of present-day Uganda. However, Kabalega, the king of Bunyoro, did not surrender to the British troops and it was not until 1897 that the British finally captured him. Meanwhile, the war devastated several areas of the kingdom and many natives starved to death.

As a punishment for Bunyoro resistance to colonialism, the British transferred land from Bunyoro to the Buganda kingdom. This led to tensions that have persisted up to this day. In fact, as late as in 2014 the

Ugandan government started a process to return to Bunyoro land that is owned by absentee Ugandan landlords (Daily Monitor, 2014).

Why then did Britain colonize Uganda? There were different reasons for their conquest. Islam was expanding from the north and Uganda was a strategic link in the British struggle to limit Muslim influence in the region. Furthermore, transportation from the Indian Ocean to the source of the Nile was a boost for trade routes between India and Egypt and then further to Europe. Many British residents also thought that Britain had a duty so save Uganda from slavery, and finally, Uganda was a market for British products as well as a possible source of raw materials. Later, Ugandan cotton became a most important export crop (Thompson, 2003).

How did the British rule Uganda? Ultimately, as a colonial power, their rule rested on force. However, as historian Gardner Thompson shows, the rule was lenient and widely accepted by the Ugandans. As evidence, he adduces that the British authorities needed no more than three administrators to rule the 340,000 inhabitants of the Lango District (Ibid.). Thompson notes that until World War II "the British had tried only to *administer*, rather than to *govern* in the sense of fully exploiting the human, financial and material resources of a territory acquired...Coercion had been replaced by consent" (Ibid.: 69).

On the other hand, critics of British rule point at some highly problematic implications of the colonial period. Traditional social structures were dismantled without a sustainable replacement, estates for cotton and tobacco production were created at the expense of traditional farms, and this change in the mode of farming also led to the spread of the deadly tsetse fly (Pulford, 2007: 107).

Uganda became independent in 1962. Since then, the young nation has endured dictatorships, ethnic conflicts, civil wars, and political corruption. During the reigns of Idi Amin and Milton Obote the death toll is estimated to have ranged between 500,000 and 600,000 people (Meredith, 2005: 238).

According to Thompson, at independence Uganda was neither a nation nor a state. The country was characterized by regionalization and "tribalism" and had no national identity or national loyalty. The government was weak, there was no sense of civic duty, and the borders of the new state were disputed (Thompson, 2003: 339). The British left Uganda with a weak economy and the crops that provided export income were vulnerable to price fluctuations on the world market. Uganda is thus an example of the problematic legacy of colonialism that Lonsdale points at: artificial states with a vulnerable economy based on primary production (Lonsdale, 2011).

Is Ugandan history after 1962 a direct result of colonial rule? "All this was, of course, an unintended outcome, quite unforeseen by the British at any time," writes historian Gardner Thompson (Thompson, 2003: 344). Does the former colonial power nevertheless have a responsibility for what happened after independence? Is there a case for rectificatory justice for earlier colonial occupation and later negligence? A similar question can be raised for other colonial regimes. For example, is there a causal link between British colonialism and the Biafra war in the 1960s, between Belgian colonialism and Mobuto's terror in Congo, between British colonial rule and Siad Barre's regime in Somalia, between French rule and Bokasssa's regime in Central Africa, between Portuguese rule and the cleptocracy in Angola, between the Belgian enforcement of the division between Hutu and Tutsi in Rwanda in the 1930s and the later genocide, and so on? That is, can the colonial powers be blamed for the tyrannical regimes, genocides, and corruption that followed independence? I will argue that under the assumption that responsibility can be shared and that colonial rule was one of many factors that led to misrule and terror, the colonial powers are at least partly responsible for what happened after they left their colonies.

Case 2: Congo

Leopold II was king of Belgium from 1865 to 1909. His conquest of Congo was grounded in a combination of personal ambition and greed. He took an interest in Henry Stanley's exploration of Congo in the 1870s and he met Stanley in person in 1878. Under the guise of humanitarian aims and help for travelers in Africa, Leopold supported Stanley in getting access to the inner Congo through the construction of roads and later railways. To get an institutional framework for his exploitation of Congo, Leopold founded the International Association of the Congo and proclaimed the Congo Free State, controlled by him. A unique colonial institution was born: a country controlled not by a foreign nation but by a foreign sovereign as his private domain.

Parallel to his efforts to get access to inner Congo, Leopold instructed Stanley to sign treaties with local kings and chiefs. "The treaties must be as brief as possible, and in a couple of articles must grant us everything," was Leopold's order. Stanley was successful and more than 450 chiefs signed treaties giving Leopold trading monopolies and territory. As Adam Hochschild notes, if by a treaty one means a mutually informed agreement, treaty is not the right word for what was going on in Congo, since many of the chiefs were not aware of the implications of signing a treaty; "The very word *treaty* is a euphemism, for many chiefs had no idea what they were signing" (Hochschild, 1999: 71f.). In any case, the endeavor opened up Congo for exploitation. Leopold's reign over Congo was confirmed at the Berlin West Africa Conference of 1884–1885 and through bilateral agreements with a number of European nations.

The veins of Congo had been opened by Stanley. Ivory was the first attractive prey for the European merchants. Elephants were hunted and their tusks collected. The ivory was then refined and shipped to Europe. Soon rubber became the major resource. From the 1890s, forced labor was used for the production of rubber for the European and American markets. Different methods for collecting rubber were used. Village women were taken as hostages and not released until their men had collected a certain amount of rubber. Sometimes villages were assigned quotas and the people punished if the quotas were not met. If the villages did not submit to the demands of the merchants, the men were shot. As proof that the punishment had taken place, the right hands of the dead men were chopped off and displayed to official representatives of the Congo Free State (Ibid.: 164f.).

Soon, stories about the atrocities committed in Congo reached Europe and America. Missionaries and others reported on the treatment of the natives. They reported on the forced labor at the rubber plantations, on the use of the *chicotte*, a whip made of hippopotamus hide, on flogging, on killing, and on mutilations. Their testimony was of course rejected by Leopold and he even started a counter-campaign. Nevertheless, the news from Congo gave rise to campaigns questioning the reign of Leopold, including that of the famous author Mark Twain (Ibid.: 241–242).

So, what was the result of Leopold's reign over Congo? How did it influence the lives of the natives? When Hochschild tries to estimate the death toll of the period of King Leopold's rule of Congo, he divides the deaths into four categories:

The first category is murder. There were many reports of murdered Africans. For example, in 1896 the *Kölnische Zeitung* reported that 1,308 severed hands had been delivered to a District Commissioner in one day; a missionary reported 6,000 murdered natives during a six-month period; and a Swedish Lieutenant in the Congo State's armed forces reported 527 people killed in four-and-a-half months when the "rubber regime" was imposed in 1894–1895.

The second category is starvation, exhaustion, and exposure. To escape the army's terror, natives fled from their villages into the forests, where many died. And due to the hard work of collecting rubber, the villagers could not produce enough food for themselves, which led to starvation and death.

Third, people died from diseases. The indigenous people were not immune to diseases that came to Africa with the colonizers. These diseases spread in different ways but not least as a consequence of forced migration of labor. A magistrate wrote in 1905: "Disease powerfully ravages an exhausted population" (Ibid.: 231).

Finally, a fourth reason behind the diminishing number of people was a falling birth rate. Roger Casement, an Irishmen who investigated the background to rubber production, reports that due to people's hardships pregnancy rates plunged.

So, all in all, how did the reign of King Leopold II influence the population of Congo? A Belgian government commission estimated in 1919 that the population of the territory had been reduced by half. The same estimate is made by Jan Vansina, historian and anthropologist. According to Vansina, during the reign of Leopold the population dropped by approximately ten million people (Ibid.: 232f.).

In 1908 the Congo Free State came to an end and the Belgian state took over the country from its king, Leopold II. Some of the worst practices of Leopold's time were abolished, although others continued. For example, when the mining of copper, gold, and tin started in Congo in the 1920s, it was still legal for the companies to use the *chicotte* as well as forced labor. Was the brutal exploitation of Congo an exception? No, according to historian Basil Davidson: "The same highly destructive system was applied in French and German equatorial Africa a little later" (Davidson, 1991: 292).

Congo continued to be a profitable colony for Belgium. It possesses some of the world's richest sources of copper, diamonds, and uranium and in 1959 10% of the world's copper, 50% of its cobalt, and 70% of its industrial diamonds were produced in Congo. The colony was totally in the hands of the Belgians. Africans were barred from education – in 1960 the total number of African university graduates was 30 – and from any political influence (Meredith, 2005).

Demonstrations and riots in 1960 led to the independence of Congo the same year. After the election of the nationalist leader Patrice Lumumba as Prime Minister, the country was torn apart. Belgian mineral interests were behind a declaration of independence by the mineral-rich state Katanga and in early 1961 Belgian officers murdered Lumumba. The country's more than 50 years of independence has to this day been characterized by civil wars, foreign economic exploitation, and political corruption (Ibid.).

Colonial regimes have often been quick to forget – or perhaps conceal is a better word – what was going on in the colonies. Belgium is no exception. In 1908 the Belgian state archives, which contained files from the Congo Free State, were destroyed. The Royal Museum of Central Africa in Tervuren in the outskirts of Brussels, which was inaugurated during the Brussels International Exhibition in 1897, contains a huge selection of African artifacts. But a small gallery informing visitors about the forced labor practices during the period was only recently added. As late as 2011, Leopold's mission with the museum was explained on its homepage as follows: "To promote Belgium's work of 'development and civilization' in Congo, and the latter's economic potential, Leopold II hoped to build some form of museum or 'showcase'" (Royal Museum for Central Africa, 2011), and a statue of King Leopold II on his horse still stands in central Brussels.

Case 3: South West Africa

Background

German colonialism started late and Germany was not as expansive as, for example, Britain and France. South West Africa, that is the present nation of Namibia, be came together with Cameroon, Togo and Tanzania German colonies in Africa. It was not until the 1880s that Germany colonized South West Africa – which was declared a German protectorate in 1884.

National chauvinism was the main reason behind German colonialism. Germany's aim was to compete with the other European powers for influence in Africa. There were also economic reasons behind German expansionism. In 1885 the German South West African Company bought the rights to exploit minerals in South West Africa, and from the mid-1890s it received land concessions and German settlers started cattle farming. This led to conflicts with the native population, who did not want their land sold to the Germans (Palmer, 2000).

During the first period of colonization only a small number of Germans moved to South West Africa. Among the first colonizers were Protestant missionaries, who went to "Hereroland," the part of the colony inhabited by the Herero tribe, and particularly active in the missionary efforts were the Rheinish Missionary Society. The Herero were at this time the main tribe inhabiting southwest Africa and when the Germans arrived they numbered around 80,000.

The German influence was partly upheld through agreements with local Herero chiefs, who took advantage of the power that the German support provided in their fight against competing tribes. For example, in 1896 the Herero Chief Samuel Maherero turned to the Germans for support against rival chiefs. Maherero's enemies were defeated and executed by the Germans and their cattle expropriated (Gewald, 1999; Palmer, 2000).

In 1896 the animal disease *Rinderpest* (also called the cattle plague), transmitted from Germany to Africa, hit the Herero communities. It is estimated that as many as two-thirds of the cattle in the territory died from the plague. The plague affected the population greatly and as many as 10,000 people died from starvation as a result. The *Rinderpest* was used by the Germans as a weapon in their efforts to strengthen their influence. Only those villages that surrendered to German rule received vaccines against the plague (Gewald, 1999: 112–121).

War

During the first years of the 20th century there were continuous tensions between German colonizers and the Herero and Nama tribes, who were struggling to keep their independence. German settlers and *Schutztruppen* showed no respect for native rights. As a consequence, rumors of a pending Herero uprising spread among the Germans. According to Gewald, "the origins of the war are to be found in the interpretations of the settlers and missionaries, rather than in those of the Herero" (Ibid.: 142). Some German settlers' farms were plundered and burned, and negotiations that had been going on for some time ended. Fear of a Herero uprising gave the Germans a reason for an attack. Around 14,000 German soldiers under the command of General von Trotha arrived in South West Africa with the aim of routing the enemy.

General Von Trotha had a tough policy towards the Herero. In a letter to the Herero people he said:

> The Herero people must leave their land. If the populace does not do this I will force them with the Groot Rohr [cannon]. Within the German borders every Herero, with or without a gun, with or without cattle, will be shot. I will no longer accept women and children. I will drive them back to their people or I will let them be shot at. (Quoted in Gewald, 1999: 172–173)

A battle took place in Hamakari at the mountain Waterberg. The Herero soldiers were defeated and those who survived the battle were driven into the Kalahari Desert by the German soldiers. There they died from hunger and thirst. Von Schliefen, the Chief of Staff in Berlin, commented: "The arid Omaheke [another name for the Kalahari Desert] was to complete what the German army had begun: the extermination of the Herero nation" (Ibid.: 146).

General von Trotha explained his aims with the following words:

> The exercise of violence with crass terrorism and even with gruesomeness was and is my policy. I destroy the African tribes with streams of blood and streams of money. Only following this cleansing can something new emerge, which will remain. (Ibid.: 174)

And his major, Estroff, remarked: "[W]e could have saved many of them and their rich herds, if we had pardoned and taken them up again, as they had been punished enough. I suggested this to general von Trotha but he wanted their total extermination" (Ibid.).

von Schlieffen commented on van Trotha's intentions:

> His plan to wipe out the entire nation or to drive them out of the country are meeting with our approval... The racial struggle that has erupted can be brought to an end only by destroying one side or reducing it to serfdom. The latter proposition is an unrealistic one given the views that are prevalent. (Palmer, 2000: 147–148)

The result

The war was over in early 1905 and the Herero nation had been destroyed. "The Herero have ceased to exist as an independent tribe," as Governor Leutwein stated in a letter (Ibid.: 146). The surviving Herero were put in concentration camps under horrendous conditions. They had to work seven days a week from morning to night "under the clubs of the raw overseers," as a missionary witnessed. "Like cattle hundreds were driven to death and like cattle they were buried," he further notes in his chronicle (Quoted in Gewald, 1999: 188).

In her book on genocides, Alison Palmer summarizes the result of the German war against the Herero nation. When the war started, the Herero population amounted to approximately 80,000 according to Palmer. After the war there was 16,000 Herero left. Of these, 14,000 were placed in the German concentration camps and 2,000 fled to neighboring South Africa and Botswana. Between 75% and 80% of the population were destroyed. All tribal land was expropriated by the Germans and many new German immigrant settlers arrived (Palmer, 2000: 144). The German genocide of the Herero tribe had long-lasting consequences. As one commentator notes:

> The lasting effects of population decimation, land dispossession and political marginalization continue to haunt the Herero identity and impede their economic, social and political progress in modern-day Namibia. (Sarkin-Hughes, 2011: xiii)

Case 4: Kenya

At the end of the 19th century what is now Kenya was the homeland of a large number of African tribes. In 1895 the British government proclaimed the area the East African Protectorate. British missionary societies and the British East African Company had paved the way for conquest. European, and especially British, settlements in the fertile lands of Kenya sprang up at the beginning of the 20th century. The European settlers occupied the best lands, for example in the Rift Valley, and this soon led to conflicts with the native population. Many Africans were employed to work on the farms as tenants and they lived in the neighborhood as squatters. During the first two decades of the 20th century approximately 70,000 Kikuyu migrated to the Rift Valley (Anderson, 2005: 24; Moutafakis, 1966).

The natives living in the areas occupied by European farmers assumed that they had a customary right, called *githaka*, to the land they were cultivating, but the white settlers saw the natives as recruited laborers. In line with the white settlers' views, Kenya's High Court judged that the settlers had property rights and the *githaka* had no juridical claim. When at the beginning of the 1950s the settlers wanted to enter into new contracts establishing the loose status of labor rights in practice, the local squatters – mainly members of the Kikuyu tribe – refused to sign. This led to the repatriation of a great number of Kikuyu to their traditional homelands or to the suburbs of Nairobi. Here they lived unemployed in shanty towns. They survived on hawking, beer brewing, and prostitution.

In practice, a system of racial division similar to the South African apartheid system was institutionalized in Kenya. Racist attitudes were common among the white settlers. Elkins writes:

> By virtue of their skin color, whites of all classes were the master race and therefore deserving privilege.... Many believed the African to be

> biologically inferior, with smaller brain sizes, a limited capacity to feel pain or emotion, and even different nutritional needs, requiring only a bowl of maize meal ... to maintain their health. (Elkins, 2005: 12)

The colonial authorities gave whites legal rights to to the land in the Rift Valley, it gave the whites, but not the Asians or Africans, democratic rights, and color bars were imposed in hotels and restaurants. The treatment of the Kikuyu resulted in feelings of humiliation and anger, which were the emotional breeding ground of the Mau Mau resistance movement (Anderson, 2005: 21–86).

The Mau Mau movement was a secret society of Africans and it was held together by oaths of allegiance to the Kikuyu people. It was seen by the British as "a sinister tribal cult affecting a largely primitive and superstitious people" (Meredith, 2005: 79). Around 1950 Mau Mau militants started attacking Africans in Kenya who were collaborating with the colonial administration as chiefs appointed by the colonial authority, civil servants, or informers, many of whom were extremely wealthy and were seen as Quislings by most Kikuyus (Elkins, 2005).

A number of ambushes were reported. The most severe took place in the northern settlement of Lari in March 1953. The families of collaborators were violently assaulted and the insurgents killed 120 people. The Mau Mau attacks were followed by a counter-attack by the colonial Home Guard against anyone who was a suspected Mau Mau sympathizer, leading to approximately 200 deaths (Anderson, 2005: 126–130).

The British colonial administration reacted strongly to the Mau Mau insurgence, and not least to the Lari massacre. Following Lari, around 2,000 Kikuyu suspected of being sympathetic to the Mau Mau were detained. Hundreds of convicted Mau Mau insurgents were hanged, in many cases without sufficient evidence, according to historian David Anderson. More reprisals would follow. A state of emergency was proclaimed and on April 24, 1954 Operation Anvil started. The city of Nairobi was besieged and no Africans were allowed to leave. Police went through the African communities looking for Mau Mau adherents and sympathizers. Fifty thousand Africans were screened and 28,000 were detained in camps. The search continued and by the end of December 1954 as many as 71,000 Kikuyu, or one in eight Kikuyu adult males, were detained in British prisons or camps (Ibid.: 313–314). The detained were harassed, beaten, and tortured and the camps were dubbed by British opposition politicians, after the German WWII concentration camps, "Kenya's Belsen" and "Kenya's Mauthausen." Nutrition was inadequate and diseases like dysentery, diarrhea, pneumonia, and typhus spread among the inmates.

Caroline Elkins writes that violence and torture characterized the camps: "A pornography of terror, including public brutality, rape, and starvation, set through the villages as well, and thousands died there," and she quotes a man who described the Mwea camp as "Hell on Earth" (Elkins, 2005: 213).

Near the end of the colonial rule of Kenya, the British colonial administration systematically destroyed documents that might show any kind of brutality or unethical behavior by British soldiers or civil servants not only in Kenya but in other colonies as well (Daily Nation, 2013). However, in 2013 thousands of documents from colonial Kenya and many other colonies, as well as documents about the slave trade, that had been hidden by the British foreign office were revealed to the public. The documents show that colonial officials in Kenya had agreed to the torture and abuse of the inmates and that these acts had been known and recognized by British officials in London. For example, the British Attorney General at the time, Eric Griffith Jones, had compared the conditions in Kenyan prison camps to those in Nazi Germany and Communist Russia. Nevertheless, he had sanctioned the treatment and commented: "[V]ulnerable parts of the body should not be struck, particularly the spleen, liver or kidneys" and "If we are going to sin, we must sin quietly" (Cobain and Hatcher, 2013; Cobain and Norton-Taylor, 2012; Cobain, 2014).

Historian David Anderson makes the following estimations of the death toll resulting from the conflict: In total, Mau Mau soldiers killed 32 European settlers, 200 British soldiers and 1,800 Kenyan "collaborators"; officially the British killed 12,000 Mau Mau soldiers, but in reality more than 20,000, according to Anderson, and many more according to Elkins (2005: 366). In total, 150,000 Kikuyu were at some time detained in a camp. According to Caroline Elkins the number may have been as high as 320,000 (Anderson, 2005; Elkins, 2005: xiii).

Although the Mau Mau movement was defeated, the colonial repression could not halt the movement towards independence for Kenya. The country became independent in 1963, with Jomo Kenyatta as its first president.

Case 5: India

In 1750 both China's and India's shares of the world's manufacturing output was larger than Europe's but in 1952 Europe's share was ten times larger than China's and 40 times larger than India's. What had happened in between? Obviously, the simple answer is that Europe – in contrast to China and India – underwent the Industrial Revolution. But how did China and India develop, or rather why did they not develop? The historian Mike Davis argues that underdevelopment in the South was created by the colonial powers in the 19th century. He illustrates his thesis with the cases of India and China. Davis's overarching view is that the "Third World," referring to the underdeveloped continents of Latin America, Africa, and Asia, was established during this period of history. According to Davis, the structure and working of the world economy was adjusted during the 19th century to fulfill the needs of Britain in particular, but also of the rest of Europe (Davis, 2002).

As we saw in Chapter 3, India was ruled in the 18th century by a British company, the East India Company. To avoid British political involvement and liability, for an annual minor tribute the British government let the Company have the privilege of ruling India and this arrangement remained in principle until 1857. As Kulke and Rothermund write, as rulers of India the East India Company could claim the heritage of the conquered Moghul Empire (Kulke and Rothermund, 1996: 239).

India was struck by severe famines in 1876–1879 and 1896–1902. During the former famine the price of wheat rose, making wheat less accessible to ordinary Indians, but the British colonial authority under Viceroy Lord Lytton was nonetheless strict in its liberal economic policy of abstaining from price regulation and price control (Davis, 2002: 31). As a consequence, the effects of the famines spiraled out of control. In a message home a British civil servant wrote: "Mothers sold their children for a single scanty meal. Husbands flung their wives into ponds, to escape the torment of seeing them perish" (quoted in Davis, 2002: 53). In all, it is estimated that in India between 6.1 million and 10.3 million people died in the famine 1876–1879, and between 6.1 million and 19 million died in the famine —1896–1902; a total of between 12.2 million and 29.3 million (Ibid.: 7).

Was the extreme death toll unavoidable? No, Davis says. He argues that one reason behind the devastating consequences of the famines was British colonial policy. After 1850, peasants were more susceptible to famines because their farming had been integrated in the world market (Ibid.: 288). He develops his argument in the following way:

1. The incorporation of smallholders' production into commodity and financial circuits controlled overseas undermined traditional food security,

2. The integration of tropical cultivations into the world market led to a deterioration of terms of trade and,
3. Victorian imperialism and centralization increased the vulnerability to climate shocks (local protection measures were not taken). (Ibid.: 290)

In this regard it is telling that although the famine 1876–1879 struck the Indian population hard, India was at the same time exporting rice to Great Britain (Ibid.: 26–27; see also Stein, 2010: 251–252 for a similar analysis).

According to Davis, the forced integration of India into the world market had as a consequence that its economic development halted. Between 1780 and 1800 the structure of the world economy changed. In 1820, Europe's share of world GDP was 26.6% and India's 15.7%; in 1890 the figures were 40.3% and 11% and in 1951 29.7% and 3.8%, respectively. Europe's share of world manufacturing output in 1830 was 34.1% and India's 17.6%; in 1900 Europe's was 63.0% and India's 1.7% (Davis, 2002: 293–294).

Of course, the main reason for the changes of regional GDP and manufacturing output is the Industrial Revolution in Europe. Industrialization meant mass production. However, there is also another side to the story. Davis writes that

> from about 1780 or 1800 onward ... every serious attempt by a non-Western society to move into a fast lane of development or to regulate its terms of trade was met by a military as well as an economic response from London or a competing imperial capital. Japan ... is an exception that proves the rule. (Ibid.: 295)

India became a market for British products and Indian farmers produced opium, cotton, wheat, and rice for the world market at the price of their own food security. From 1875 to 1900 annual Indian grain exports went up from 3 million to 10 million tons (Ibid.: 299). Opium exports from India to China were secured by the British through the Opium Wars against China in 1839–1842 and 1856–1858 (Ibid.: 300).

From the middle of the 19th century a "deindustrialization" took place in India. Before, India had exported textiles; afterwards, they exported raw cotton for manufacturing in England. The proportion of workers in agriculture increased and in manufacturing decreased and by the late 19th century 75% of the population was dependent on agriculture. This had devastating implications. Burton Stein writes:

> Famine and disease were the more lethal consequences of change during the century of British imperial dominance that had begun in 1840, but chronically inadequate nutrition and consequent morbidity revealed a degradation of the socio-cultural fabric of the entire subcontinent. (Stein, 2010: 235–236)

But India was not only a market for British textiles. To avoid Indian competition the expanding Indian textile industry was outrivaled. Through duty-free imports of British textiles the Indian factories were put out of business (Maddison, 2002: 7; Barratt-Brown, 1963). In this way, as Immanuel Wallerstein argues in line with Davis's thesis, India was incorporated into the capitalist global economy and the Indian economy was adjusted to fit the needs of Britain (Wallerstein, 1989).

Davis concludes his work with the following words:

> If the history of the British rule of India were to be condensed into a single fact, it is this: there was no increase in India's per capita income from 1757 to 1947. Indeed, in the last half of the 19th century, income probably declined by 50 percent. (Ibid.: 311)

However, Davis's "immiseration thesis" is contested. Bernard Waites refers to statistics showing an increase in the area of tilled land and of food grain in India between the middle of the 19th century and 1920 (Waites, 1999: 176). However, this increase was mainly for the cultivation of crops for export. After 1920 the food crop acreage in fact declined (Barratt-Brown, 1963: 175).

Could India have developed in another way? Economist Angus Maddison speculates about the possible consequences if India had not been ruled by the British for two centuries (Maddison, 2002). In one of Maddison's scenarios, India would have, like China, maintained indigenous rule with a few foreign enclaves. If that had happened, Maddison assumes, India would have been split up by civil wars and the traditional, conservative society would have prevailed. Due to a smaller drain on resources from India to foreign powers, Maddison assumes that the average standard of living would have been a little higher. Alternatively, in a scenario where India became independent from Britain in the 1880s it is "likely that both income and population growth would have ... accelerated," Maddison writes (Ibid.: 11).

Waites also stresses internal reasons for Indian backwardness: for example, traditional Indian values and the caste system, which were obstacles to development, a factor that Davis does not mention (Waites,

1999: 183). But, as Barrat-Brown shows, one main reason that development in India was held back and the traditional caste society prevailed was the indirect rule practiced by Britain. The British ruled through local princes and landlords, who were rich and privileged and had no interest in changing the status quo. Thus, the traditional feudal system in India was preserved by British rule (Barratt-Brown, 1963: 178).

The significance of the five cases

In the preceding chapter I first gave a broad overview of the history of colonialism and of different accounts of how this historical period should be evaluated. In this chapter five cases of colonial histories were examined. Of these cases, three were British colonies, one German, and one Belgian. The five cases illustrate different aspects of how colonialism affected the colonies in ways that have implications for the present discussion of rectificatory justice. I will now comment on the significance of the five cases.

Colonial occupation

Let me start with the original colonial occupation. In the case of Uganda, as with many other cases of colonization, the territory was occupied by means of both war and agreements. It took some years of fighting before the natives' resistance was broken. The agreements that paved the way for colonial domination were in many cases unfair and based on cheating and manipulation.

The wars of occupation violated traditional principles of a just war. According to these principles, originating from the natural law tradition, war must be waged for a *just cause*, which in practice means war in self-defense or war to rectify an injustice and as a *last resort* when all alternatives to war have been tried (Dower, 2009). For obvious reasons colonial occupations cannot have a just cause.

However, both in Africa and in India, colonial influence was also based on agreements with local rulers. Although some of these agreements were based on fraudulence, others were of mutual benefit to the parties. At least in the cases when the local rulers were legitimate, the influence of the colonial powers was less challenging from a moral point of view.

Thus, colonialism was based on both military occupation and agreements, some fair and some unfair. How does this cohere with the principles of rights, justice, and the common good for the global order that John Rawls elaborates in his book *The Law of Peoples* referred to in Chapter 2? Rawls's principles summarize a common morality for international relations and I will use them in my discussion of the moral assessment of colonialism.

Colonial occupation violates at least two of John Rawls's principles of a Law of Peoples. First it violates the first principle: "Peoples are free and independent, and their freedom and independence are to be respected by other peoples." It also violates Rawls's fourth principle, which coheres with the principle of just war: "Peoples are to observe a duty of non-intervention" (Rawls, 1999: 37). In cases when a fair agreement was made between a colonial power and a local king, it is less evident that it conflicts with Rawls's principles.

Exploitation

After a colonial power had obtained control of a territory, the extraction of its natural resources began. What took place in the Congo during the reign of King Leopold II is perhaps an extreme case. As we recall, the Belgian king did not spare any means to extract the natural resources of Congo, with human tragedies as a consequence. Similar things happened in Latin America in the 16th century and onwards when Spain and Portugal extracted natural resources such as gold, silver, and cotton.

The colonialists extracted natural resources with the help of forced labor. Can we say that they therefore *exploited* the colonies? The answer to this question is not as obvious as it appears. We can quite plausibly assume that if the colonialists had not extracted the natural resources of the colonies, no one would have done it, because the natives lacked both the knowledge and the means to do it. Were the colonized then exploited because someone else – the colonialists – took advantage of the resources?

In order to answer this question let me narrate the following hypothetical case:

> You are an energetic and innovative person. You go down to an island in the South where you find some natural resource to extract. The island is inhabited by natives who earn their living through hunting and fishing. You have brought a drill and a spade and you find in a deserted area a valuable metal in the ground. You do not interact with the natives, but extract the metal yourself and bring it back home and sell it with a good income. Have you done anything wrong? (Case A)

Yes, one might argue. The valuable metal belonged to the natives who had lived on the island for generations. But why did the resources belong to the natives just because they happened to live on the same spot?

The fact that they lived on the island was a coincidence, an instance of the natural lottery, which is arbitrary from a moral point of view. Is it not more reasonable to concede with John Locke and Hugo Grotius, philosophers contemporary to the colonization of America and Asia, that humankind received the earth in common, with a common interest in its resources, which may be extracted in order to serve the needs of humankind (Locke, 1977 [1690]; Grotius, 2004 [1712])? The natives did not have the means to extract the metal so they lost nothing they had access to. If you had not been there, the metal would still be in the ground. Therefore, it is a blessing when someone takes the initiative to extract natural resources to produce oil, gold, rubber, cotton, and so on, benefitting the common good, if these resources otherwise would not have been extracted.

The argument that you did not exploit the natives when you went down to the island and extracted the metal is based on two premises: first, natural resources belong to humankind in common and a people has no special right to resources just because they happen to inhabit the area were the resources are found. Second, it is in everyone's interest that natural resources are extracted and, thus, a person who has the energy and initiative to do so has also a right to benefit from it.

Let me change the story a bit:

> You find out that there are vast natural resources to extract and you can by no means do it by yourself. You have brought a rifle and you now use it to threaten 20 unarmed natives. You tell them that you will kill them if they do not work for you. As a consequence, they are forced to work and in this way you are able to take home large amounts of the valuable metal. (Case B)

Now it appears that your activities in the southern island have become problematic from a moral point of view. By threatening and forcing the natives you are harming them, and you do that in order to enrich yourself.

The story does not end here. The following happens:

> There is a plague that kills all the animals on the island so the natives have lost their means of survival. You see a chance to let them all work for you and you do not need to pay them more than what is sufficient for their survival. In this way you have access to many workers whom you can pay very little and you receive huge incomes from selling the metal. (Case C)

Now, you did not threaten or force the natives to work for you. They did it freely in order to survive.

In which situation did you exploit the natives? When you by yourself extracted the natural resources (Case A), when you forced them to work for you (Case B), or when working for you was the only available means of survival (Case C)?

Exploitation is a vague concept used in various meanings. Obviously it is negatively value-laden. Exploitation is something morally wrong or, more precisely, unfair. When A exploits B, "A takes unfair advantage of B," say Wertheimer and Zwolinski (2013). What then is unfair about exploitation? Exploitation means that A takes advantage of B's weakness or lack of alternatives. Exploitation entails that A gains from an action that harms B or coerces B (Ibid.). In this case exploitation is obviously morally harmful. But can a relation between A and B be characterized as exploitation even if B gains? Yes, when A takes advantage of B's weakness or vulnerability, it is a case of exploitation. Then, the moral value of the act is mixed. The act is both morally problematic, because it implies exploitation, and morally beneficial, because B gains.

How then can we characterize the three cases above? Case A is hardly a case of exploitation. You extract the natural resources but you do not affect the natives in any way. Case B describes a coercive act; the natives are forced to work for you, and it is obviously a case of exploitation. In Case C you take advantage of the natives' vulnerable situation caused by a plague. It is assumed that the natives will die if they cannot work for you, so to work for you is a better option for them than any alternative. Thus, they gain from the relation but the relation can nevertheless be characterized as a form of exploitation because you take advantage of their weakness.

Let me now relate this argument to what happened in Congo during Leopold II's reign. This period in Congo's history is most similar to the hypothetical Case B. Africans were forced to collect ivory tusks and work on rubber plantations. As we noticed, forced labor was also used in other parts of Africa during the 19th century, in Latin America after the advent of the colonists in the 15th century, and in Asia, for example in Indonesia. Many colonial practices were also similar to Case C. Colonized people worked in mines and on plantations for meager wages and under severe conditions because the alternative options were even worse. The colonialists took advantage of their vulnerable situations.

How should we morally assess the extraction of natural resources that took place during colonialism? Under the conditions that the resources were abundant and the colonized peoples could benefit from the extractions, no injustice or exploitation was done. However, if the natural resources were limited and thus nothing left for the colonized peoples, and/or if the colonized peoples could not benefit from the extractions, injustice was done to them. They, at least, have the same right to natural resources as the colonial powers, including the natural resources found in the homelands of the colonial powers themselves. There seem to be empirical examples of both kinds. For example, extractions of minerals in the Congo have not benefited the Congolese people up to this day. In spite of the fact that enormous amount of gold, silver, and minerals for consumer electronics have been extracted in the Congo, the standard of living of the Congolese is among the lowest in the world.[1] Malaysia is a contrast. Here the rubber plantations that were initiated by the British during the colonial period have been taken over by Malaysia and are presently in different ways benefitting the Malaysian economy (Oxford Business Group, 2012).

Genocide

The German war against the Herero tribe in southwest Africa occurred parallel to Leopold II's ravaging of Congo. Here an African tribe was almost exterminated by German military efforts. In International Humanitarian Law genocide means

> any of the following acts committed with intent to destroy, in whole or in part, a national, ethnical, racial or religious group, as such: (a) Killing members of the group; (b) Causing serious bodily or mental harm to members of the group; (c) Deliberately inflicting on the group conditions of life calculated to bring about its physical destruction in whole or in part; (d) Imposing measures intended to prevent births within the group; and (e) Forcibly transferring children of the group to another group. (Convention on the Prevention and Punishment of Genocide, Article 2, United Nations, 1948)

The criteria for a case of genocide is therefore both an intention to "destroy…a group" and actions leading to this result. Did the German war against the Herero fulfill these conditions? Yes. From the quotations of German Chief of Staff von Schlieffen and General von Trotha above one can conclude that they in fact intended to exterminate the Herero tribe, and the intention was followed by actions that slashed the tribe's numbers by approximately 80%.

The extermination of groups of people like that of the Herero happened in many places during the history of colonialism. Whether these atrocities can be labeled genocide or not has been a matter of dispute. For example, is the Belgian King Leopold's killing in Congo a case of genocide or not? The intention was not to wipe out ethnic groups. On the other hand, some ethnic groups resisted the Belgian colonizers and in those cases the colonizers intended to destroy them (Yale University, 2010).

However, the definitional requirement of *intent* to destroy a group has been questioned. For example, Maybury-Lewis suggests a widening of the concept to include "genocidal massacres." He shows that colonialism and imperialism implied genocidal actions in a number of cases: besides the above-mentioned, the Spanish and Portuguese conquering the Americas, the warfare against Native Americans in North America, British colonization of Tasmania and Australia, and so on.

When summarizing these cases of genocide or genocidal massacres, Maybury-Lewis writes:

> Imperialist genocide against indigenous peoples was thus of two kinds. It was practiced in order to clear lands that invading settlers wished to occupy. It was also practiced as part of a strategy to seize and coerce labor that the settlers could not or would not obtain by less drastic means. It was often inspired furthermore by the rulers' determination to show who was master and who was, if not slave, then at least obedient subject; and it was often put into effect as deliberate policy where the masters felt that their subjects had to be taught a lesson. Acts of resistance or rebellion were often punished by genocidal killings. (Maybury-Lewis, 2002)

This description fits well with what the Germans did to the Herero population.

Resisting independence

The case of the British suppression of the Mau Mau uprising is an example of how a colonial power violently resisted a struggle for independence. Here the fierce Mau Mau insurgence against British rule was met with different forms of violence: military action, detention camps, torture, and so on.

Britain normally reacted more peacefully towards its colonies' claims for independence than other colonial powers. The British practiced "indirect rule," which meant that domestic affairs were left to traditional authorities. Britain expected that the colonies would grow to maturity and they introduced constitutional rule and elected legislative constituencies.

Although the constituencies were "color blind," that is, in principle open to all inhabitants, voting rights required either property or education, which in practice excluded most natives (Chamberlain, 1998: 44).

When, after World War II, the British colonies demanded independence, the normal procedure was to organize conferences with native leaders in London or other places and plan for a peaceful transfer of power and elections. However, there were some exceptions to this peaceful process. In the Gold Coast, later Ghana, resistance leader Kwame Nkrumah was arrested several times by the British authorities, and the same happened to resistance leaders Kenneth Kaunda and Harry Nkumbula in Northern Rhodesia, later Zambia. In India, Mahatma Gandhi led non-violent resistance under the label "*satyagraha*" (truth force) from 1915 onwards. The British tried to resist the movement, sometimes with violent means. In Amritsar in 1919 British troops attacked unarmed demonstrators, killing 379 and wounding 1,200, and many of Gandhi's actions were met with force and Gandhi himself imprisoned (Stein, 2010).

The history of the dissolution of the second-largest empire, the French Empire, was more violent. Perhaps this had to do with France's different approach to its colonies. Assimilation was the leading idea behind the French Empire. It meant that the colonies were considered as parts of France. Inhabitants of the colonies who acquired French citizenship had the right to elect deputies to the National Assembly and to vote for the president. When the colonies wished to secede from the French Empire, France reacted violently.

In Algeria, the French government tried to curb the FLN rebellion in the middle of the 1950s. In 1956, 500,000 French troops were sent to Algeria. The Algerian rebellion was also resisted by *pieds noirs*, French nationals living in Algeria (Meredith, 2005). Finally, in 1962 Algeria got independence. The total number of deaths during the Algerian war of independence is estimated at between 100,000 and 1 million (Wikipedia, 2012).

Madagascar is situated at the opposite end of Africa. Here rebellion against French rule broke out in 1947. When French forces attempted to curb the rebellion, it is estimated that 20,000 people were killed (Chamberlain, 1998: 173).

Vietnam was colonized by the French at the end of the 19th century. During World War II Vietnam was occupied by Japan. In 1946 French troops returned to Indochina. No agreement with the Vietminh troops, headed by Ho Chi Minh, was reached and a war of independence started. The war lasted until 1954, when the French troops were defeated in Dien Bien Phu. France had to leave Vietnam but, with the support of the United States, Vietnam was divided and Vietminh got control only of the northern part. The colonial war now merged with the Cold War between the West and the East, the main combatants being the United States and the Soviet Union. During the French colonial war against the Vietminh between 300,000 and 1 million people died (Wikipedia, 2012).

Last, but not least, Portugal resisted independence in its African colonies Mozambique, Angola, and Guinea Bissau until the 1970s. After World War II the Portuguese government encouraged emigration to the colonies, or the "overseas provinces" as they were called, and hundreds of thousands of Portuguese settlers went to Mozambique and Angola. In Angola the resistance movements MPLA and Unita formed in the 1950s, and Frelimo, the liberation movement in Mozambique, was founded in 1962. After almost two decades of war, the Portuguese withdrew from its colonies, and in both Angola and Mozambique civil wars broke out when Portugal left (Meredith, 2005).

The era of colonialism ended in some places peacefully and in others after wars of independence. We have noticed that colonial empires differed with respect to how to react to movements for independence. In most cases, Britain made efforts to achieve a peaceful path towards independence, while France and Portugal opposed claims for independence with violence.

The right of colonies to independence was declared by the United Nations in the Declaration on the Granting of Independence to Colonial Countries and Peoples, adopted by the General Assembly in 1960. § 4 says:

> All armed action or repressive measures of all kinds directed against dependent peoples shall cease in order to enable them to exercise peacefully and freely their right to complete independence, and the integrity of their national territory shall be respected. (United Nations, 1960)

The United Nations' Declaration states that the colonies' claims for independence are legitimate. The use of violence by the colonial powers to resist movements of independence was thus a violation of the United Nations' Declaration.

Economic subjugation

During colonialism India became integrated into the world economy. India was assigned by the colonial power the roles of both supplier of raw materials to the world market, and market for industrial goods. As a consequence, India's own potential for industrial production was undermined and annihilated. This, in its turn, had long-term economic consequences for India, which for decades after independence was one of the most underdeveloped nations of the world.

The fact that colonialism is one of the factors behind the failure of present-day developing nations is shown by Daron Acemoglu and James Robinson, as referred to in Chapter 5, which deals more thoroughly with the relation between colonialism on the one hand and dependence and underdevelopment on the other.

Negligence

Finally, Uganda is an illuminating example of how negligence by the colonial power had devastating consequences for the colony after its independence. As its post-colonial history shows, Uganda was not prepared for independence. After about 70 years of colonial rule there were not enough educated people, no civil society, and no reliable political structure – all of these are requirements for stability and development. As in so many other colonies, the failure of the colonial power paved the way for internal strife, political corruption, and poverty. A tribal society was suddenly and unpreparedly transformed into a modern society. This is the basis for what the Ugandan philosopher Edward Wamala calls "Africa's integrity crises" (Wamala, 2008). As John Rawls points out in his eighth principles of a Law of Peoples, lack of human capital and technological resources prevent a people from having "a just or decent political and social regime" (Rawls, 1999: 37).[2]

But is the failure of former colonial powers to prepare their former colonies for independence really morally blameworthy and a reason for rectification? Are we not responsible only for our actions and not for our negligence? In responding to this objection I will elaborate on Peter Singer's argument about the child in the pond (Singer, 1972). Singer tells a story about a child who is playing near a pond and asks how we should react if we see that it is at risk of falling into the pond and drowning. If you see a child and then push it so that it drowns, you are clearly responsible for its death. If, when passing, you see the child walking dangerously near the pond and do not intervene to stop it from falling in, you are at least partly responsible for the child's eventual drowning. If you as parents of the child never told it anything about the risk of drowning in the pond and you let your child play near it, you are also partly responsible for your child's death if it falls into the pond and drowns.

Singer applies the story of the child near the pond to our duties to the poor. Let me instead apply it to the relationship between colonial power and colony. All three situations could be applied to this relationship, but let me elaborate on the third. The third situation is in some aspects similar to the relationship between Britain and Uganda at the time of independence. Given, as was argued above, that the colony was totally unprepared for independence, and it was in the might of the colonial power to prepare the colony for it, through, for example, offering education and institutional support, the colonial power was – like the negligent parents – partly responsible for the mess that followed independence. There is therefore responsibility for negligence: for not having prepared the colony sufficiently.[3]

Conclusions

The cases above illustrate the various result of colonialism that have a bearing on today's discussion of global justice. Colonialism involved violation of international morals as well as of human rights. Even if some of the deeds at the time were not illegal because there was no international convention or law regulating wrongs, they are nevertheless highly challenging from the moral point of view today. Therefore, they invite further reflection on the implications of the moral legacy of colonialism. So, the significance of these five cases is that they in different ways illustrate the moral and political failure of colonialism and the reasons for rectification.

5
The Legacy of Colonialism

In the previous chapter, some significant and morally challenging implications of colonial rule were presented. The point of departure of this chapter is the question of how colonialism and imperialism shaped the present global structure. The primary question is: How were the present poor former colonies affected by the fact that they were colonized by foreign powers for hundreds of years? Did it accelerate their development or was it an obstacle to their progress? The secondary questions are: How did the exploitation of the colonies affect development in the now wealthy nations? Were colonialism and imperialism important for their development or did they play only a minor role? Both these questions are highly controversial and, needless to say, experts in the field are far from unanimous. Hence, my aim is to review some of their answers and discuss the implications for my main question in this book: Is there is a valid argument for rectificatory justice after colonialism and imperialism?

Why do nations fail?

My point of departure is a recent seminal contribution to the understanding of poverty and development. In the book *Why Nations Fail* (2012) economists Daron Acemoglu and James Robinson devote a chapter to the role of colonialism in the present-day underdevelopment and economic dependence of nations in Africa, Latin America, and Asia.

What were the economic implications of colonialism? How did the former colonies develop after independence? Acemoglu and Robinson answer these questions by providing some examples. Their first example is the Dutch colonization of Indonesia. When the Dutch East India Company reached the Banda Islands, it found a lively trade in spices.

Instead of engaging in the trade, the Company conquered the island, massacring around 15,000 natives. Many native leaders were killed and the Dutch governor, Jan Pieterzoon Coen, established a large-scale plantation economy, which, according to Acemoglu and Robinson, "condemned the islands to underdevelopment" (Acemoglu and Robinson, 2012: 249). To prevent the Dutch from profiting from their take-over of the islands, many indigenous peoples destroyed their plantations of nutmeg and other spices. Acemoglu and Robinson write: "But as in Moluccas, Dutch colonialism fundamentally changed their economic and political development. The people of South East Asia stopped trading, turned inward, and became more absolutist" (Ibid.: 250).

Regarding Africa, Acemoglu and Robinson argue that African economies were shaped by the slave trade. More than 10 million people were shipped from Africa to America. African nations were transformed into slave-hunting nations and the economies of Africa were accordingly changed. The slave trade had huge demographic consequences. It is estimated that in West Africa, the main source territory for slaves, the population in 1850 was only half of what it would have been without the slave trade: around 25 million instead of around 50 million. Although the slave trade was abolished by Great Britain in 1807, slavery continued on the African continent and it is estimated that in West Africa around 30% of the population were still enslaved in 1900. Acemoglu and Robinson summarize the implications of colonialism in the following words:

> [We have] also shown that in several instances the extractive institutions that underpinned the poverty of these nations were imposed, or at the very least further strengthened, by the very same process that fueled European growth: European commercial and colonial expansion. In fact the profitability of European colonial empires was often built on the destruction of independent polities and indigenous economies around the world, or on the creation of extractive institutions essentially from the ground up, as in the Caribbean Islands, where, following the almost total collapse of the native populations, Europeans imported African slaves and set up plantation systems. (Ibid.: 271)

The debate on colonialism and underdevelopment

There are different voices in the discussion of the legacy of colonialism. In this part I will relate and discuss some of these views.

The Brazilian economic historian Andre Gunder Frank has developed a theory of the interdependence of development in the "metropolis" and underdevelopment in the "satellites." He uses Chile and Brazil as illustrations. Frank writes:

> My thesis is that these capitalist...contradictions and the historical development of the capitalist system have generated underdevelopment in the peripheral satellites whose economic surplus was expropriated, while generating economic development in the metropolitan centers which appropriated that surplus – and, further that this process still continues. (Frank, 1967: 3)

According to Frank, the world economy can be described as a chain connecting metropolises and satellites. For example, the poor peasants in northern Brazil are connected to the rich shareholders of a British cotton or sugar company and the peasants' poverty is directly related to the wealth of the shareholders. The peasant works at a *hacienda*. He produces a surplus that is appropriated by the owner of the *hacienda*. The owner can be an individual or a large company. In order to maximize the surplus, the peasant's wage should be as low as possible. Thus, he or she remains poor. The surplus is the basis for the accumulated capital that ultimately makes up the profit for the owners and banks.

Frank distinguishes between domestic and overseas metropolises. The countryside in the satellite is dependent on the regional and/or central cities that on the one hand gain the surplus from the farms and on the other hand control the farming. However, the domestic metropolis is itself a satellite of an overseas metropolis, like London or New York. Even this relation is characterized by dependence and domination (Ibid.: 25). Frank argues that these relations of exploitation and acquisition produce wealth in the metropolis and "consolidate" underdevelopment in the periphery.

Frank's book is mainly based on an analysis of Latin American economic history. African historian Walter Rodney presents a similar thesis from an African point of view. According to Rodney, economic development took place in Africa before Africa became the subject of colonialism (Rodney, 1972: 69). Slavery and the slave trade halted this development and as a consequence the slave trade was the basic factor behind African underdevelopment, Rodney argues. Why? Because through the slave trade the most able-bodied and healthy men and women were taken away from their home countries.

The economic relations between Europe and Africa were either "destructive," as in the slave trade, or "extractive." Raw materials were extracted from Africa and exported to Europe. According to Rodney, the

Europeans disregarded all African attempts to gain education and technology and as a consequence Africa remained rural and underdeveloped. Like Frank, Rodney argues that there is a relation between underdevelopment in the colony and development in Europe. He writes:

> From an African viewpoint that amounted to consistent expatriation of surplus produced by African labor out of African resources. It meant the development of Europe as part of the same dialectical process in which Africa was underdeveloped. (Ibid.: 149)

Rodney's argument is challenged by Bernard Waites. According to Waites, the exploitation of the colonies played only a marginal role in the development of Europe. He writes:

> For Europe as a whole, commerce with the "periphery" was simply too small a part of total economic activity for its profits to have played a significant role in capital accumulation during industrialization. (Waites, 1999; 19)

For example, between 1800 and 1938 only 18% of total European export was destined for countries in Asia, Africa, and South America (Ibid.: 20). On the other hand, Waites also maintains that the trading of colonial products contributed to the wealth of the North. For example, in 1850 colonial trading contributed to 31% of the Dutch public revenues (Ibid.: 92).

How then did Europe influence Africa? In some parts of Africa, like Congo, Equatorial Africa, and Mozambique, the colonial power handed over the exploitation of natural resources to concessionary companies. These companies practiced often forced labor and harsh punishments for workers that did not fulfill their quota (Ibid.: 136–137; see also Hochschild, 1999).

Did then the European presence generally benefit African economic development or not? It is clear that the slave trade and the harsh exploitation of human and natural resources by the concessionary companies in the 19th century resulted in a sense of humiliation among Africans. Economically, Waites concludes that "the balance of the evidence indicates that colonialism did not impoverish Africans." On the other hand, he also maintains that "it would be unrealistic not to recognize basic and fairly intractable constraint on the promotion of capitalist development by the colonial regimes" (Ibid.: 215, 219). In comparison with Rodney, Waites has a less negative view of the impact of colonialism on African economic development.

How are Frank's and Rodney's views related to the argument for rectificatory justice developed in this book? As will be recalled, my point of departure was the question of whether there are reasons to widen the global justice discussion by including the question of rectification for past wrongs during colonialism. Is the present unjust global structure a result of decisions and actions in the past that demand rectification? Based on Frank's and Rodney's analyses one could set forth the following hypothesis:

> Present underdevelopment in the Third World and development in Europe can be explained by a history of exploitation that goes back to colonial times. Those who are responsible for this exploitation have reasons to compensate for these past (and present) actions.

However, this hypothesis is based on a highly controversial premise. Certainly the economies of Africa, as well as of other colonized continents, were adjusted to supply Europe and later North America with crops and raw materials. However, according to Bernard Waites, among others, the evidence does not support the argument that exploitation of the colonies was a major reason for development in Europe. Colonialism might even have been an economic burden for Europe. It is not unthinkable that the British economy would have fared even better if, instead of using the colonies as suppliers of raw material, it had supported economic development in the colonies and then benefited from them as markets for their products (Vernon, 2012: 51).

On the other hand, the colonies supplied the colonial powers with much-needed raw materials and capital. For example, argues historian Hilary Beckles, the Industrial Revolution in England was fueled by incomes generated by the slave trade and Caribbean sugar. He writes:

> Without the infrastructure represented by the Caribbean sugar economy and its related slave-trading and commodity-trading networks, eighteenth-century England's economic growth would not have reached the level that enabled the use of the term Industrial Revolution. (Beckles, 2013: 101)

As Michael Barratt-Brown shows, there are some simple economic mechanisms that explain why colonialism contributed to lasting underdevelopment in the colonies. During the first period of colonialism resources flowed from the colonies to Europe. Later, in India and China (which both were on the brink of manufacturing industrialization), the emerging industries were efficiently eliminated by the colonial powers.

Similarly, Basil Davidson refers to the "the steady destruction of African handicraft industries" in the wake of imperialism during the first decades of the 20th century (Davidson, 1991: 304).

In general, the colonies were left with primary production serving the needs of the colonial regime. The high profits earned due to extremely low wages in the colonies were remitted overseas and thus not used for investment in the colonies. This, it seems, is the basic formula for why colonies remained underdeveloped and dependent. In colonies with large white settlements, like Australia, South Africa, and North America, the natives were either killed off or forced into reservations. Here the picture looks different precisely because the white settlers kept the surplus and used it for productive investment (Barratt-Brown, 1963: 159–163).

What would have happened if Africa had not been colonized? As Rhoda Howard-Hassman writes, this question invites uncertain counterfactual speculations. With Ghana as her example she writes:

> [W]ithout European incursion, Ghana would have developed in a capitalist direction... [but] perhaps had Ghana been left alone, the economic outcome might simply have been the continuation of a subsistence-level peasant society. Ghana might have been simply undeveloped rather than underdeveloped. Perhaps in another scenario of noncolonial development... [the development] might have resulted in a slave-based economy. (Howard-Hassman, 2003: 195–196)

The discussion of the implications of colonialism is extensive and it goes beyond the limits of this book to make a full assessment of the different positions. We can notice, however, that the question of the implications of colonialism for the colonies and for the colonial powers is controversial. Both Frank and Rodney argue that colonialism implied underdevelopment in the colonies and development in Europe. Frank's and Rodney's theses of the relation between colonialism and underdevelopment are indeed controversial and perhaps overstated but it seems nevertheless difficult to dispute that there is a connection between on the one hand the economic and political relations established between the colonial powers and their colonies and on the other hand the post-colonial relations between rich and poor nations. Thus, the present global economic order was to some extent shaped by colonialism. There seem to be reasons to side with Acemoglu and Robinson in their analysis of the role of colonialism in the failure of many of the former colonies. Their view is also supported by Bräutigam and Knack, who state:

> There are many reasons why governance is poor in much of sub-Saharan Africa. Colonialism did little to develop strong, indigenously rooted institutions that could tackle the development demands of modern states. (Bräutigam and Knack, 2004, 255)

The lack of educational opportunities for Africans during colonialism was one factor behind the failure of colonialism in Africa. For example, in the late 1950s in Kenya, Tanganyika (present Tanzania without Zanzibar), and Uganda, with a combined population of 24 million people at the time, only 2,000 individual school certificates were issued annually and in 1958, of 3 million people in South Rhodesia (present Zimbabwe) only 13 African children achieved standard 12 (the last year in the four-year secondary course) (Davidson, 1991: 319). How could an uneducated population be expected to run an independent nation?

What should the colonial powers have done?

We have seen that the colonial powers left their colonies with tumbling and dependent economies and deficient institutions for education and health care. What should the colonial powers have done? What would a reasonable and fair colonialism look like? The question is perhaps nonsensical. Is not colonialism by definition unfair? Yes, but let me then rephrase the question; Given colonialism as a historical fact, what should the colonial powers have done in order to minimize the need for rectification? Let me illustrate the question with another story:

> You walk in the wilderness and meet a young man who lives there. He is poor and barely surviving. You tell him that he can work for you. You employ him but pay a meager wage and force him to work at least 12 hours a day under poor conditions. After having worked for you for almost all his life, when he gets old he is able to work for himself. You profited from his work but he did not get any education and only sufficient health care to keep him alive when working for you. As a consequence, his life as a free person is miserable. When he blames you that you did not help to prepare him for this situation and demand that you compensate him, you respond that he got a better life working for you than he would have had in the wilderness. Thus, there is no reason for blame or compensation. Is your response justified?

It is contentious whether the story is analogous to what happened when European colonialists occupied the colonies. In some cases, for example Congo and South West Africa, colonialism certainly implied a deterioration of the natives' lives. But let us assume that the story pictures the reality in some other colonies. Is your response justified in a case when the natives fared better under colonialism than before? It seems to me that the man has good reasons for his complaints and that your response is unjustified. You had the opportunity to treat him in a decent way, provide him with education and health care, and prepare him for his life as a free man and still benefit from the exchange. You could have done that but you did not. Your negligence was therefore indeed morally wrong.

Mutual respect and equal relations

Human beings as well as nations have a general duty to treat others with respect. This idea, among others, is developed by John Rawls in his treaty *The Law of Peoples*. Rawls here presents "principles of justice among free and democratic peoples" (Rawls, 1999: 37). For the question I am discussing, his use of the term "peoples" instead of states is an advantage. Peoples, according to Rawls, are actors in the Society of Peoples. They are "group agents" and act as moral agents towards other peoples (Pettit, 2006: 46). Many former colonies were at the time of colonization normally not states in the modern sense, but rather groups of tribes and kingdoms. However, due to colonization they became states at independence.

A people can expect to receive from other peoples "a proper respect and recognition of their equality," Rawls writes (1999: 35). Furthermore, peoples should according to a Law of Peoples, that is, a moral law for international relations, be free, independent, and equal, have the right to self-defense, honor human rights, and have a duty to assist other peoples that due to unfavorable conditions lack the possibility to develop decent political institutions (Ibid.: 37). In spite of the fact that the different colonial powers treated their colonies differently, some more oppressively and exploitatively than others, a common factor is that they did not treat them as peoples in Rawls's sense. The colonies were treated as means for the colonial powers' ends; to take home raw materials, to have a market for their products, to increase their international power, and so on. Generally speaking, they did not fulfill any of the principles included by Rawls in a Law of Peoples.

Colonialism had different facets. Some colonial histories were more brutal than others. Sometimes colonies were even said to have a "civilizing" impact. But even the kind of colonialism that is sometimes called "civilizing colonialism" is questionable because the colonial power did not treat the colony as an equal.

In a similar vein, Lea Ypi argues, in line with Kant's ideas of equality between peoples, that what is wrong with colonialism is that it implies inequality between peoples. She writes: "[W]hat made the colonialism practiced by European states particularly abhorrent was its violation of standards of equality and reciprocity in setting up common political relations" (Ypi, 2013: 174). Of course, Ypi is also aware of the manifold colonial harms that were done, but the lack of mutual respect and reciprocity in the relation between a colonial power and a colony implies that even well intended and benevolent colonialism, like colonization motivated by a civilizing mission, is a basic moral wrong (Ibid.).

The same criticism applies to commercial colonialism. I argued above that the fact that a people happens to inhabit a particular territory does not necessarily imply that it has the right to obstruct others from exploiting the resources of the territory. However, what was wrong with commercial colonialism is that the extraction of the colonies' natural resources was not based on mutual and fair agreements but on force or deception and manipulation.

Conclusion

As a consequence of colonial dominance and exploitation, the former colonial powers have a debt to pay. It is a "debt that has been rolling up throughout the period of colonization" and remains today, say Lea Ypi et al. (2009: 124).

The moral problem with colonialism is – generally speaking – first, that the colonies were harmed in different ways, as exemplified in Chapter 4; second, that colonialism implied a structural and economic dependence, hampering economic development in the colonies and leading to enduring underdevelopment, as Acemoglu and Robinson show; and third, that colonial relations were characterized by paternalism and dominance.

As a consequence of the three kinds of moral wrongs associated with colonialism, rectification after colonialism has to take several forms. First, colonial powers should acknowledge the harms done, apologize, and compensate. Second, they should support the economic and social development of their former colonies. And finally, the interactions between former colonial powers and their colonies should be changed into relations characterized by equality, reciprocity, and respect.

Colonialism not only had enduring economic and social consequences. It also affected the mentality and worldview of the colonized. The cultural and psychological effects of colonialism are the topic of the next chapter.

6
Restoring the Epistemic Framework

Epistemic injustice

Colonialism had not only economic and political consequences but also intellectual and cultural consequences. Colonial relations had the character of master–servant relations and these relations ran parallel with race and ethnicity; the white person was the master, the non-white the servant.

Enduring social relations of superior and subordinate have a tendency to create cultural images of the other and of oneself. The master, the white person, is looked up to and the servant, the colored person, is someone to look down on.

The cultural images resulting from colonialism have been analyzed in the vast academic and cultural genre called post-colonial studies (Said, 2003; Loomba, 2005). It would take another book to analyze and comment on different positions within the field of post-colonial studies. I will here limit myself to discussing one thought-provoking contribution to the field: the Indian social theorist Rajeev Bhargava's ideas on how colonialism led to epistemic injustice (Bhargava, 2013).

According to Bhargava, colonialism comprised physical violence, occupation of lands, and the flight of resources from the colonies to the colonial powers; disempowering the former and enriching the latter. But colonialism implied more than that. Cultures and minds were also "colonized."

When explaining the colonization of cultures and minds, Bhargava introduces the concept "epistemic framework":

> An epistemic framework is a historically generated, collectively sustained system of meanings and significance, by reference to which

> a group understands and evaluates its individual and collective identity. (Ibid.: 401)

Naturally, an epistemic framework is important – indeed necessary – for any culture. It provides its members with basic tools for understanding the world and themselves. Now, Bhargava argues that colonialism replaced the epistemic framework of the colonized peoples with the colonizers'. This aspect of colonialism he calls "epistemic injustice." He explains:

> Epistemic injustice is a form of cultural injustice. It occurs when the concepts and categories by which a people understand themselves and their world are replaced or adversely affected by the concepts and categories of the colonizers. (Ibid.)

How then did this happen? According to Bhargava, cultural and epistemic injustices can take different forms and the epistemic framework of the colonized could be lost by different processes.

First, when the dominant epistemic categories are those of the colonizers, the traditional, domestic categories become "scattered and diffused." Second, even when the epistemic framework of the colonized groups remains, it is considered worthless and inferior and is marginalized in the society. The third kind of epistemic injustice happens when the content of the epistemic framework is transformed. Bhargava gives an example: For the colonizer, the colonized appeared as a collective, a mass of people and not as individuals. They then transferred this view to the epistemic framework of the colonized, portraying it falsely as "collectivist." This resulted in colonial policies that were "based on the idea that the conception of an individual was simply absent among the colonized and that only group identity mattered in their traditions" (Ibid.: 415).

To conquer the culture

What happened then when the colonizers left? According to Bhargava "a new, second phase of colonialism began." The domestic academic elite took over the Western epistemic framework and even identified "with the aggressor" (Ibid.: 416). The intellectuals know by heart the imported Western theories and categories but are ignorant of their own traditions. Some of them face the challenge of restoring their own traditions, which have been marginalized and despised for a long time.

Bhargava writes: "[T]he slow, painstaking process of partial recovery of the voice and history of the colonized can begin by putting together and reinterpreting traces of evidence and meaning present in largely forgotten texts" (Ibid.: 417). However, the recovery of their own traditions should according to Bhargava not lead to the exclusion of Western ideas. Instead, the people should aim for "bi-culturalism."

When reading Bhargava, I was reminded of what my master's student from Pakistan said in my class on global justice, as mentioned in Chapter 1. I raised the question whether colonialism had left any morally relevant traces in the present. She explained:

> Yes, certainly! Everything Pakistani is today considered of less worth compared to the West: we consider our own history as shameful and we feel that we are still slaves under the British rulers. These feelings have also a cultural impact today; to be beautiful is to have blond hair, not black, to be civilized is to eat with knife and fork, not to eat in our traditional way, and our traditional languages are superseded by English.

Bhargava elaborates on the epistemic background of this experience. Epistemic injustice is, according to Bhargava, a kind of cultural injustice and means that "concepts and categories" providing self-understanding and orientation are replaced or marginalized by a dominant power, in his case the colonizer. For the colonizer, Bhargava writes, it was "important to conquer not only the land and goods of the colonized but also their culture and minds" (Ibid.: 114).

Some challenging questions

Bhargava's contribution is well argued and convincing, but also challenging. His argument is quite brief and general and in need of clarification and distinctions.

According to Bhargava,

> The current conjecture in the world is witness to a dramatic, almost irreversible breakdown of the hegemony of mainstream intellectual traditions of the west. Ideas and practices associated with the modern west have been long criticized. (Ibid.: 413)

This kind of generalization of "Western ideas" seems to be less than helpful to the analysis. Among Western ideas one finds neo-liberalism, as well as Marxism, fascism, and egalitarianism. What is the purpose of lumping together so many different ideas in this way? Is it really helpful to categorize ideas as "Western" or "Eastern"? Bhargava's analysis of how colonialism has led to epistemic injustice is not dependent on such a rough characterization.

Bhargava argues that each group has its own "system of meanings and interpretations" (Ibid.). That could be interpreted as implying a kind of relativism, because if each group has its own epistemic framework it is hard to see how they could communicate with each other. However, that strong interpretation does not seem to be Bhargava's view, because – as we have noticed – he also argues for the possibility of "bi-culturalism," which means a "potentially common tradition." He even foresees "the renewal of western traditions by nonwestern people" (Ibid.: 417). This more universalistic view is in agreement with, for example, Amartya Sen's argument that different cultures and religions share some common values, such as freedom (Sen, 2000). Interestingly, both Bhargava and Sen use the example of the 3rd-century Indian emperor Asoka in their arguments – Bhargava's for the need to recapture lost or marginalized perspectives, Sen's to show that universal views of freedom and tolerance are inherent to Indian tradition.

My final point takes me to both Bhargava's and my own conclusions in this book. Bhargava argues that the concept of global justice would benefit from "rejuvenating" from the "outsiders" (Ibid.). He does not explain what this would mean in practice, but from his article one can assume that he has in mind that the voices of the "wretched of the earth" should be listened to, and that ideas and concepts of global justice should be reinterpreted by scholars from the South. I agree that our understanding of global justice would benefit from their experiences and views. However, the discussion on global justice can also benefit in other ways from Bhargava's perspective. Colonialism implied, as Bhargava spells out, not only economic exploitation and political domination for hundreds of years, but also a changed mindset of the colonized subjects, implying a loss of cultural means for identity formation and self-respect. What should the colonial powers do to repay this huge debt? How could that type of wrong be rectified? How should we globally dispel the enduring relations of dominance, epistemic and others, and establish relations characterized by equality and mutual respect?

7
Rectification for Slavery

Introduction

The aim of this chapter is to analyze arguments for rectification for the slave trade. I start with excerpts from the Abuja and Durban Declarations that highlight the need for remembrance of slavery and the slave trade. In contrast to the Durban Declaration, the Abuja Declaration asks for rectification, including compensation, to Africa. Then I give a short overview of the history of slavery in Africa and the slave trade, and finally I discuss whether present-day African nations should be compensated for the harmful economic impact of the slave trade.

In 1993 African leaders met in Abuja in Nigeria. The so-called Abuja Proclamation demanded that former colonial powers and states involved in the slave trade should compensate for past injustices. At the UN World Conference against Racism, Racial Discrimination, Xenophobia and Related Intolerance in Durban in 2001, slavery and the slave trade were in focus. The delegates expressed their sorrow for this "dark period in history" and demanded that it should be commemorated. However, there was no unanimity over claims for rectification. In fact, a group preparing the Declaration demanded that a development fund should be created for compensation for the damages caused by the slave trade and colonialism but this claim was not included in the final Declaration (Tan, 2007).

In Chapter 1 I included some essential paragraphs from the Durban Declarations (Durban I in 2001 and the follow-up conference in Geneva in 2009). Here follow some paragraphs from the Abuja Proclamation.

The Abuja Proclamation

The Abjuja Proclamation was the Declaration of the first Abuja Pan-African Conference on Reparations for African Enslavement, Colonization and Neo-Colonization, sponsored by the Organization of African Unity and Its Reparations Commission, April 27–29, 1993. The Proclamation is introduced with the following words:

> recalling the Organization of African Unity's establishment of a machinery, the Group of Eminent Persons, for appraising the issue of reparations in relation to the damage done to Africa and its Diaspora by enslavement, colonization, and neo-colonialism.

Then it states:

- Convinced that the issue of reparations is an important question requiring the united action of Africa and its Diaspora and worthy of the active support of the rest of the international community...
- Fully persuaded that the damage sustained by the African peoples is not a "thing of the past" but is painfully manifest in the damaged lives of contemporary Africans from Harlem to Harare, in the damaged economies of the Black World from Guinea to Guyana, from Somalia to Surinam...
- Respectfully aware of historic precedents in reparations, ranging from German payment of restitution to the Jews for the enormous tragedy of the Nazi Holocaust to the question of compensating Japanese-Americans for injustice of internment by the Roosevelt Administration in the United States during World War II...
- Cognizant of the fact that compensation for injustice need not necessarily be paid only in capital transfer but could include service to the victims or other forms of restitution and readjustment of the relationship agreeable to both parties...
- Emphatically convinced that what matters is not the guilt but the responsibility of those states and nations whose economic evolution once depended on slave labor and colonialism, and whose forebears participated either in selling and buying Africans, or in owning them, or in colonizing them...
- Convinced that the pursuit of reparations by the African peoples in the continent and in the Diaspora will itself be a learning experience in self-discovery and in uniting experience politically and psychologically...

- Convinced that numerous [acts of] looting, theft and larceny have been committed on the African People... [the Commission]
- Calls upon those in possession of their stolen goods artifacts and other traditional treasuries to restore them to their rightful owners the African People.
- Calls upon the international community to recognize that there is a unique and unprecedented moral debt owed to the African peoples which has yet to be paid – the debt of compensation to the Africans as the most humiliated and exploited people of the last four centuries of modern history.

The Abuja Proclamation emphasizes that slavery and the slave trade have had enduring consequences up till the present day, and it mentions poverty among blacks both in Africa and in America and the enduring economic problems in Africa as examples of this. The Proclamation states further that while damages caused by the slave trade and colonialism are still manifest, there is a need for compensation. The argument for compensation is underpinned by references to the payment by Germany to the Jews after the Holocaust and the Unites States' payment to Japanese-Americans who were detained in the US during World War II.

The Durban Declaration against Racism, Racial Discrimination, Xenophobia and Related Intolerance from 2001 was approved by the conference delegates. The introductory part of the declaration underlines the horror of slavery and the slave trade and relates it to colonialism. Like the Abuja Proclamation, the Durban Declaration argues that this period in history had enduring consequences in terms of poverty and inequality. The Declaration also stresses that the memories of the victims should be honored and that reoccurrence of such historical horror must be prevented. The Declaration asserts that the states that were once responsible for slavery and the slave trade have a duty to apologize for their past involvement and to contribute to restore "the dignity of the victims," and it emphasizes the need for development programs based on equality and mutuality in order to overcome the present poverty.

According to the Durban Declaration, colonialism did not end with independence for the colonies and the withdrawal of the colonial powers. This period in history had lasting reverberations, which continue to affect the former colonies as well as the former colonial powers and their mutual relations. The same is true of slavery. Slavery has existed throughout the history of mankind but the Declaration primarily refers to the transatlantic slave trade from Africa and Asia to the Americas beginning in the 15th century and abolished, but not ended, by the British parliament in 1807.

The question of rectification for colonialism and slavery was a much debated issue at the conference. Although the delegates managed to agree on a final Declaration, there were persisting disagreements among the delegates. The Western delegates (European Union and US) argued against any formulation that declared that slavery and the slave trade *at the time* was a crime against humanity, because such a formulation could lead to claims for reparations. They reasoned that while international regulations prohibiting slavery were introduced later, at the time of the slave trade it was not according to international law considered a crime. Consequently, they also opposed the inclusion in the Declaration of legal claims for rectification (Beckles, 2013).

The African delegations were divided. The Durban conference was preceded by the so-called Gorée initiative. To prepare for the Durban conference a group of African scholars and NGOs met in Gorée in Senegal at the initiative of the Inter-African Union for Human Rights. The Gorée initiative stated that

> the principle of just and fair reparations for the Slave Trade and enslavement of Africans is the usual result of the recognition of this crime. In the specific case, it is a crime against humanity ... reparations should not be considered as a sanction, but rather as a step forward in reconciling the human family. (Quoted in Beckles, 2013: 183)

During the Durban conference some African leaders, including those from South Africa, Senegal, and Nigeria, while of course condemning slavery and the slave trade, tried to avoid any mention of rectificatory claims. Instead, on the initiative of the President of Senegal, they announced a New African Initiative, referring to an "African renaissance" with a new self-confident African continent taking responsibility for its own future development. This initiative was supported by the Western nations, and the World Bank intervened and promised financial support for development projects.

The Gorée initiative was, however, objected to by the Caribbean states and several African NGOs in Durban. They insisted that there was an outstanding moral duty for the former slave-trading nations to compensate the victims, including their descendants, for the slave trade.

A crucial formulation in the final Declaration from the Durban conference was the following: the signatories "further acknowledge that slavery and the slave trade are crimes against humanity and *should* always have been so" (Para. 1). With the word "should" the Declaration makes it clear that slavery at the time when it was practiced was not a crime against humanity, even if from today's horizon it is considered such a crime. Therefore, as a consequence, no one could claim compensation. The Caribbean delegations, on the other hand, insisted that slavery and the slave trade had always been crimes against humanity, irrespective of whether they occurred yesterday or 300 years ago (Beckles, 2013: 172–193).

Slavery and the slave trade

At the time of the transatlantic slave trade, slavery was nothing new for the African continent. Africa had for centuries delivered slaves to the Greek and Roman Empires and to Arab countries to the north and it continued to do so when colonialism created a new market for this trade. However, the slave trade spiked after the discovery of the Americas. It was not long before the demand for slaves from Africa rose. At first, the colonizers of America used the native Indians as a workforce. However, it soon became apparent that they could not withstand forced labor. Indians could not sustain the colonization and Basil Davidson writes that as early as 1518 a "well placed" Spaniard reported that when the island Hispaniola was discovered it was inhabited by over a million Indians, but after only 20 years the number was down to 11,000 (Davidson, 1991: 207). Work force had to be sought somewhere else.

In the 17th century the slave trade accelerated. Slaves were captured by African kings, armed bands, and Portuguese warlords. Paul Lovejoy describes how enslavement was conducted: African states raided neighboring states to capture slaves, African kings engaged in warfare against neighbors to capture prisoners of war to sell to the Europeans, criminals were convicted and enslaved, and African and European warlords raided villages and kidnapped young men and women. The slave trade was profitable and many merchants were involved. The African kingdoms tried to control it in order to exclude private merchants, but without success (Lovejoy, 2000: 78–90, 104).

African slaves were a valuable resource on the American market. In contrast to the Indians, they could adjust to the harsh working conditions. In return for slaves, African kings and merchants got silver, textiles, and, not least important, firearms. Firearms were especially attractive returns and the increasing access to weapons led to further wars and enslavements campaigns.

The slave trade was at the time a large business sector. For example, in the 1750s, 330,000 British seamen were engaged in it (Beckles, 2013: 45). How many slaves were captured and where did they come from? The answers to these questions are debated. Historian Paul Lovejoy has conducted a detailed investigation of the slave trade. According to Lovejoy's estimates, the total number of slaves exported from Africa to America in the period from 1450 to 1900 was 11.3 million. More than half of them were exported in the 18th century. The majority of the slaves came from West Africa (the bays of Benin and Biafra) and southwest Africa, but a large number also came from southeast Africa (Lovejoy, 2000: 19, 81, 146).

What did it mean to be a slave? As Lovejoy defines the term, a slave is someone's property, subject to coercion without any possibility to influence his or her destiny, an outsider denied heritage and a right to reproduction (Ibid.). Thus, a slave is treated as a commodity and not as a person. Needless to say, the status of slaves made them vulnerable to mistreatment, humiliation, and exploitation. Slaves were treated as cattle, both after their capture and during their transport to America. On the overcrowded transatlantic ships, slaves were kept below decks and the death rate was 10–15% (Davidson, 1991: 214). Upon arrival in the new continent, the slaves were branded with the initials of their owner (Beckles, 2013: 42).

Marcus Rediker reports that in order to prevent the slaves from deserting in the African ports or during the passage across the Atlantic, the captain would throw one slave into the water to be attacked by sharks. He reports the following story:

> A captain seized upon a woman and sacrificed her as a proper example to the rest. The woman was tied with ropes and lowered into the water. When the poor creature was thus plunged in, and about half way down, she was heard to give a terrible shriek, which at first was ascribed to her fears of drowning; but soon after it was found that a shark which had followed the ship, had bit her off from the middle. (Rediker, 2007: 40)

The slaves were seen as cargo rather than as humans. Hilary Beckles recounts the story of the "Zong case" in 1781. A ship named "Zong" carrying 470 chained slaves was delayed for various reasons. Because of the delay both Africans and crew got sick and many died. According to insurance regulations, accidental deaths of slaves and slaves killed or thrown into the water after rebelling, but not natural deaths, were covered by the insurer. As a consequence, in order to save water and to be able to claim insurance money, the captain Luke Collingwood decided to throw living slaves overboard. By the end of the journey 131 Africans had been dumped in the sea (Beckles, 2013: 71–73).

By the end of the 18th century protests against the slave trade were growing and the opposition became more organized, especially in Great Britain. Slavery was questioned both for moral and for economic reasons. Slavery did not fit well in the emerging capitalist economy and the economic gains from slavery for the leading economic power Great Britain had diminished (Ibid.: 108). As a consequence of the opposition, the slave trade was prohibited by Great Britain in 1807 and other Western powers soon followed suit. However, it was not easy to stop a trade with such global dimensions. Not only did the slave trade continue in many parts of Africa but, as a consequence of its abolition overseas, the internal it actually increased during the 19th century. As a matter of fact, as Lovejoy points out, anti-slavery ideology became a "banner" for the European colonization of Africa at the end of the century. Missionaries and others argued that they had a "civilizing" mission aimed at ending the African slave trade with the Arab countries and elsewhere (Lovejoy, 2000: 286).

So, what is the legacy of slavery and the slave trade? What were the lasting economic consequences of the fact that millions of young and industrious people were taken away from their homeland and shipped to the Americas? This is a debated issue among historians. According to the "minimalist" position, the rate of abduction of slaves was lower than the natural rate of population increase and the loss of people was compensated for by the high birth rate in the mostly polygamous African societies. According to the "maximalist" position, although not more than 9 million slaves entered the Americas between 1700 and 1850, a total of 21 million people were captured in Africa and the ones who never reached America were used for domestic slavery or suffered death in captivity. As a consequence, in 1850 the Sub-Saharan African population was estimated at half what it would have been without slavery (Waites, 1999: 105–106).

As we have seen, African kings recruited slaves through wars against their neighbors. Hence, the slave trade added fuel to internal conflicts between African kingdoms. Through the slave trade Africa, and in particular West Africa, lost a big proportion of its most able population. The slave trade had other economic consequences in that it undermined other, more productive, endeavors. The young workforce could have been used to develop their home countries and work in agriculture, manufacturing, and trade instead of being sent to America. Because of all these effects, the slave trade had enduring consequences. It undermined a productive and sane economic development, weakened African kingdoms, and paved the way for European imperialism at the end of the 19th century.

Another lasting consequence of slavery was a sense of subjection and humiliation among Africans. Rhoda Howard-Hassman quotes one of her African students, who says:

> Europeans who bought Africans treated them as subhuman: they raped, tortured, mutilated, and murdered their slaves with impunity. To know that one's ancestors were, or might have been, enslaved in such a dreadful way is painful. (Howard-Hassman, 2008: 75)

Victims

Who then were the victims of the slave trade? And are there any victims today who – if there is a justified case for rectification – should be compensated?

Victims of the slave trade could be found on both sides of the Atlantic. When slaves arrived in South and North America, they were treated like animals and suffered from degradation and overwork. This has led to a vibrant discussion in the United States about ways to compensate the present black population for the long-ranging consequences of slavery (Brophy, 2006).

In Africa the immediate victims of slavery were the families and compatriots of the slaves who were left behind and suffered the social and economic consequences of the "drain" of millions of their sons and daughters and brothers and sisters. The crucial question for rectification is, however, whether these consequences now lie in the past or still reverberate in the present. Did slavery and the slave trade have enduring social and economic costs that present Africans are still having to pay?

Arguments for rectification for slavery and the slave trade

Both the Abuja Proclamation and the Durban Declaration describe slavery and the slave trade as past injustices that have had lasting consequences. The Abuja Proclamation demanded rectification, while the Durban Declaration more vaguely spoke of restoration and a need for contributions to poverty relief. According to both declarations, the legacies of the slave trade are both economic and ideological. It disrupted the African economies with effects that can still be observed today and it implied humiliation of an entire population and fueled enduring racism.

In the next section I first discuss the argument that the long-lasting social and economic consequences of slavery and the slave trade that still hamper development in Africa is a reason for rectification. Slavery and the slave trade also had enduring cultural and ideological effects, which are discussed in the following section. Finally, I comment on the present implications of these economic and ideological effects.

Rectification for lasting economic stagnation?

According to the argument for rectification, African states should be compensated for slavery, or more precisely for the transatlantic slave trade, because it caused long-lasting economic stagnation in Africa, or at least in the parts of Africa that were involved in the slave trade. Hence, present-day African states (and their citizens) are still victims of the slave trade and deserve rectification.

The argument is based, first, on the factual premise that *the slave trade caused long-lasting economic stagnation* and, second, on the normative premise that *victims of economic stagnation should be compensated.* A condition for the normative premise is that the economic stagnation was caused by human agency. Indeed, people who are suffering from economic stagnation caused by, for example, a natural disaster may receive economic relief from the government, but compensation as an act of rectificatory justice requires that the harm was caused by human agents or institutions (which is an instrument of human action). There must be someone who can be held responsible.

In accordance with the model for rectification presented in Chapter 9, rectification for lasting economic stagnation caused by slavery and the slave trade requires that if X, an agent, did A, caused long-lasting economic stagnation, to Y (Africans) at t1, that is, during the period of slavery and the slave trade, then A at t2 should acknowledge the harm, apologize and compensate the victims.

Who then was morally responsible for the slave trade, that is, who were the agents? The slave trade involved a chain of activities from the capture of a slave, transportation to a slave market, sale, and transportation over the ocean to the final destination: an American plantation, farm, or home. The supply and marketing of slaves were typically controlled by Africans and in this sense native African kings and merchants were actively involved in the slave trade. At the slave market, European traders took over, with the blessing of their governments. This means that the slave trade was managed in collaboration between Africans and Europeans. This fact has implications for the question of who should be assigned responsibility today. The responsibility is shared by present European and African states. This co-responsibility was also acknowledged by Ghanaian tribal leaders in 2007, who publically apologized for the kidnapping and sale of slaves by their forefathers.

On the other hand, this sharing of responsibility does not seem entirely fair. The project or institution of the transatlantic slave trade was orchestrated by the colonial powers, and in particular Great Britain. Therefore, one should distinguish between those who had a major responsibility, that is, colonial politicians and merchants, and those who had a minor responsibility, carrying out the project as subcontractors, that is, the African kings and merchants.

The argument that the former slave-trading nations should compensate Africa today, rests on the controversial factual premise that the slave trade, as a matter of fact, was a causal factor behind long-term economic stagnation in parts of Africa.

Did then the slave trade lead to underdevelopment in Sub-Saharan Africa? After a thorough investigation of the impact of the slave trade on different conditions for economic development, the economist J. E. Inikori's answer is yes. I will here summarize his argumentation. He bases it on three factors: (1) the demographic impact of the fact that, between 1500 and 1890, millions of people in their most productive stage of life were exported as commodities; (2) the long-term political effects in Africa of the slave trade; and (3) the lasting implications for the African economies.

As was noted above, there are different estimations of the number of slaves. In line with Lovejoy, Inikori estimates that between 1500 and 1890 about 22 million slaves were exported to the Americas and to Muslim countries in the north. Their age was between 16 and 30 and the sex ratio around 2 males to 1 female. To this number should be added the number of captives that never made it across the Atlantic. A large number of captives – one estimation is around 25% – died before they arrived (Inikori 1982, 23).

The demographic implications were not limited to the number of slaves. There was an unusual frequency of wars during this period. As we saw, the slave trade motivated military operations against neighboring nations and slave-raiding. These military operations and wars also had demographic consequences.

When summarizing the demographic implications, Inikori writes:

> When proper account is taken of all the new factors affecting demographic processes in West Africa from 1500 [to] 1880, the evidence points strongly to a significant declining population from 1650 to 1850...It seems clear, therefore, that the existing evidence strongly supports the conclusion that the population of sub-Saharan Africa was declining from the seventeenth to the nineteenth century. (Inikori, 1982: 29–30)

The slave trade also had political and cultural implications on African kingdoms which affected their development, Inikori argues. He writes: "[T]he political and cultural spheres of these kingdoms and empires were all structured in accordance with the economic conditions provided by the export slave trade" (Ibid.: 16). One political effect, as we have just seen, was conflicts and wars between kingdoms. There were raids into neighboring countries to acquire captives for export. Another, no less important, factor was the conflicts between kingdoms and empires for influence and control over the slave trade. These conflicts were clearly obstacles to economic development, Inikori argues. Slaves were often traded against arms, which increased the tendency to go to war (Ibid.: 45–51).

The slave trade had both direct and indirect detrimental effects on economic development, Inikori argues. The direct effects were the loss of a productive workforce. But, further, while the economic focus was on the slave trade, other economic activities were neglected. Africa could have produced goods and raw materials that instead were produced in America. Inikori writes:

> The irony of the situation is that the export slave trade lowered Africa's comparative advantage, while increasing that of the Americas, in the development of commodity production and trade with Europe. (Ibid.: 53)

There was obviously a potential global demand for these products, but Africa was not a supplier due to the fact that its economy was oriented towards the slave trade.

The lack of population pressure necessary for the transformation of manufacturing and agriculture is another economic factor that Inikori points at. Inikori argues that, according to economic theory, population pressure leads to incentives for higher productivity and new technologies. In contrast, the low population density in Africa following from the export of millions of people led to extensive farming and local self-sufficiency. He summarizes:

> The underdevelopment of African agriculture between 1600 and 1900 was thus due to underpopulation and lack of external demand for agricultural commodities, both of which were the direct product of the export slave trade. (Ibid.: 56)

Parallel to the export of slaves, Africa imported cheap manufactured goods from Europe. This flow of textiles and other goods, which continued after the end of the slave trade, undermined domestic production. African manufacturing was, in contrast to European, not protected by customs or tariffs and could not compete with the imported goods.

In conclusion Inikori writes:

> In the end, underpopulation and the political and social distortions arising from the slave trade created conditions entirely hostile to the process of economic transformation. To make matters worse, the stimulating influence of commodity export trade could not operate as the slave trade prevented the development of growth of all other forms of trade. Sub-Saharan Africa thus developed over the slave trade era as a periphery of other economies in the Atlantic area. And once that position was firmly entrenched, it tended to be self-perpetuating, particularly under colonial rule when there were no independent national governments to reverse the trend. (Ibid.: 59–60)

Following Inikori, it seems that the slave trade undermined economic development in Africa in different ways. Furthermore, the slave trade was an incidence within a series of European intrusions that undermined African economies. As we saw, the slave trade had different kinds of devastating consequences for Africa. It weakened Africa and paved the way for colonization from abroad. The new European rulers adjusted African economies in the 19th century in accordance with their own needs, and there is a causal link between what happened then and the present underdevelopment and dependency of many African economies. This is an example of enduring injustice that requires rectification. Thus, rectification is perhaps not primarily motivated by the slave trade *per se*, because there are at present no living victims, but by a chain of European trespasses and intrusions, including the slave trade, which resulted in long-lasting underdevelopment in Africa.

Lasting violations of human dignity

In the last section I discussed the argument that slavery and the slave trade had long-term economic consequences in Africa. Another lasting effect of slavery and the slave trade was the disregard and violation of human dignity following the institution of slavery. Human beings were treated as cattle by the slave traders. There are plenty of eye-witness reports showing how the slaves were caught, imprisoned, renamed, and transported. The slave lodge in Cape Town in South Africa, now a museum, is one setting where one can learn about how the slaves were treated.

Without any doubt, slavery and the slave trade had lasting cultural and human consequences. The slave trade can be seen as a symbol of, as well as a cause of, a categorization of human beings that was established during colonialism; the white as master and the non-white as servant. Even if the institution of slavery has been abolished and colonialism is a past period in history, the power structure and priorities that it represents is still with us. As one of the participants in a seminar in Uganda said: "History is important for your identity – for who you are. Failure to make up for colonialism implies for us a continued sense of subjection." I presume that this statement summarizes the experiences of many black people. Cultural and human implications of colonialism and slavery such as these are a main focus of post-colonial studies (Loomba, 2005; Fanon, 2004).

Who then are the present victims of the long-lasting human consequences of the slave trade? The immediate victims of the slave trade are long since dead. But even later generations of black people are victims because they are disrespected due to the color of their skin, and this lack of respect is a legacy of slavery and the slave trade.

But what could rectification mean for this kind of legacy of the slave trade? Who should be compensated and how? Descendants should not be compensated for harms suffered by their ancestors. Neither should present black people be compensated because of injustices done to their forefathers. Instead, to overcome the lasting racist consequences of the slave trade we should aim to establish relations between blacks and whites that are characterized by human dignity, equality, and mutual respect.

But is it really fair to focus on the slave trade driven by the Western nations when we know that other forms of slavery were also practiced at the time? In her book *Reparations to Africa* Rhoda Howard-Hassman discusses demands for reparations for the transatlantic slave trade. She thinks that the Abuja and Durban Declarations and other African claims for rectification are guilty of one-sidedness. She writes:

> This focus on Africa's relations with the West, but not on its relations with other regions, raises some uncomfortable questions. Not only the Western world, but also the Muslim world, enslaved Africans. (Howard-Hassman, 2008: 71)

However, the fact that other wrongs were committed should not restrain us from criticizing specific wrongs. A more reasonable position is rather that the critique of the Western slave trade should be supplemented by a critique of similar atrocities committed by others.

Conclusion

The Abuja Proclamation argued for rectification for slavery and the slave trade, and the UN conference on racism in Durban emphasized in its final Declaration that present-day racism is related to colonialism and slavery and that there is a need to restore "the dignity of the victims" of colonialism and the slave trade. In this chapter I have discussed two arguments for rectificatory justice: first, that African nations should be compensated for slavery, or more precisely for the transatlantic slave trade, because it caused long-lasting economic stagnation in Africa, and second that there is a case for rectificatory justice due to the degradation and humiliation of human dignity caused by slavery and the slave trade.

My conclusion is first that the argument that African nations should be compensated for the slave trade is based on the somewhat controversial assumption that the slave trade had devastating long-term economic effects. However, irrespective of present economic traces of past injustices, there is a case for apology for what once happened. Furthermore, the slave trade was the beginning of a range of aggressions that resulted in enduring injustices up until this day. There is an outstanding duty for the former colonial powers to do what they can to change the resulting unequal relations in global politics and economy.

Second, slavery and the transatlantic slave trade entailed grave violations of the human dignity of the slaves. The institution of slavery implied a master–slave relationship. This had lasting implications for racial attitudes and the possibility of mutual respect between whites and blacks. There is still a need to pay attention to stereotypes and to establish relations characterized by mutual respect.

What claims for rectification and compensation for colonial wrongs have the victims of colonial injustices raised so far? Have the former colonial powers ever acknowledged past wrongs or apologized? These questions are in the foreground of the next chapter.

8
Claims for Justice after Colonialism

Colonialism lasted for almost 500 years. During this period European nations occupied countries in other continents, massacred large numbers of the indigenous peoples, and dominated those who survived, using many of them as slaves or as forced labor. The economies of the occupied territories were adjusted in the interests of the colonizers. One could expect that this lengthy period should have resulted in massive demands for rectification when it finally ended in the 1960s and 1970s. However, this did not happen. As we will see in this chapter, victims of colonialism have indeed claimed compensation, and there are examples of apologies from former perpetrators, but the numbers are far less than might be expected.

In later chapters I will discuss the philosophical arguments for rectification for colonial injustices and what rectification could mean in practice. In order to situate my argumentation in a historical and political context, I will in this chapter briefly describe existing claims for rectification. I will start with some cases of rectification to former colonies, then give some examples of initiatives for rectification for the slave trade, and finally give an account of some instances of rectification to indigenous populations.

Rectification to former colonies

The Boers

The Boer War was a colonial war between two European population groups. The Boers had emigrated from the Netherlands to South Africa in the 17th century and had lived there since then. As a consequence of their long inhabitation, they claimed to be an indigenous population. At the end of the 19th century the Boers resisted British dominance and a war broke out in 1899. The British engaged in a harsh suppression of the Boers, mobilizing 450,000 men. Large numbers of the Boer population were put in camps, where 27,927 of them died (Ferguson, 2004: 280; Gann and Duignan, 1978: 129).

In 1999 the British queen Elizabeth visited South Africa. During her visit she addressed the Boers and apologized for British violence towards and suppression of the Boers. As we saw in Chapter 3, the British also suppressed indigenous African tribes, killing thousands of black people. During her visit, black leaders requested that the queen also address the British devastation of African tribes during the 19th century, but she refused to do so (Howard-Hassman, 2008: 141).

South West Africa

In September 2011 a delegation from the Herero and Nama peoples in Namibia, led by Chief Kuiama Riruako, arrived in Berlin. The purpose of the visit was to take home 20 skulls that had been brought to Germany after the genocide against the Herero and Nama tribes in 1904–1907. "For us it means the return of our relatives, grandmothers and great-grandfathers," Ida Hoffman, a member of the committee, said to journalists (The Telegraph, 2011).

In Chapter 4 the genocide of the Herero tribe by the German colonialists at the beginning of the 20th century was described. The visit of the delegation to Berlin focused attention on the massacres committed by German soldiers under the lead of General Lothar von Trotha. Von Trotha was under the command of Emperor Wilhelm II when he ordered the extermination of the Herero nation in retaliation for threats to Germans in South West Africa. Before the massacres, the Herero population was estimated at 80,000; three years later only around 16,000 survived.

The visit of the delegation to Berlin was not the first time that the genocide was commemorated. Descendants of the Herero tribe have claimed rectification several times. When German Chancellor Helmut Kohl had visited Namibia in 1995, Herero soldiers had presented him with a petition demanding payment of war reparations to the Herero people (Gewald, 1999: 1). A similar claim had been made to German President Roman Herzog when he visited Namibia in 1999. In 2001, the Herero People's Reparations Corporation had filed a lawsuit in an American federal court against both the Federal Republic of Germany and German corporations that had benefitted from German colonialism. The Namibian government, though, refused to support the lawsuit, arguing that the whole nation had suffered from German colonialism and they did not want to highlight the suffering of just one particular tribe. They also feared that the lawsuit would endanger the relations between Namibia and Germany, especially serious given Germany was Namibia's main donor (Kurowska, 2008).

Finally, in 2004, on the centenary of the genocide, the German minister for Economic Development and Cooperation Heidemarie Wieczorek-Zeul apologized on behalf of the German government but she did not promise any economic compensation to Namibia or to the descendants of the victims (BBC News, 2004). In 2012 the German parliament rejected a proposal from the Linke party that an apology and compensation should be given to the descendants of the victims in order to achieve reconciliation.[1]

Congo

The Belgian king Leopold II's reign over Congo between 1885 and 1908 was one of the cruelest episodes in colonial history. The quest for raw materials cost millions of African lives (see Chapter 4). But in spite of its shameful past, Belgium has never officially taken responsibility for what happened.

There is to date only one case of an official Belgian apology to Congo, but not concerning the ravaging of Congo during Leopold IIs reign. In 1961, when Congo became independent from Belgium, Patrice Lumumba was elected president. However, his plan to nationalize the foreign-owned mines led to his assassination. Belgian officers were involved in the assassination and in 2002 Belgium issued an official apology (Howard-Hassman, 2006: 144).

Uganda

Having conquered the kingdom of Buganda in 1890, British colonizers aimed also to conquer the kingdom of Bunyoro, situated in the northern part of present Uganda. However, Kabalega, the king of Bunyoro, did not surrender to the British troops and it was not until 1897 that the British finally captured him. Meanwhile, war devastated parts of the kingdom and many natives starved (see also Chapter 4).

In 2004 – more than a hundred years later – Solomon Iguru I, king of the Bunyoro territory in Uganda and a descendent of King Kabalega, announced that he would sue Britain for crimes committed during the war against his forefather (Pulford 2007, 120–121). In an interview the prime minister of Bunyoro-Kitara declared: "We want justice as the first thing... Certainly, they should compensate us. It doesn't have to be cash really but if a programme could be worked out to address these injustices, I think we would be okay" with it (Ibid.). However, the British government has not made any efforts to compensate or apologize.

In April 2014, in a similar request, representatives of the Lamogi clan, belonging to the Acholi people in Uganda, whose ancestors fought with the Bunyoro against the British colonizers, claimed compensation from the British government for injuries inflicted during a rebellion in 1911. According to the accusations, the British troops killed clan members and used chemicals in their efforts to suppress the rebellion, both of which had long-lasting effects in the region. After the rebellion was crushed, the British displaced Lamogi inhabitants, and the "effects are still haunting the people of Lamogi," according to MP Gilbert Olanga (Acholi Times, 2014).

Kenya

During the war of liberation against the British that finally led to Kenya's independence in 1963, between 150,000 and 320,000 Kenyans, primarily belonging to the Kikuyu tribe, were placed in detention camps. Many were tortured and killed (see Chapter 4).[2]

In 2005 the Kenyan Justice Minister Kiraitu Murungi asked for a formal apology from the British government for "barbaric crimes against humanity," but received no response (BBC News, 2005). Six years later a court case started that would turn out to be more successful.

In April 2011 four of the thousands of victims of the British war against the Mau Mau movement in Kenya around 50 years earlier came to London. The four appealed to a British court for compensation for the harms they had suffered in British detention camps. They had been victims of castration, torture, and rape. They were now elderly and one of them died before the trial ended.

In a court decision in October 2012 the Kenyans were given the right to sue the British government. When information about the treatment of prisoners in Kenya that was held secretly by the British Foreign Office was revealed, the British government started negotiations with thousands of Kenyans who had been victims of torture in the camps for compensation, and in June 2013 the British government decided to pay over £19 million in compensation (Cobain and Hatcher, 2013; Guardian, 2013a) (see also Chapter 14).

Libya

Libya was an Italian colony between 1912 and 1943. The Italian colonization was resisted by the Libyans and Italian troops violently crushed their resistance. Indigenous Libyan tribes were suppressed through mass deportations, use of chemical weapons, and killing of prisoners of war. As a consequence, about half of the Bedouin population was forced to leave their settlements and placed in concentration camps and approximately 40,000 of the 100,000 internees died in the camps (Duggan, 2007: 496).

In 2008 Italy decided to pay $5 billion in compensation for the atrocities suffered by the Libyan population during Italian colonization (Political Apologies and Rectifications 2014).

Algeria

When visiting Algeria several French presidents have admitted responsibility for atrocities committed there during the time of French colonization. For example, when President Chirac visited Algeria in 2000, he apologized for France's use of torture in trying to curb the Algerian war of liberation. One year later he admitted French responsibility for the deaths of hundreds of thousands of people during the same war (Political Apologies and Rectifications, 2014)

The massacres of demonstrators and subsequent repression resulting in between 15,000 and 45,000 deaths carried out by French troops in the Algerian town of Setif in 1945 have been a particular issue and Algerian presidents have requested that France should apologize for mass killings of Algerians. However, in 2006 the French Interior Minister Nicolas Sarkozy refused to apologize (Howard-Hassman, 2008: 144).

When President Hollande visited Algeria in 2012, he mentioned French colonial history in Algeria in his speech. He said: "For 132 years, Algeria was subjected to a brutal and unfair system: colonization…I acknowledge the suffering it caused," but he did not apologize, let alone sanction reparations (Deutsche Welle, 2012).

Indonesia

On the occasion of the Indonesian celebration of the 50th anniversary of the country's independence from the Netherlands in 1995 (according to Indonesian historiography, independence preceded the colonial war 1945–1949, but according to the Dutch, Indonesia won independence in 1949), the Dutch queen Beatrix visited Indonesia. In a speech she regretted the pain of the war and the fact that the Netherlands had not been prepared to grant Indonesia independence sooner. However, she did not apologize for its colonization (The Low Countries, 2011).

In 1947, during the war of liberation in Indonesia against the Dutch colonial regime, Dutch troops committed a massacre in the village of Rawagede. Four hundred and thirty-one of the villagers were killed. The killings did not become a court case until 2009, when ten survivors sued the Dutch state in court. Dutch government representatives publicly apologized for what had happened in Rawagede but argued that statutes of limitation applied. The Netherlands agreed to pay 850,000 Euro to the community and 180,000 to the plaintiffs and their families. In a ceremony in December 2011 the Dutch ambassador apologized on behalf of the Dutch government for the massacre (Radio Netherlands Worldwide, 2011) and in 2013, the Dutch government formally apologized for its colonial misdeeds. At a ceremony at the Dutch embassy in Indonesia the Dutch ambassador said:

> On behalf of the Dutch government, I apologize for these excesses. The Dutch government hopes that this apology will help close a difficult chapter for those whose lives were impacted so directly by the violent excesses that took place between 1945 and 1949. (Deutsche Welle, 2013)

Malaysia

In Malaysia about 10% of the population is of Indian descent. Many of them are socially and economically deprived. On November 25, 2007 a big demonstration took place outside the British embassy in Kuala Lumpur. The demonstration was organized by the newly formed Hindraf organization, which stands for Hindu Rights Action Force (Malaysiakini, 2007). Although Hindraf's specific target was the British authorities responsible for taking Indians to Malaysia for quasi-slave work during colonial times, the protest seemed also to be targeted against present discrimination of Indians in Malaysia An Indian lawyer affiliated to Hindraf filed a suit against Britain of US$4 trillion for "withdrawing after granting independence and leaving us [Indians] unprotected and at the mercy of a majority Malay-Muslim government that has violated our rights as minority Indians" (Ibid.).

Haiti

Haiti became a French colony in the 17th century. In 1803 slaves in Haiti rebelled and put an end to French colonial rule. French property was confiscated. Thirty-five years later, as an independent state, Haiti paid 90 million francs in gold to compensate French landowners, a payment that had considerable detrimental effects on the Haitian economy.

Two hundred years after the slave rebellion the Haitian President Aristides demanded repayment of the compensation by France. The sum was estimated at US$21 billion in present value. The French government dismissed the proposal and refused to acknowledge any reasons to repay, arguing that the reason the Haitian economy was bankrupt was corruption. The French Foreign Minister de Villepin also commented that the European Union had given Haiti €2 billion in foreign aid (Beckles 2013 214–215; Williams, 2003).

Rectification to victims of slavery

The slave trade was arguably the practice that caused the most suffering during colonialism. The primary victims were the slaves themselves, but their descendants also suffered from the consequences of the slave trade – as well as the African nations that lost many of their most productive inhabitants. Claims for rectification for the slave trade have been raised on both sides of the Atlantic.

As a result of the Abuja Pan-African Conference on Reparations for African Enslavement, Colonization and Neo-Colonization, supported by the Organization of African States (OAS), in 1993, the delegates issued the Abuja Proclamation demanding compensation for the African slave trade from American and European governments (Political Apologies and Rectifications, 2014). In line with the Abuja Proclamation, historian Ali Mazurui argued for restitution in the form of a "skill crusade" from the West to Africa, that is, the massive migration of well educated Westerners to Africa with the aim of lifting Africa out of poverty.

In preparation for the UN Conference on Racism in Durban in 2001, several members of the US Congress argued – but without success – that President George W. Bush should formally apologize for the slave trade at the conference (Political Apologies and Rectifications, 2014)

At the commemoration of the 200th anniversary of the abolition of British slave trade in 2007, Prime Minister Tony Blair expressed his sorrow for British participation in the trade. However, he did not apologize (Howard-Hassman, 2008: 141). In the same year Christian leaders from Europe went to Zimbabwe and apologized for harms done during the slave trade (Ibid.: 142). In a similar vein, The British Anglican Church has on many occasions apologized for British participation in slavery and the slave trade. For example, when the Archbishop of Canterbury visited Zanzibar in 2007, he condemned the slave trade and apologized on behalf of Britain (Political Apologies and Rectifications, 2014)

American presidents Bill Clinton and George W. Bush took up the slave trade in speeches when visiting African countries in 1998 and 2003, respectively. They both regretted what had happened but neither of them apologized (Howard-Hassman, 2008: 143). President Clinton also rejected proposals in the congress to compensate the descendants of slaves with the argument that it had happened a long time ago. However, in 2009 the US Senate passed a resolution to apologize to African-Americans for slavery and discrimination, though the resolution did not authorize any payment of compensation (Political Apologies and Rectifications, 2014). Moreover, the resolution addressed only black Americans, not African states.

The slave trade was a joint effort of African kings and European slave traders (see Chapter 7). In 2007 Ghanaian tribal leaders performed traditional ceremonies of apology and atonement in relation to the slaves that had been kidnapped by their forefathers and sold to slave traders (Political Apologies and Rectifications, 2014).

In 2014, 15 leaders of Caribbean states demanded that European slave-trading nations should apologize for their involvement in the slave trade and compensate the descendants of slaves, who still live in poor circumstances (see Chapter 14).

Rectification to indigenous populations

On all continents, when colonizers took over land they often drove out the indigenous people, killed them, or placed them in camps or reserves. These systematic violations of human rights have led to a number of apologies from political leaders.

During the 18th century the British colonization of Australia, Tasmania, and New Zealand led to the formation of six colonies. New Zealand got independence in 1856 and the other colonies joined and formed Australia in 1901.

Australian officials have on different occasions acknowledged the violent history of the British colonization of Australia and the genocide of Aborigines in the 18th, 19th, and 20th centuries. The Aboriginal population of ca. 1 million people at the time of the arrival of the colonizers was reduced by 90% by the terror, massacres and diseases that followed. Many Aboriginal children were taken from their parents and placed in white foster homes. The treatment of the Aborigines was publicly regretted by Prime Minister Paul Keating in a speech in 1992 (Political Apologies and Rectifications, 2014).

In 2009 the Australian Prime Minister Kevin Rudd issued an apology to the Aboriginal population. The apology was followed by an action plan to support the Aborigines, including educational projects about Aboriginal history and a national database of children who had been taken from their homes that would assist them in finding their biological families (Ibid.).

In 1840, during the colonization of New Zealand, the British government signed the Treaty of Waitangi with native Maori leaders, guaranteeing the Maori rights to their land. This treaty was broken by the colonists and the New Zealand government considered in 2005 how this could be rectified. A tribunal was set up and discussions on how to apologize to the Maori people have been going on since then (Young, 2008). Furthermore, claims from Maori tribes for compensation are being settled by the New Zealand government in the form of compensation to the tribes (Tahana, 2013).

During Britain's colonization of Canada the indigenous population was oppressed and abused in different ways. For example, a parliamentary act of 1857 decided that the Canadian government should establish residential schools with the purpose of assimilating the indigenous children into Canadian culture and traditions (Political Apologies and Rectifications, 2014). In 2004 Ontario Premier Dalton McGuinty apologized for what had been done to the Ontario indigenous population, and in 2005 the Canadian government decided that Can$5 billion should be used to improve their lives. In 2008 a Truth and Reconciliation Commission was set up with the aim of exploring and revealing the past, and in particular the working of the Indigenous Residential Schools (Stanton, 2011).

During the colonization of the United States, the Native American population was terrorized and the United States government broke many treaties with the Native Americans. In 2004 a process started in the US Senate for an apology to the Native American population. In 2010 the US Congress apologized to the Native Americans for "ill-conceived policies," "breaking of covenants," and violence committed against them (Associated Press, 2010).

Conclusion

In this chapter I have given an account of the various claims for rectification and apologies after colonial wrongs. The examples were divided into cases where former colonies have claimed rectification, claims for rectification for the slave trade, and claims for rectification to indigenous peoples. This account raises two main questions.

First, why have the demands for redress been so few in spite of the fact that the number of trespasses and violations of human rights were so huge? At least the following reasons seem plausible: When the colonies gained independence, the former colonial powers tried their best to turn the page on the past and to hide the evidence of what had been going on, with the result that it was difficult for the victims to obtain documented evidence of what had happened. This happened, as we saw, in the case of the British files documenting the war against Mau Mau in Kenya, but also in many other cases, as has recently been revealed (Daily Nation, 2013).

Second, the elite in the newly independent nations had often been allied with their former masters and had nothing to gain from claiming rectification. Even if not allied, governments in former colonies could be afraid of losing investments and support from the former colonial power if they claimed rectification. This was, for example, the motive for the Namibian government in not supporting rectificatory claims.

Third, for many former victims it could seem pointless to claim rectification; what would it amount to in practice when the prospects of success were so dim?

The second question is: Why have the former colonial powers been so reluctant to apologize? Plainly because they do not want to run the risk of having to compensate victims of previous injustices. There is a significant difference between a political leader declaring that her nation regrets trespasses in the past and formally apologizing for those transgressions. While the first act is a moral declaration, the second will have juridical implications and may lead to claims for monetary compensation (Beckles, 2013: 16). Many leaders of former colonial powers have been hesitant to follow this latter path.

9
The Meaning of Rectificatory Justice after Colonialism

Introduction

In this chapter I discuss the meaning of rectificatory justice and how it applies to rectification for colonial harms. I will first clarify the conceptual question, that is, the question of which term is the most appropriate to use. Then I will sketch a theory of rectificatory justice. When the theory of rectification is applied to the history of colonialism a number of questions need to be answered.

First I address the question: Who, or which entity, is responsible for rectification for colonial harms and what does that responsibility entail? Second, I discuss whether it is anachronistic and perhaps even unfair to blame a nation for historical harms. Perhaps the actions that we today consider blameworthy were not at the time considered immoral? Is it then fair to claim rectification for them today? Third, I try to answer the question: What does rectification mean in practice? I discuss this question in connection with Renée Hill's theory of a "Just Compensation Rule" and David Miller's categorization of claims for rectification. My fourth question is: Should there be statute of limitations with regard to rectification? In other words, is it reasonable to claim rectification for harms that one's forefathers suffered, and should descendants be obliged to rectify for the wrongs of their ancestors? Finally: What is reasonable rectification? and: How can reasonable rectification for colonial harms be accomplished?

Justice is a multifaceted concept. Aristotle distinguished between *distributive* and *rectificatory* justice. Distributive justice (*dianemetikon dikaion*) focuses on the fair distribution of scarce resources and goods. Rectificatory justice (*diorthotikon dikaion*), on the other hand, is backward-looking and focuses on correction for past deeds. Aristotle explains rectificatory justice as follows:

> [F]or in the case also in which one has received and the other has inflicted a wound, or one has slain and the other been slain, the suffering and the action have been unequally distributed: but the judge tries to equalize things by means of the penalty, taking away from the gain of the assailant... therefore, corrective justice will be the intermediate between the loss and gain... Now, the judge restores equality. (Aristotle, V: 4: 115)

Given that colonialism involved inflicting wounds and slaying, Aristotle's view can provide us with an *a priori* argument for rectificatory justice after colonialism.

A theory of rectificatory justice can also draw on more recent works in philosophy. Robert Nozick's entitlement theory is an example of a historical, backward-looking theory of justice. According to Nozick, a person is entitled to his or her property provided that it was acquired in a just way. Hence, property rights depend on justice in acquisition and justice in transfer (Nozick, 1974: 151). Nozick's theory is a philosophical justification of libertarianism, and he applies his theory to the question of just holdings of property. However, Nozick's line of thought that historical injustices trigger later claims of rectification can also be used to justify other claims for rectificatory justice. Given that present global inequalities and the concentration of property and wealth in the rich part of the world are at least partly the result of unjust historical acquisitions, that is, plunder, slavery and occupation, one could, in line with Nozick's entitlement theory, argue for a "rectification of injustice in holdings" (Ibid.: 152). David Lyons's discussion of whether American states are, in accordance to Nozick's argument, obliged to give back land that was seized from Native American tribes during the colonization of America is a case in point (Lyons, 1982).

Nozick sketches a "principle of rectification." Claims for rectification are based on historical information about injustices, the actual course of events after the injustice, and estimates of what would have occurred if the injustice had not taken place (Nozick, 1974: 152–153). The estimation of what would have occurred if injustice had not taken place is of course speculative and the principle suffers from the problem of counterfactual estimations, as Jeremy Waldron has argued (Waldron, 1992). Nozick himself argues that in the absence of reliable historical information of what compensation would amount to when rectification is proper, a "rule of thumb" could be to apply the difference principle developed by John Rawls, that is, to maximize the position of the least advantaged group. His reasoning is based on the assumption that the members of this group (or their descendants) are probably those who have suffered most from previous injustices (Nozick, 1974: 231).

So far, we have come across two accounts of rectificatory justice. Aristotle argues primarily for equalizing a wrongdoing in order to achieve a *status quo ante* (the situation before the wrongdoing) and Nozick, in his defense of property rights, argues for rectification of past injustice in the acquisition and transfer of property. They have in common the view that past injustices have implications for the present discussion of justice.

However, the simple idea that if A has harmed B, A has to somehow correct his or her act later, that is, the basic idea of rectificatory justice, presupposes a line of complicated assumptions when applied to specific historical incidences, and I will in this chapter discuss some of the questions that a principle of rectificatory justice raises.

Conceptualization of historical justice

In this section the terminology and conceptualization of historical justice are in focus. First, there is a need for some conceptual clarification. In the discussion on historical, "backward-looking," justice, the terms "rectificatory justice," "corrective justice," "compensatory justice," and "restorative justice" are often used in the same or at least similar senses. We saw, for example, that in the translation of Aristotle, rectificatory and corrective justice are used interchangeably. That we use different words with similar meanings in casual speech does not usually cause any misunderstanding. However, when the aim is to construct a theory, terminological precision becomes more important.

The basic ideas behind **backward-looking justice** are that there is a situation where harm is done to someone, the condition of the harmed is as a consequence changed for the worse, the harm is made up for by the perpetrator, and the result is a state similar to that before the harm was done. The *status quo ante* is restored. This is also the literal meaning of **restorative justice**. Someone is harmed and the harm is healed.

The terms **compensatory justice** and **rectificatory justice** have wider implications than **backward-looking** or **restorative justice**, and hence are less precise with regard to the aim of the compensation or rectification. To compensate for a loss or harm does not necessarily mean to restore the *status quo ante*. Instead, the aim is to *make up for* the loss or harm, in the sense that justice allows for some other outcome than the one that preceded the harmful act. For example, if a dam project requires that a village is removed, the villagers could be compensated in different ways: they could be allowed to move to a similar village somewhere else or to a new neighborhood that is different from the old village or they could receive monetary compensation. In all cases compensation is achieved and the term compensatory justice may be used for all alternatives but only the first option is an instance of restorative justice.

In discussions of historical justice after periods of oppression and injustice, the kind of harm done is one factor behind the choice of terminology. If, for example, an invader steals valuable pieces of art or historical artifacts, historical justice would require that the art and artifacts are returned. In that case, reparatory or restorative justice would be at least partly realized. Partly, because the theft is in itself a violation that also needs to be rectified. If, on the other hand, the historical harm refers to genocide or slavery, **rectificatory justice** is a more appropriate term than restorative justice. The harm is so enormous and the consequences so extreme that there is no way to restore the *status quo ante*. Hence, in dealing with justice after colonialism, which involved both genocide and slavery, the term restorative justice is too narrow.

The term compensatory justice is less appropriate than rectificatory justice in this context due to its unfortunate material connotation. Compensation to victims is often calculated in terms of money but most cases of claims for historical redress include more than material compensation (Satz, 2007; Torpey, 2003). Historical justice can also imply apologies, the restoration of relationships, and reconciliation. The term rectificatory justice is broader and more inclusive than either restorative or compensatory justice. What then is the meaning of rectificatory justice?

Requirements for rectificatory justice

What does rectification require? As we noticed, Aristotle proposes that rectificatory justice aims at equality. Aristotle's almost arithmetical account of rectificatory justice is utterly demanding. He is right to point out that justice demands some kind of compensation or rectification for wrongs done, but in many cases *equalizing* for past wrongs seems to be too much to ask. For example, in the context of wrongs done during colonialism we are talking about a lengthy period of a variety of harms, such as unjustified acquisition of land and artifacts, slavery, and genocide. It is beyond the power of the compensating parties to equalize these kinds of injustices. Compensation could never fully make up for – equalize – the harms done.

However, equality can mean different things and refer to different values. It can for example mean "treating people as equals" (Kymlicka, 2002: 3). With this interpretation of equality, a possible goal of rectificatory justice is not necessarily equalizing for past wrongs. The goal is instead that relations between perpetrators and victims that previously were characterized by a master–slave relation be changed into relations where the parties are entitled to equal worth and mutual respect. As I will show in Chapter 11, there is a relation between rectification and reconciliation; and as I argue in the last chapter, the establishment of equal relations between former colonial powers and former colonies is perhaps the key element in the process of rectificatory justice after colonialism.

So, what precisely is required for rectification to be achieved? To start with, we have a situation where someone (an individual or group) is harmed. According to Renée Hill, rectification means that a harm is compensated for, and the injured party is "made whole," implying that he or she is "as well as before the transgression occurred" (Hill, 2002: 398). Hill does not include apology as a condition for rectificatory justice. Her argument is that apology requires an inner motivation on the part of the perpetrator and it is impossible for a legislator to judge whether such an inner disposition is present or not (Ibid.). Hill's perspective is strictly legal. However, if we look at rectification from a moral point of view, Hill's suggestion is too narrow. The previous harm was perhaps abusive, and resulted in lasting tensions and distrust between victims and perpetrators. To overcome the tensions, something more than compensation is required. Rectificatory justice also requires that the perpetrator acknowledges and apologizes for the harm done.

Why then is acknowledgement and apology required for rectification? An apology is performative; something happens when someone apologizes. When a perpetrator acknowledges and apologizes for a past injustice, the victim is assured that the perpetrator is aware of what he or she has done and is prepared to change his/her behavior. Most often, acknowledgment and apology seem to be more important for victims than compensation. In the case of political rectification, when, for example, a government or a state should rectify for past injustices, acknowledgement might include truth commissions, and setting up memorials and museums. These kind of commissions and institutions will ensure a public acknowledgement.

In discussions of rectificatory justice it is often argued that the rectificatory process should lead to rehabilitation of the victim and to a renewed relation between perpetrator and victim characterized by mutual respect. Even if this is a desirable consequence of rectification, it is not a requirement. It might be impossible for the former victim to respect the former perpetrator because of what happened in the past, even though the perpetrator has done everything in his or her power to rectify it. In such a case, rectification is achieved even if a new relation is not established.

Another question is how rectificatory justice is related to retributive justice. Both rectificatory and retributive justice are backward-looking in the sense that they refer to some previous wrong. Rectificatory justice refers to a state of affairs; a previous wrong is rectified. Retributive justice, on the other hand, refers to a person or group that deserves to be punished for some wrong committed. However, there is often a link between retributive justice and rectificatory justice. Retribution is normally connected to some kind of rectificatory duties. For example, a perpetrator who is convicted can be obliged to compensate the victim.

A model of rectificatory justice

I have so far in this chapter discussed conceptual questions and some requirements for rectificatory justice. I will now try to structure and clarify the notion of rectificatory justice by proposing a model (RJ).

Model RJ

Case P

X (the **agent**: person, group, state, etc.) did A (**harm**: stealing, wounding, oppressing, killing, etc.) to Y (the **victim**: a person, group, state, etc.) at t1 (**time**).

Given Case P, rectificatory justice requires at t2 that:

1. X acknowledges the harm (A) done to Y,
2. X apologizes for A,
3. X (or X's descendants) compensates Y (or Y's descendants) with B (something valuable: money, etc.) or returns what was taken at t1.

The model is a first, tentative explication of the meaning of rectificatory justice, which will be elaborated in what follows.

Are the three requirements both necessary and sufficient for rectificatory justice? As will be explained later, depending on the circumstances, when the victim is better off than the perpetrator at t2, only acknowledgement and apology might be necessary for rectification. In other cases, compensation would also be required. The three requirements seem to be sufficient, that is, if they are fulfilled, rectification is achieved. What else could be needed?

Now, let me discuss the challenging questions indicated in the introduction of the chapter.

Who is responsible for rectification?

As we noted in Chapter 3, within the framework of colonialism there were many different agents involved. These were individuals, for example conquistadors and slave traders, companies like the East and West India Companies, and official representatives of the colonial powers. Which agents have responsibility today for rectification for past injustices? The view of rectificatory justice so far developed implies that each responsible agent has a duty to rectify and, if we accept transgenerational commitments that this duty also falls on the descendants of the responsible agents. But such a strict view is untenable. It may be difficult or even impossible to trace the descendants of the conquistadors, and companies active during the colonial epoch may no longer be in existence.

A possible solution to the problem of establishing who owes rectification is to assign responsibility to the colonial states involved. As the colonial states were themselves deeply involved as agents, and were the homelands of the acting individuals and companies, and as they also provided the juridical framework for the colonial activities, responsibility falls back on them. But what does responsibility for rectification mean in practice? In answering this question I will refer to David Miller's distinction between **outcome responsibility** and **remedial responsibility**.

When we ask for outcome responsibility we ask which agent "can be credited or debited with a particular outcome – a gain or a loss either to the agent herself or to other parties" (Miller, 2007: 87). Remedial responsibility, on the other hand, asks "whether there is anyone whose responsibility it is to put that [particular problematic] state of affairs right" (Ibid.: 98). Who should make right what once was made wrong? There is an obvious link between outcome responsibility and remedial responsibility: the one who caused the harm is a primary candidate to make it right, but even other agents may have remedial responsibility because, for example, they are connected to the wronged party or they benefitted from the wrongful acts. If we assume that the historical account of the implications of colonialism that was described in Chapters 4 and 5 is correct, former colonial states have outcome responsibility. They then also share remedial responsibility today. But there might also be other states that have remedial responsibility due to, for example, connections with the former colonies, their present welfare, or some principle of distributive justice. (The relation between global rectificatory justice and global distributive justice will be explained in Chapter 14.)

There are at least two possible objections to the assigning of outcome responsibility today to the former colonial states for the negative consequences of colonial wrongs. One is that the colonial state may no longer exist. This objection has relevance in a parallel discussion about rectification for harms caused by the Soviet Union to the Baltic States. Does remedial responsibility in this case fall back on present-day Russia? It is at least contentious, because Russia is a different state from the Soviet Union. Even if Russia was the main part of the Soviet Union, the Soviet Union also included other states, including the Baltic States themselves. However, this objection is not relevant in the case of colonialism. There is a continuous identity between the former colonial powers Britain, France, Belgium, and so on, and the presently existing states. Even the former colonies exist today as politically independent states. Accordingly, the beneficiaries of rectification are the peoples of the former colonies and the present heirs of the former colonial states have remedial responsibility.

The second objection with regard to outcome responsibility applies to the case in which the colonial power at the time of colonialism was a totalitarian state and its policies lacked popular support. Then, one could argue, since the policies were not democratically established, the present-day democratic government need not take responsibility for the acts of its totalitarian forefathers. However, this view disregards that there is a "trans-generational continuum" of national responsibility irrespective of forms of government (Thompson, 2002: 74). One can, in line with Janna Thompson, argue that states' obligations and agreements remain stable over time. The same goes for responsibility for past wrongs. She writes:

> To be worthy of respect, a nation has to be prepared to fulfill its historical responsibilities. This means that its members have to be prepared to keep its commitments and make reparations for its past wrongs – including wrongs that were done in past generations. (Ibid.: 68)

The sense of trans-generational responsibility is illustrated by a personal experience I had some years ago. Together with some British friends I visited the summer palaces in Beijing. On many old castles and mansions there was a sign saying: "This building was burnt down by the British in 1860." My British friends were not unaffected by this. On the contrary, they experienced a trans-generational continuum of responsibility and they felt ashamed for the deeds of their forefathers.

Finally, a terminological remark. I have generally used the term "state" and not "nation" in my discussion on rectificatory justice. I have argued that states are responsible for rectification. Is it as states or as nations that the former colonial powers should assume responsibilities?

A state is a formally constituted body with territorial sovereignty, an "institutional moral agent" that is self-asserting, has an identity over time, and has a "conception of itself as a unit," as Erskine argues (Erskine, 2003: 27). A state acts towards other states on the basis of decisions taken by legitimate bodies (if they are democratic states, that is) and it is possible to assign responsibility to the state. Besides, states have international recognition and status according to international law. International agreements are made between states, relations between states are regulated in international conventions, and as a consequence states are assigned both moral and legal responsibility. These kinds of formal and legal agency speak in favor of using states as the more appropriate subject of rectification.

On the other hand, a reason for discussing global rectificatory justice in terms of nations is that nations have a historical continuity. David Miller defines a nation as

> a body of people who share a common national identity, involving cultural values [and] attachment to a territory...and who aspire to institutions of political self-determination which they may or may not actually enjoy. (Miller, 2007: 143)

In a similar vein, John Stuart Mill argues that national sentiments are based on the

> identity of political antecedents; the possession of national history, and consequent community of recollections; collective pride and humiliation, pleasure and regret, connected with the same incidents in the past. (Mill, 1962)

Accordingly, the argument for using the term *state* is that a state is a moral agent, and the argument for using the term *nation* is that the notion of nation has a historical connotation which is of relevance to the discussion on historical justice. Historical continuity seems more obvious for a nation than for a state. A nation has, in contract to a state, a collective identity and memory. On the other hand, as Richard Vernon argues, nations change as much as states. Nations as defined in terms of values and cultures are far from permanent, but instead continuously changing as much as state institutions (Vernon, 2012: 96).

When Miller assigns responsibility to *nations*, it is primarily because of the historical identity and inclusiveness that the term represents, and when Vernon assigns responsibility to *states*, it is because of the institutional and legal standing of states. Even if a nation represents a historic continuity, claims for compensation, apologies, and changed policies can only be addressed to states as moral agents and it is the political bodies of a state that can decide on these claims. Thus a combination of the two views seems most appropriate: The answer to the question *why* there is a reason for rectification is that a nation has a historical debt. The answer to the question *who* should act in the present by way of apologizing or compensating is the state as a moral agent. Hence, in line with Miller's distinction, nations have outcome responsibility and states have remedial responsibility.

Does rectificatory justice imply anachronism and unfairness?

Rectificatory justice means that previous harms are rectified at a later stage. But, someone might object, in the case of the colonizer, the harms were done a long time ago. Even if we today consider some of their actions as wrong, they had different values and were perhaps even motivated by good intentions. This means that one applies other criteria for moral judgments than would have been appropriate to apply at the time of the action. Is it not unfair to demand rectification on the basis of moral norms that were not known by the wrongdoers or, at least, not a part of the common morality, that is, moral standards shared by most people in the society? A parallel in law would be that one should not be judged for past actions in accordance with laws that did not exist at the time of the action. Hence, the objection says, it is unfair to ascribe present-day moral criteria to historical agents who were not aware of them. This implies that historical rectification is due only for historical wrongs that (1) are today considered (by morally competent persons) morally wrong, and (2) were known (by morally competent persons) as morally wrong at the time of the harmful actions. The addition "by morally competent persons" is motivated by the fact that at a given time not everyone is aware of the content of the common morality.

However, these objections to rectificatory justice are in my view not as potent as they might seem. First, one can in fact demand rectification for actions that were done in ignorance, that is, without the perpetrator being aware of the violation of moral norms. Let me support this view with the help of following story:

> Imagine that your parents were racists and supported white supremacy in South Africa. Through their education it became natural for you to look down on black people and to consider them as inferior. As a consequence, you treated your black servant in an arrogant and degrading manner. Now, 50 years later, you have different values and realize that you were wrong then. Recently you met your former servant and he blamed you for having shown such despicable behavior to him 50 years ago. You responded that he has no grounds for blaming you because you had different values at that time, but now you have changed.

Is this response well founded? No, for the following reason. If you now realize that you were wrong at that time and that your servant was harmed because of your behavior, you certainly owe him an apology for what you did, because you know now that you were wrong then and you are the person who 50 years ago harmed the servant. Similarly, the fact that time has passed since the colonial nations treated their colonies in ways that we now deem to be morally wrong and harmful, is not a valid excuse for refusing to rectify and apologize for past misdeeds.

However, there are reasons to believe that even at the time of colonialism, many of the deeds were in conflict with the common morality, or at least with some interpretations of it. Let me give a few examples. One might think that the Spanish conquest of America in the 16th century was considered morally acceptable at the time, and of course it was defended by prominent members of the court and of the Church (Elliot, 1984). However, the treatment of the indigenous population was fiercely questioned by others, for example, as we noted in Chapter 3, by the Catholic priest Bartolomé de Las Casas. In a letter addressed to Prince Philip, de Las Casas begged him to persuade King Charles I to change Spanish policy:

> It is my fervent hope that, once Your Highness perceives the extent of the injustices suffered by these innocent people and the way in

> which they are being destroyed and crushed underfoot, unjustly and for no other reason than to satisfy the greed and ambition of those whose purpose it is to commit such wicked atrocities, Your Highness will see fit to beg and entreat His Majesty to refuse all those who seek royal license for such evil and detestable ventures.... (de Las Casas, 1992: 7)

Although de Las Casas did not succeed in his efforts, his message shows that he refers to the moral sentiments of the day.

Similarly, in the 17th and 18th centuries, the British government imposed slavery on Africans in Africa, which was not allowed in Britain. Why not in Britain? Because it was deemed immoral. As Hilary Beckles writes: "The English state, then, knew that slave trading and slavery were crimes but was prepared to risk seeking their normalization in the interest of nation building" (Beckles, 2013: 21).

The abolitionists trying to end slavery and the slave trade at the turn of the 18th century, and the media campaign waged by missionaries and journalists against King Leopold II's brutality in Congo at the end of the 19th century are other examples of the fact that the suppression of indigenous peoples and slavery was questioned from a moral point of view at the time (Lovejoy, 2000; Hochschild, 1999).

These examples of moral criticism of colonial injustices in the past weaken the objection that present claims for rectificatory justice are unfair and anachronistic. Even at the time when the atrocities took place, they created moral objections. Second, as the above story shows, even those actions in the past that we today find morally wrong but at the time were not considered wrong by the perpetrators can generate claims for rectification. And, finally, from the point of view of the victims who suffered from the atrocities, the question of whether rectification is unfair would be puzzling, to say the least.

Who should rectify and who should be rectified?

A basic idea behind rectificatory justice is that victims of historical injustices can claim apology and compensation. Who then – if any – can today claim rectification for injustices under colonialism? And if rectification is pending, can descendants of the victims claim rectification? In this part I will discuss both the requirements for rectification to individuals and to nations.

Let me start with the question of rectification to individuals. Réene Hill tries to answer the questions who deserves compensation and on what grounds by framing – what she calls – a "Just Compensation Rule." Hill makes a distinction between injuries affecting a person's wellbeing (injury p) and compensation for property rights violations (injury pr). According to Hill, "Compensation must be tied to clear injury" and, thus, compensation for the former kind of injury could never go to descendants but only to the person who was affected. "The injury is like a hole which the compensation strives to fill," Hill argues (2002: 403). In contrast to this, descendants of the victims could be compensated for lasting injuries to property, either from the perpetrator him/herself or from the descendants of the perpetrator if they still benefit from the original injury (Hill, 2002: 405).

That victims of injustices are owed rectification is uncontroversial, but what about their descendants? Do they inherit a right to rectification? Hill argues that compensation to children for parents' personal injuries is "un-compelling" (Ibid.: 403). Chandran Kukathas agrees. It is not reasonable to identify descendants to victims who should be eligible to compensation for historical injustices. Individuals have always and in all societies been subject to injustices and if this implies compensation to the descendants "...victims of past injustices might include everyone," Kukathas argues (2006: 335). Hence, it is according to Kukathas reasonable to limit claimants of compensation to those who themselves have been injured.

Contrary to Hill and Kukathas I would argue that in some cases even descendants to persons who were harmed in the past could deserve compensation not only for property rights violations but also for other kinds of harm, namely if their lives were seriously negatively affected by the harm done to their parents. The reason is, as was already pointed out, that they also are victims of previous wrongful acts and it would be arbitrary to exclude them only because they belong to the next generation. Clearly, it might be more difficult to establish that there is a causal relation between their present lives and what was once done to their ancestors. However, the miserable lives of – for example – some aborigines, Herero and American natives today illustrate the connections between harm done to ancestors and present living conditions of descendants. (In Chapter 10 I will discuss some further objections to the rights to compensation for descendants.)

Let me now move on to the question of rectification to states for past wrongs. Can former colonies also claim rectification for injustices in the past? Colonialism affected entire communities with enduring negative consequences for later generations. Rectificatory justice after colonialism involves contemporary states on both sides. The former colonial powers were states that still exist today: Portugal, France, Great Britain, Belgium, and so on. The former colonies were at the time of colonization territories inhabited by indigenous peoples and tribes. Decolonization implied that the colonized territories became independent states, and when the borders were drawn, ethnic, religious, and cultural differences were frequently neglected.

In which cases is a former colonial power today responsible for wrongful actions in the past so that it is morally obliged to rectify? In answering this question I will follow David Miller's categorization. Miller distinguishes four different categories of possible claims for rectification, and I will apply his categorization to the question of rectification for colonial wrongs.

In the first category, **objects, land, or other resources** have in an unjust way been seized by a colonial power in the past. The controversies over Lord Elgin's acquisition of marbles from the Parthenon in Athens, presently in the British Museum, and artworks taken by British colonizers to Europe after they had seized and burned the historical kingdom of Benin in 1899 are cases in point (Returning Africa's Stolen Artifacts, 2011). These artworks were created by native artists and can be seen as parts of a national treasury. They were taken without consent and the former owners and their descendants can rightly claim that the objects are to be returned and, *vice versa*, the present descendants of the colonizers have no rights to them (Miller, 2007: 152).

The second category entails **exploitation of the colonized**, leading to long-lasting enrichment and present benefits for the exploiter. Miller here refers to colonialism and imperialism. He argues that even in the latter case, rectification for the previous injustice is justified. By enriching themselves at the expense of the colonized, some nations took unfair advantage of their weakness in the past and this implies that there is a reason for rectification today. A later generation is not entitled to assets that their forefathers wrongly acquired in the past, since they do not have a valid title to them.

The third category entails cases where a colonial power which in the past exploited its colony does not benefit from these past practices today even though the former colony **still suffers** from the past exploitation. Then, one could argue, the former colonial power does not, as in the first two categories, unduly benefit from goods that it is not entitled to and hence, it is not compelled to recompense the former colony. However, there are still reasons for rectification. Miller here refers to "nations as intergenerational communities" (Ibid.: 154). It is inconsistent of nations to claim that only historical successes and not past wrongs are part of their "national inheritance." Hence, the descendants of a former imperialist nation that caused harm to its colonies are liable for the historic wrongs, even if they do not benefit from them anymore, Miller argues.[1]

Finally, the fourth category entails cases of **previous injustices** when neither the former perpetrator nor the former victim gains or suffers from the historical wrongs today, but the memories of the misdeeds are still alive. Miller argues that even in relation to this category of claim, the heirs of the perpetrator owe some rectification to the heirs of the former victims. However, while the past acts have not left any material injustices in the present, rectification does not have to involve compensation but can be limited to an apology (Ibid.: 156–158). In this case acknowledgment of the past may include truth commissions, memorials and museums.

Miller does not discuss a possible fifth category of claim, resulting from a nation's **taking advantage** of another nation's wrongful actions. For example, what present duties of rectification (if any) fall on a nation that was not itself a colonial power, but nevertheless gained from colonial injustices? Take Sweden as an example. Surely, Sweden had a few tiny colonies: New Sweden in Delaware for less than 20 years in the 17th century and Saint Barthélemy in the Caribbean for 90 years until 1878.[2] But more importantly it benefitted from colonialism. It gained for example from trading with colonial powers and its ships were used for transportation to and from colonies, including transportation of slaves. Does Sweden therefore also have a duty of rectification? The question is: What is the responsibility of bystanders who take advantage of the injustices done to others?

Daniel Butt argues that "even those countries which did not directly act as colonial powers may have compensatory duties in the current day" (Butt, 2009: 129). I tend to agree with Butt, but only on the condition that the country in question did not actively combat colonialism. If a country actively opposed colonialism, it seems odd that it should owe rectification for its benefits. However, when it comes to Sweden, this was not the case. On the contrary, Swedish trading companies, like the Ostindiska Kompaniet (Swedish East India Company), were actively involved in the colonial venture. Using Miller's terminology, one could argue that even Sweden shared outcome responsibility for colonialism and as a consequence it also shares remedial responsibility.

How does Miller justify his categorization? He bases his argumentation on two principles. According to the first principle, one has no right to bequeath goods or wealth to one's descendants that were unjustly acquired (Ibid: 152). This principle seems to be uncontroversial. According to the second principle, nations are intergenerational communities and therefore later generations may inherit duties of rectification from their forefathers. How does Miller justify this latter principle and what does the view of nations as intergenerational communities entail?

According to Miller, there is continuity between generations. The present generation inherits gains and debts from the previous generations, and tries to "enrich the lives of the future ones" (Miller 2006, 154). However, Miller's rather conventional view of succeeding generations is questioned by Daniel Butt. As an alternative Butt uses the notion of "overlapping generations." Generations do not succeed each other, they overlap. In each year there are a number of children born and a number of people who die. A nation is, Butt argues, a "conglomerate collectivity." Hence, the identity of a generation is not the sum of a specific number of individual entities, which implies that there is continuity between generations. The identity of the conglomerate remains, even though specific individuals are added or withdrawn. If we, like Miller, see generations as wholes that succeed each other, it undermines the idea of trans-generational responsibilities. In contrast, Butt's view of overlapping generations strengthens the view of a nation's enduring responsibility for past injustices (Butt, 2009: 184).

Are obligations to rectify for past injustices limited in time?

Colonial rule ended in Latin America over a century ago (almost two centuries ago in some cases). Many African countries celebrated the 50th anniversary of their independence in 2010. The Portuguese colonies Mozambique, Angola, and Guinea Bissau were among the last major colonies to gain independence. After years of fighting they finally won their independence in the mid-1970s, that is, less than 40 years ago.[3] Can all these former colonies still demand rectification for harms suffered during colonial rule or do the reasons for rectification dwindle over time? Is there a time limit for justified demands for rectification for past wrongs and, if so, what is it?

The British delegation to the Durban Conference in 2001 argued that too long a time had passed since the slave trade for any legal action to be taken against those responsible (Beckles, 2013: 196). The philosopher Renée Hill also argues that there are time limits for rectification. According to Hill, it is not reasonable to claim compensation for harms that happened more than roughly 50 years ago. After this period the consequences of the injuries are "accommodated" and the harms are forgotten, she argues (Hill, 2002: 400).

It is certainly likely, and in most cases desirable, that memories of past injustices fade over time. However, sometimes memories remain alive for a long time, as is illustrated by the yearly commemorations of the Holocaust and by the fact that former members of Mau Mau went to Britain to demand justice 60 years after their detention.[4] Even when it is too late for legal action, moral rectification could still be made.

As the Herero genocide in 1904–1907 illustrates, a people can remember and suffer from past injustices for a long time. In his analysis of the consequences of the genocide Sarkin-Hughes writes:

> The lasting effects of population decimation, land dispossession and political marginalization continue to haunt the Herero identity and impede their economic, social and political progress in modern-day Namibia. (Sarkin-Hughes, 2011: xiii)

The implications of the genocide are enduring. Thus, the genocide generates two kinds of duty. First, a duty on behalf of Germany to apologize for the genocide that took place over one hundred years ago. Second, remedial responsibility to aid and support the present descendants of those who survived of the enduring consequences of the genocide.

As Daniel Butt emphasizes, a refusal to acknowledge and rectify for past injustices is in itself a wrong that adds to the original harm (Butt, 2009: 185–187). Turkey's refusal to apologize to the Armenians for massacres after World War I is a case in point, as is the negligence of many colonial powers to rectify for colonial harms.

In conclusion, traces and memories of past injustices fade over time, and should then be forgotten. But that is not always the case. There are cases of enduring harm, and hence enduring reasons for rectification.

Reasonable rectification

There are reasons for rectificatory justice after colonialism, but what kind of rectification can the victims claim? Rectificatory processes can have different faces. They include public apologies, truth commissions, affirmative actions, the foundations of museums and setting-up of memorials for remembering and commemorating past injustices, and of course monetary compensation (Barkan, 2000: Torpey, 2003; Brophy, 2006). The common aim is to realize justice, achieve reconciliation, and enable conflicting groups to cooperate in the future.

According to my model, rectification implies the following:

Given Case P at t1, rectificatory justice requires at t2 that

1. X acknowledges the harm done to Y,
2. X apologizes for A,
3. X (or X's descendants) compensates Y (or Y's descendants) with B (something valuable: money, etc.) or returns what was taken at t1.

As was argued above, official acknowledgements for political injustices in the past may take the form of truth commissions, memorials and museums. The third requirement is compensation to the victims. What does compensation for colonial harms imply? Reasonable rectification requires that the victim of an injustice is satisfied and prepared to leave the past behind. What, then, amounts to a satisfactory compensation?

Monetary compensation has often been offered to individuals who are victims of injustices. For example, Japanese-Americans detained during World War II were after the war offered $20,000 each as compensation (Brophy, 2006: 8). A more recent example of economic compensation is the British compensation to the members of Mau Mau. The British government agreed in 2013 to pay £19 million to the more than 5,000 victims who are still alive.

Welfare economics offers one way to estimate compensation for past wrongs. According to welfare economics, monetary compensation is sufficient and an agent is completely compensated if his preferences are equal as before the wrong, or with the language of economics; he is "indifferent between his life as it was before the loss and his life as it is now after the loss but with additional goods" (Satz, 2007: 178). As Debra Satz points out, there are a number of problems with this view if it is applied to compensation for historical wrongs.

First, some harms or losses cannot be compensated with money. Satz takes missing educational opportunities as an example. Black American children who due to discrimination and poverty are deprived of good schools cannot be fully compensated with money when they are adults. Money cannot compensate for the missing life chances, the lacking possibilities to develop their capabilities and the violation of their dignity that the inferior schools implied.

Further, welfare economics assumes that compensation can be provided according to a single preference scale. This view presupposes a simplified view of human preferences. Not everything could be compensated for with money. Satz mentions the example of the Sioux tribe, which in 1980 refused to accept US$122 million as compensation for the seizure of the Black Hills in 1877. They refused because of the symbolic and historical importance of the Black Hills for the tribe, which could not be substituted with money. Instead they claimed the mountain back.

Third, the economic view misses the relational aspect of historical wrongs. There is a perpetrator and a victim, responsibilities and distrust, and the aim of rectification is to repair the relationship. A restored relationship could not be bought for money (Ibid: 179–183).

There is also a fourth problem with the economic view of compensation. Welfare economics assumes that monetary compensation can be based on a subjective scale of preferences. But is a historical wrong always sufficiently compensated for even if the victims or their descendants are satisfied? Perhaps they are wrong? Perhaps they over- or underestimate what once happened? Take as example an oppressed people that live in utmost poverty. They are offered a minimal compensation – say $100 per person as compensation for a past injustice. Their acceptance of the compensation is the result of adaptive preferences, meaning that their preferences are formed by present oppressive circumstance so they do not expect more. According to welfare economics, complete compensation is achieved. However, in this case one could still argue that the victims are not compensated for what once happened even if they think so themselves.

Compensation for colonial wrongs to groups or states might take various forms depending on the kind of wrong. When, for example, pieces of art and cultural artifacts were taken from the colonies, for example at the British siege of Benin in 1899, compensation would – among other things – require that these be returned to the former colony. However, in other cases, when colonialism involved the unjustified acquisition of land, slavery, or genocide, it could be beyond the power of the rectifying perpetrator to economically compensate the former colony. No compensation would be sufficient. Does that imply that rectificatory justice is unfeasible? No. Justice does not necessarily mean *full* compensation for harms. What then constitutes reasonable, that is sufficient and feasible, rectification? To answer the question one must have knowledge of the circumstances and the context. The dictum "ought implies can" is applicable here. An estimation of what is reasonable compensation after colonialism – and hence morally required – should also be grounded in an analysis of what is possible to achieve.

To find out what constitutes a reasonable rectification the following variables should be taken into account:

1. harm done,
2. impact of time; assuming that the need for rectification is dependent on a time factor: the more that has passed since the harm was done, the more the victims have adjusted to the new situation, the less need to rectify,
3. present situation of the former victim; what kind of compensation is most valued and appropriate in its present situation?
4. present situation of the former perpetrator; how many resources can it set aside for compensation without endangering its own future?

As the first two variables have already been considered, let me comment on the third and the fourth variables. The Durban Declaration suggested debt relief and development funds as instruments for compensating nations that had suffered the consequences of the slave trade and colonialism (United Nations, 2001). In other words, if a former colony is dependent on the export of particular products for its development, then perhaps the best way for a former colonial power to compensate is to enter into favorable trade agreements with its former colony, and to contribute to its capacity to produce other goods.

A problem with economic compensation for colonial wrongs is that the situation of the former colonies might have changed after their independence. Consider the following possibility: Assume that two colonies, A and B, are treated equally wrong by a colonial power. After independence the two former colonies develop differently. In a number of years, thanks to hard work, rich natural resources, and good ideas, the former colony A prospers so that the economic traces of colonialism vanish. In contrast, the other former colony B is still shaped by the legacy of colonialism, the people are afflicted by diseases and ignorance, and remain in poverty. Then one could say that there are traces of colonialism left in B but not in A. Is it not then reasonable that B and not A should be compensated by the former colonial power? If the reason for rectification is the past wrongs and if A and B were treated equally badly, they could demand equal compensation. But to compensate A seems unnecessary given its economic prosperity.

The idea behind compensation is that there is a causal relation between present-day economic distress and colonialism. If there is no such relation, then there is no reason for compensation. Hence, B should be compensated only if its present poverty is caused by colonialism and not by, for example, idleness. Thus, to know if the theory of rectification is applicable in this case we need empirical information about the causes of poverty. On the other hand, both A and B may suffer from cultural traces of colonialism such as enduring feelings of inferiority and humiliation. If this is the case, the former colonial power still has a duty of rectification for a history of subjugation through, for example, apologies and memorials. But does not the fourth variable above – that compensation is dependent on the capacity of the former colonial power – make justice relative?

Let me give an example mentioned by one of my interviewees in Mozambique. If Portugal were required to rectify for injustice done to Mozambique when it was a Portuguese colony, including for the war Portugal fought against the liberation front Frelimo from 1962 to 1975, it would demand a huge amount of resources from Portugal's side. However, one could argue that it is not reasonable to demand that Portugal pay large sums in compensation to Mozambique at the present when its economy is in a crisis. That would be a too substantial a sacrifice. But in connection with the transfer of ownership of the Carbora Bassa dam, which had been built during the colonial period by Portugal, Portugal could have done so without demanding payment as compensation for past injustices. However, this was not Portugal's view and Mozambique had to pay Portugal to get control of the dam (Valy, 2007). Hence, Portugal missed the chance to compensate Mozambique for previous injustices.

There is another problem with the fourth variable. Let us assume that two colonies A and B were treated in a similar way and during the same time span by colonial powers X and Y, respectively. However, let us also assume that later (t2) X and Y faced very different economic situations. X can give sufficient compensation to A, but Y cannot give as much to B. From the point of view of B this seems wrong. Why should B be satisfied with much less than A when their colonial experiences were alike?

To deal with this problem, let me introduce a distinction between ideal and non-ideal rectificatory justice. Ideal rectificatory justice means that all requirements for rectification are fulfilled. Non-ideal rectificatory justice means that all requirements for rectification *that in a given concrete situation are possible to accomplish*, are fulfilled. Ideally, former victims should be fully compensated for previous harm. In the real world, however, what counts as sufficient compensation has to vary depending on the present capacity of the former perpetrator. If not, rectification, and as a consequence reconciliation, could in some cases never be achieved.

Finally, what then amounts to reasonable rectification? As the reasoning above shows, there is no definitive answer to this question. The harm done, the impact of time, the present situation of the former victim, and the present situation of the former perpetrator are all factors to consider. As will be argued in Chapter 11 a further goal of rectificatory justice is to restore moral relations and attain reconciliation. As a consequence, when compensation is required for rectification, there must be a situation where compensation is no longer pending, that is, a time when the former perpetrator has offered sufficient resources or other means to compensate the former victim. Then the compensatory requirements for rectification are fulfilled.

10
Rectificatory Justice – Philosophical Challenges

Introduction

Demands for affirmative action to compensate black Americans, the abolition of apartheid and the initiation of the truth and reconciliation process in South Africa, the collapse of the Soviet bloc, and the restoration of democracies in Latin America have triggered interest in how to handle past injustices. Philosophers have contributed to the discussion and some have criticized the idea of rectificatory justice.

In this chapter I discuss three main objections to rectificatory justice. The first is Jon Elster's argument for ethical presentism and ethical individualism, and I examine whether his theory challenges the idea of collective historical rectification. The second is Jeremy Waldron's objection that historical rectification presupposes tricky counterfactual premises, and I assess whether this undermines the argument for rectificatory justice after colonialism. The third is George Sher's argument that descendants of people who suffered injustices in the past have no right to rectification because they would not exist if the injustice had not taken place.

Ethical individualism and rectification

My argument for rectificatory justice after colonialism presupposes both that at least some injustices from the past matter morally today, and that states have reasons to claim rectification for past injustices. But, one might ask, is not morality concerned with present and future *individuals*? We cannot do anything about the past but we can act today in ways that affect the lives of present and future individuals. This questioning of a collective and historical approach to justice is supported by Jon Elster's argument for "ethical individualism" (EI) and "ethical presentism" (EP) (Elster, 1993). Elster writes: "I defend the views that for purposes of distributive justice, groups don't matter and the past doesn't matter. Justice is concerned with living individuals and with future individuals" (Ibid.: 1). Elster's argument seems to challenge claims for justice that refer to *past* wrongs and also the belief that there are *groups* on both sides in a rectification process.

Before we take a closer look at Elster's arguments, we should note that he states that "for purposes of *distributive* justice groups don't matter and the past doesn't matter" (my emphasis). Thus, he claims that his argument is about distributive justice, but among the views he criticizes are arguments for affirmative action for blacks in America and compensation to developing countries for what the industrialized countries did to them in the past, that is, arguments for *rectificatory* justice. So, Elster's arguments are relevant to my discussion because they target some vital premises behind the idea of rectificatory justice.

According to EI, only living individuals and not groups count as moral agents and moral recipients. Hence, for example, whites as a group have no duty to compensate blacks as a group for injustices in the past. To argue for collective guilt and compensation is to assume that because a person has a special attribute, for example being white, which is associated with specific harmful acts, for example slavery, that person has in fact committed the act. Such a view of collective responsibility is clearly mistaken.

Elster argues that only individuals and not groups matter morally. To compensate groups like black Americans or women for past injustices goes against EI. Then all members of the group, for example all blacks or all women, will be compensated irrespective of whether they themselves were victims of injustice or not. It implies that some individuals will profit from past wrongs that have harmed others. Only individuals who themselves have suffered from past wrongs are entitled to compensation. And the other side of the coin is that only those individuals, for example whites or men, who themselves have benefitted from past injustice have reasons to compensate the victims.

Elster's argument of collective compensation seems to conflict with my argument in Chapter 9 that *states* could be on both sides in a rectification process; as both debtor and creditor. Is not a state a group and does not obligation to compensate for past wrongs imply that also individuals who neither contributed to the past injustice nor benefit from it today are obliged to compensate? Would that not imply that an injustice is done to them?

There is no controversy regarding rectification to individuals. It is consistent with EI that individuals who have committed a wrong are obliged to rectify and individuals who are victims of past wrongs can claim compensation. This also applies to wrongs committed during colonialism. What we must discuss more carefully is whether states can be responsible for harms done and whether states can be claimants of rectification.

I have argued that states that were previously colonized can claim rectification for previous harms, as well as for those harms that are enduring, and that states that once had colonies have a duty to rectify. Is there a difference between groups in Elster's meaning and states? A group is a sum of people who share some characteristics that are arbitrary from a moral point of view. Just because a person happens to be male or white does not make him guilty of any harm that other males or whites might have caused innocent people. What then is the difference between a state and a group in Elster's sense? A state is a formally constituted body with territorial sovereignty. A state acts towards other states on the basis of decisions taken by political and executive bodies and it is possible to assign responsibility to a state. States also have international recognition and status according to international law. International agreements are made between states, relations between states are regulated in international conventions, and as a consequence states are assigned both moral and legal responsibility. A state can also be seen as the institutionalized body or representative of a nation or people.

So the notion of states as claimants and responsible agents for rectificatory justice differs from Elster's "groups." Elster refers to groups as a sum of individuals sharing some characteristics. Hence, his critique of group arguments for affirmative action and historical compensation has little bearing on my discussion on rectificatory justice between states. As a matter of fact, it is surprising that Elster does not consider states as agents in his discussion on historical justice.

But Elster might object that if a state is obliged to compensate for past injustices, both present citizens who perhaps were not even born at the time when the injustice was committed and recent immigrants must contribute to the rectification. Does that not imply that innocent individuals have to rectify for others' wrongs? As was explained in Chapter 9, the answer is no, because citizenship implies responsibility. As citizens we both benefit from the values associated with citizenship and are obliged to follow the laws and pay the taxes, including those taxes that are used to pay off historical debts. Put in a positive way:

> As citizens or members of a nation, we have certain civic responsibilities that are independent of our choosing and past responsibility. The duty of justice is one of the civic responsibilities of citizenship. (Tan, 2007: 298)

Therefore, it is not as "innocent individuals" that recent immigrants also have a duty to contribute to a state's historical debt, but as new citizens who through citizenship share both the values and the responsibilities of their new status.

Past wrongs and present rectification

My argument for rectificatory justice presupposes that past deeds have implications for the distribution of responsibilities and obligations today. Does this view come into conflict with ethical presentism? As we noted, Elster argues that the past does not matter for present discussions on distributive justice. As a consequence, policies of affirmative action motivated by historical injustice are mistaken, according to Elster. However, Elster suggests one important exception. He writes that "injustice done to individuals who are no longer alive may constrain present distributions *only if it has left morally relevant traces in the present*" (Ibid.: 5, my emphasis).

Elster compares two situations. In the first, A's grandfather did bad things to B's grandfather and presently A is benefitting from this history and B is suffering from it. The second situation is similar to the first, with the exception that the past harms have no reverberations for A and B. In the first situation, there is a reason for rectificatory justice, for example according to Robert Nozick's theory, but not in the second situation, Elster argues.

Elster's condition provides us with a criterion for deciding which historical injustices are relevant in the present discussion and which are not. For example, would a principle of rectificatory justice imply that the Scandinavian countries should compensate England and France for what the Vikings did to their ancestors in the 9th and 10th centuries? The answer is no. Not because the harms inflicted by the Vikings took place in the past but because – as far as one can notice – the Vikings' ravaging has not left any morally relevant traces in the present.

But a view that demands rectification if past wrongs have left morally relevant traces in the present opens up epistemic difficulties, Elster argues. For example, a policy of affirmative action that benefits the black population in the US at the expense of whites, based on the view that slavery in the 18th and 19th centuries still influences the lives of both white and black Americans, presupposes that one could identify which individual black Americans are suffering from, and which individual whites are benefitting from the past injustices. However, that is not possible. There might even be individual blacks who are better off and individual whites who are worse off because of that history. Since we cannot know who has gained and who has lost, a general policy of group compensation is unjust (Ibid.).

How then is Elster's argument relevant to the question of rectificatory justice after colonialism? EP implies that only those individuals who suffered from colonialism ought to be compensated. For example, those individuals who have suffered from racism in the United States or from British colonialism in Kenya deserve rectification. However, for the reasons Elster explains, this should not imply that all blacks in the United States or all Kenyans are owed rectification. On the other hand, the risk of *not* compensating individuals who deserve compensation should outweigh the risk of compensating those who do not. It is also questionable from a moral point of view to argue that the reason not to compensate for past wrongs with clear traces in the present is that we lack a clear metric to identify all and only the right recipients.[1]

Past injustices matter today if they have left morally relevant traces in the present, Elster argues. As I argued above, colonialism has left different traces in the present. There are victims and their descendants who still suffer from wrongs inflicted by colonial powers, and many of the present global injustices have their roots in the colonial structures. Hence, my argument for rectification for colonial injustices does not come into conflict with Elster's notion of EP. The past injustices are not separated from the present. Instead history matters because the past is still with us in the form of a global institutional order shaped by the colonial past.

The diminution of transferability

Another objection to the idea of rectificatory justice is the difficulty of distinguishing which losses or harms are due to the act of a perpetrator and which are due to the subsequent choices of the victim. With George Sher we can call this argument "the argument of diminution of the transferability [of compensation]" (Sher, 1980: 12). Arguments for compensation for past wrongs are normally based on counterfactual assumptions. Sher gives the following example: Because of discrimination against black people, X could not be admitted to law school. Now, if X had not been deprived of this opportunity, his life would be different and his daughter Z would probably also have benefitted from her father's being a lawyer. Hence, one could argue that both X and Z deserve compensation as victims of racial discrimination.

Sher then raises the question of what exactly the victims of discrimination are entitled to in this kind of situation. What X would have acquired in a just world without racial prejudice is to a large extent dependent on his own choices. Having started his education, he might, for example, have chosen to become a business lawyer or a human rights lawyer and his future would look different as a consequence of this choice. Should, in the real situation with a history of racial prejudice, compensation be provided for the loss of a career as a business lawyer or as a human rights lawyer? Neither, Sher argues. What should be compensated for is the loss of opportunity to enter law school. What would have happened thereafter would have been dependent on X's own choices, and the outcomes of choices are not a basis for compensation. "But the opportunity is not worth as much as the goods themselves" (acquired after correct choices in the hypothetical world), Sher argues (Sher, 1980: 12). In this way, what should be compensated for is less than the possible goods achieved due to an educational opportunity. The reason is that only compensation for "disparities of entitlements which are the automatic effect of the initial wrong act" are justified, Sher argues. By "automatic effects" he seems to mean those effects that are directly caused by a perpetrator or by unjust circumstances (Ibid.: 13).

Next, Sher applies his argument to the idea of compensation for "ancient wrongs." The result is a "diminution of the transferability" of the compensation. We have noticed that the transferability of X's entitlements is limited by X's omissions and actions. The same applies to the daughter Z's omissions and actions and so on. The result is a continuous limitation of historic entitlements over time. The transferability of entitlements decreases with every generation, as does the justification for the claims for rectification for ancient wrongs. At a certain point there is nothing left. As a consequence of the diminution of transferability, only recent claims for compensation have any substance, Sher argues. Applied to compensation for wrongs during colonialism, Sher's argument implies that the further back in history an injustice was done and the more choices have been made by the colonized themselves after independence, the less responsibility the colonizers have for rectification.

How does Sher's argument affect the idea of rectificatory justice after colonialism? In responding to Sher I will refer to arguments developed by Janna Thompson and Daniel Butt. Sher treats ancient wrongs as if they were independent incidences. Against this, Jaana Thompson argues that typically injustices happen over time. She takes the fate of the Australian Aborigines as an example, but the same can be said of other colonial wrongs that I have discussed in this book. Thompson writes: "particular injustices are interdependent components of a history of disrespect," and it is this history that is relevant to claims for rectification (Thompson, 2002: 82). Thus, to refer to Sher's own example, it is not only the deprivation of a chance for education for one particular person, but the enduring deprivation of education and other possibilities for the black population as a whole that are the grounds for present claims for rectification after slavery and discrimination. In a similar vein, it is the cumulative effects of colonial domination, including "a history of disrespect," that are at stake here.

Daniel Butt is also critical of Sher's argument. He argues that when applied to the history of colonialism, the "automatic effects" of injustice were comprehensive and left little opportunity for the colonized peoples. Butt writes: "[I]t is hard to acquire alternative entitlements once one has been unjustly deprived of large quantities of one's natural resources" (Butt, 2009: 113). The colonial structure provided the colonies with little freedom of action and their deterioration is to a large extent explained by colonialism and to a lesser extent by the subsequent choices of the victims. The far-reaching implications of the slave trade for Africa explained in Chapter 7 is a case in point.

Colonial rule often had a profound impact on the community and identity of the colonized peoples. Their capacity to rule themselves and develop a unity and a public ethos was dissolved. Hence, the failures of these peoples to form stable governments and prosper economically after independence are to a large extent explained by the previous colonial rule. As a consequence, responsibility for the problems facing these nations after independence falls back on the colonial powers.

To sum up: Sher's "diminution of the transferability" argument suffers from "atomism." Its focus is on independent choices and actions. Therefore, it lacks relevance to the discussion of rectificatory justice after colonialism, as it neglects both a history of disrespect and the automatic pervasive effects of colonialism that limited the range of possible alternative actions for the colonized peoples.

Counterfactual argumentation

What would have happened if America, Africa, and Asia had never been colonized? Would the continents have remained poor or would they have developed? How would the quality of life of their peoples have been today compared with the present situation? Can we assume that their alternative historical path would have been better than what actually happened? Do the claims for rectification after colonialism depend on the questionable assumption that these countries would have fared better without colonialism?

One argument against claims for historical justice focuses on problems connected to counterfactual explanations. This argument is developed by Jeremy Waldron (1992), among others. His critique of rectification for historical injustices can be summarized as follows: counterfactuals are impossible to verify, entitlements fade over time, and injustices are evened out by circumstances. The main target of Waldron's criticism is Nozick's entitlement theory, but his critique is also relevant to my argument for rectificatory justice after colonialism.

Counterfactuals that are impossible to verify

Waldron first contests the view that past injustices generate a demand for full reparation. He assumes that the aim of rectification (AIM) is to alter the present situation (A) so that it comes as close as possible to how it would have been (B) if the injustice (C) and its consequences had not occurred (AIM/B = A-C). Full reparation means therefore that the victim of injustice receives the resources that he or she would have had if C never had happened.

This view of rectification is based on counterfactual calculations. Waldron argues that these calculations rest on fragile ground because they are dependent on beliefs of how people, for example the ruling elites, would have acted between the time of the injustice and the present. Since these people would have had various opportunities and made various choices, it is impossible to estimate the alternative outcomes. There are no strong reasons for assuming that they would act as "idealized agents of rational choice," Waldron argues (Ibid.: 13).

Counterfactual calculations are also built on assumptions that other negative events, for example invasions from abroad, would not have occurred, Waldron argues. To exemplify this point: without British dominance at the end of the 19th century, the kingdom of Buganda might have been attacked by the neighboring Muslim Mahdiyah state in present Sudan, with possibly grave consequences for the kingdom. What would have been the implications of such an invasion and how grave would the consequences have been compared with the British dominance? An argument that is dependent on counterfactual assumptions suffers from indeterminacy: which alternative scenario should we chose as the baseline (Ibid.; Elster, 1993)?

Let me comment on Waldron's first objection to rectification. Given Waldron's assumption that rectification would mean *full* reparation for past injustices, or compensation in *proportion* to the loss, his argument is sound. Full or proportional rectification would require preposterous counterfactual calculations. However, such claims are rare in the discussion on rectification and of limited relevance to my argument. Rectificatory justice in my view rather implies that former colonial powers acknowledge and apologize for past injustices, and that they contribute in different ways to the former colonies' development: by supplying resources, supporting their trade, international position, and so on. In these and other ways they can rectify for what they did, and no counterfactual estimation is necessary. Compensatory measures are not proportionate to former injustices but instead dependent on contextual circumstances and on what is considered reasonable and appropriate. Thus, it is sufficient to establish that a colony was subjected to grave and lengthy injustices to ground a claim for rectification, which implies both compensation and future-oriented changes of relations between former colony and colonial power. See also my discussion in Chapter 5, where in relation to a story about a man in the wilderness I argue that claims for rectification are based on what in fact happened, not on a counterfactual comparison.

Changing entitlements

A historically based view of rectification runs the risk of neglecting that times are changing, Waldron subsequently argues. This is an obvious problem with Nozick's theory. A condition for Nozick's view of rectification is that entitlements are invariable and are always subject to full rectification. Waldron questions this idea and argues that entitlements fade over time. Waldron exemplifies his reasoning in the following way: P is the original owner of a piece of land. When Q seizes the land, an injustice is done to P. However, when the new situation prevails, P adjusts to it. The circumstances change. Originally, P was dependent on the land and Q's occupation was wrong. However, in the later situation, P is no longer dependent on the land. On the contrary, P lives his life well, or at least subsists, without the land. Why should in this situation P claim the land back? At least, the fading of entitlements makes the original claim of P to get the land back less forceful – "a justification that does fade over time" (Waldron, 1992: 18). Waldron applies this argument to the – in his view unfounded – claims of Australian Aborigines to reclaim land that the colonizers took from them (Waldron, 2007).

Does Waldron's argument against rectification affect my argument for rectificatory justice? First, it should be noted that Waldron's target is different. He discusses Nozick's entitlement theory, while my discussion relates to colonial wrongs. Waldron argues that the time factor is important for rectification. Because people adjust their lives to new circumstances, their dependence on land and other entitlements that was a reason to condemn the original seizure becomes less relevant when the dependence fades. However, this schematized situation does not resemble colonial occupation. It is true that the colonized peoples had to adjust to a new situation in order to subsist, but the dominance was enduring, albeit in new forms and structures. After formal independence, a sense of humiliation could remain and memories of past injustices affected present lives. Hence, there is continuity between the past and the present.

So, I conclude that Waldron's argument from changing entitlements might be a relevant objection to Nozick's argument for rectification for past violations of property rights, but it does not challenge my argument for rectification for wrongs done during colonialism.

Sensitivity to changing circumstances

A moral theory must be sensitive to circumstances. A problem with Nozick's entitlement theory is, according to Waldron, that it lacks sensitivity to changing circumstances (Waldron, 1992: 20ff.). Entitlements do not necessarily persist through time unchallenged. Waldron provides the following example: Assume that there are plenty of water holes in the desert. A has acquired a water hole in a just way and, thus, it belongs to A. A is entitled to the water hole and it is wrong for B to occupy it. But circumstances change. There is a drought, which dries out the other water holes, and finally there is only A's waterhole left. In this new situation, with different circumstances, it is wrong for A to exclude others from access to her water hole because they will then die of thirst. Waldron's point is that entitlements are not absolute but dependent on other morally relevant circumstances.

What we ought to do depends on a weighted perspective of all morally relevant factors. Thus, due to changing circumstances, what is morally right to do at one time is not necessarily so at another time. Entitlement to a water hole prevents others from access in a situation with plenty of water, but should not prevent others from having water in another situation framed by drought, Waldron argues. In this second situation other morally compelling reasons like the right to survival or to subsistence will trump entitlements. Waldron is clearly right here.

What then are the implications of Waldron's argument for a theory of rectificatory justice after colonialism? The argument is not directly relevant to my view on rectificatory justice, since my argument is not dependent on Nozick's version of entitlement theory. However, we can reformulate the argument so that it targets the argument for rectification after colonialism better. Changing circumstances have consequences for our moral duties. Assume, for example, that a former colony claims rectification at time (t2) for an injustice committed by the colonial power at (t1). At (t2) the colonial power has a moral duty to compensate the former colony. However, the former colonial power is hit by an earthquake and hundreds of thousands of people die, the infrastructure breaks down, and so on. Is it also in this new situation, at time (t3), a moral duty for the former colonial power to compensate the former colony for the previous injustice? No, because the duty to rectify is dependent not only on the historical injustice but also on other circumstances, for example the capacity of the former colonial power to rectify, as was argued in the previous chapter. In the situation after the earthquake the former colonial power has less capacity to compensate. Thus, at (t3) it has no moral duty to do so. But the debt remains due for payment at a later time (t4) when the capacity is restored.

To take another example of changing circumstances, assume that a former colony claims rectification, including monetary compensation, at independence, time (t1), but after independence the colony develops by its own efforts and its people achieve a high standard of living. If the claim was rejected by the colonial power at (t1), does it then still have a duty to monetary compensation at (t2) in spite of the new economic situation of its former colony? As was argued in Chapter 9 with reference to David Miller, there is still a pending moral debt, but it might at (t2) be paid by an apology rather than by monetary compensation.

The rights of descendants and the non-identity problem

In the discussion on rectificatory justice after slavery and the slave trade it is argued by some that descendants of slaves deserve compensation for what was done to their ancestors (Brophy, 2006). But do descendants have rights to such compensation? One objection to this idea is based on Derek Parfit's account of the "non-identity problem." According to Parfit, "if any particular person had not been conceived when he was in fact conceived, it is *in fact* true that he would never have existed" (Parfit, 1984: 351, Parfit's emphasis). For example, those descendants of slaves who were conceived after slavery would not have existed if slavery had not happened. George Sher applies Parfit's "non-identity problem" to the question of compensation to descendants of injustice (Sher, 2005). His argument starts from the assertion that children of victims of injustice would have been different children if the injustice had not taken place. The reason is biological. Reproduction is like a lottery and if the circumstances are slightly different, for example that conception takes place at some other time, the resulting child will have a different genetic profile. Thus, if the parents had not suffered from the injustice, a different child would have been born, which implies that it is the wrong child who would be compensated. The existing child would not have existed if the injustice had not taken place, and hence there are no valid claims for rectification.

Sher's view that a child born after an injustice done to his or her parents is a different person from a descendant of the same parents had the injustice never taken place is of course correct, but there are nevertheless arguments for compensation to children of victims of injustice that are not affected by Sher's argument. First, it does not apply to a child born before the injustice was done. Hence, if compensation to descendants is due, at least the children born before the injustice deserve it. Furthermore, as Sher himself points out, if the perpetrator fails to compensate the parents for the original injustice and this failure is repeated after the later child is born, this is a further injustice to the parents for which also this child may claim compensation. Thus, the subsequent failure of the victimizer to compensate for the injustice once done to the parents implies also subsequent injustice to the children born after the original injustice, for which they deserve compensation (Ibid.: 192–193).

Third, one could argue that descendants deserve compensation because their parents were harmed. Harms can have long-ranging reverberations in a family and as a consequence the children will also suffer from them. However, one must distinguish between harms to descendants that are the consequence of previous harms to their ancestors and harms that have other causes. For example, what are the implications for children's rights to compensation if we assume that the parents are unable to care for their children for other reasons than the previous injustice, or that the parents themselves undermine the welfare of their children? Andrew Cohen argues that given that children are entitled to support from their parents, children have the right to claim compensation from the former perpetrator only in cases where previous injustices prevent the parents from supporting their child (Cohen, 2009).

This argument – that descendants deserve compensation because their parents were harmed – is supported by Thompson's discussion of injustice against "family lines" (Thompson, 2002: 137–139). She takes slavery as a case in point, but other instances of forced labor and forced migration are also cited as examples of injustice against family lines. Her point contra Sher is that a right to reparation is claimed by an ancestor as a member of a family line. The family line establishes a link between the victim of an injustice and his or her son and daughter, and from this angle the exact genetic make-up of the offspring is unimportant. Thompson writes: "For their claim rests not on their being the particular individuals they are, but on their membership of a family line to which an injustice was done" (Ibid.: 139).

In conclusion: the non-identity problem does not pose a serious objection to my argument for rectificatory justice after colonialism. Sher's argument that a child born after an injustice done to his or her parents is a different person from a descendant of the same parents had the injustice never taken place and that this child therefore does not deserve compensation does not take into account "family lines." Furthermore, and in my view more to the point, it has no impact on the argument that colonialism had lasting implications for the relations between former colonies and colonial powers, that it affected whole communities, and that virtually all people born in the former colonies were affected by enduring injustices.

Conclusion

In this chapter I have discussed some philosophical objections to the idea of rectificatory justice. I considered Jon Elster's notions of ethical individualism and ethical presentism and found that my argument is consistent with both. The idea of rectification to states does not conflict with EI. And, since colonialism has in different ways left morally relevant traces in the present, EP is also compatible with my argument for rectification.

Next I discussed George Sher's argument for the diminution of transferability. According to Sher, rectification is due only for the original harm and not for the subsequent choices made by the victims themselves.

However, Sher's argument also lacks relevance to my argument for rectification after colonialism. Its focus is on independent choices and actions. Therefore it neglects both a *history* of disrespect and the automatic pervasive effects of colonialism that strictly limited the range of possible alternative actions for the colonized peoples.

Many arguments for rectification, for example Nozick's, depend on counterfactual calculations, that is, comparisons between the present situation and what would have happened if the historical wrongs had never been done. Estimation of compensation is based on the difference in outcomes. As Jeremy Waldron argues, such counterfactual calculations rest on fragile grounds. However, they presuppose that compensation should be proportional to the loss. My argument for rectification after colonialism does not presuppose such an estimation and therefore is not vulnerable to Waldron's objection. Neither is Waldron's argument regarding changing entitlements and changing circumstances a threat to my argument for rectification after colonialism. Even if the colonized peoples adjusted to new circumstances, many of the injustices of colonialism are enduring.

Finally, George Sher argues that the non-identity problem undermines the rights to compensation of descendants born after an injustice is done. Neither is this argument a more valid objection to rectificatory claims after colonialism because it does not take into account the collective and enduring nature of colonial harms.

11 Ways Forward: Rectification, Forgiveness, and Reconciliation

Introduction

In this book I argue for global rectificatory justice. Colonialism has in different ways shaped the present global order and the legacy of colonialism requires both rectification for past injustices and forward-looking remedies. How should the relations between former colonies and former colonial powers be shaped in the future? Do demands for rectification for past wrongs merely open wounds that have already healed? Perhaps forgiveness and reconciliation are better alternatives than rectification?

Over the last decades we have witnessed a number of examples of restorative processes after injustices and dictatorships: after the end of apartheid in South Africa, after the overthrow of military dictatorships in Latin America, for the rehabilitation of the Roma people in Europe, and so on. In parallel with demands for rectificatory justice, questions of forgiveness and reconciliation are often raised. In Chapter 7 we saw some examples of apologies for injustices during colonialism. Germany has apologized for the genocide of the Herero in the beginning of the 20th century, Australia's government apologized in 2009 for the atrocities towards Aborigines when the continent was colonized, and most recently and intriguingly, in 2013 the British government apologized and compensated former interns in British detention camps during the Mau Mau uprising.

Although rectificatory justice, forgiveness, and reconciliation cover similar conceptual realms, that is, how to deal with harms done in the past, and in some ways overlap, there are also crucial differences, which I will come back to. First, I will say something about the meaning of forgiveness and reconciliation.

Forgiveness for past wrongs

Can rectification be substituted by forgiveness? Forgiveness is often seen as a requirement to move forward for individuals who have been wronged. Broken relations and psychological wounds can be healed by forgiveness. Forgiveness is also often considered a virtue, not least in Christianity. Jesus says, according to Matthew: "If you forgive those who sin against you, your heavenly Father will forgive you" (Matthew, 6:14). Many believe that it is commendable to forgive and that forgiveness implies that good prevails over evil.

Typically, forgiveness is part of individual ethics. Someone is harmed, for example cheated or assaulted, and the response to this injustice could be revenge or forgiveness. However, forgiveness has also recently become an alternative path for conflict resolution in social ethics, illustrated most vividly by the South African Truth and Reconciliation Commission.

After apartheid South Africa faced the difficult challenge of how to respond to the past. There were strong moral reasons for claiming rectificatory justice for those who had suffered under the racist laws and to take the former perpetrators to court. The black population had been maltreated for many years and their leaders had been imprisoned, tortured, and killed. Some black leaders demanded that the perpetrators should be tried in courts but others, among them the leading figure in the South African Truth and Reconciliation Commission, Bishop Desmond Tutu, argued for forgiveness and reconciliation. He proclaimed forgiveness as an ideal solution when perpetrators had publicly acknowledged their crimes. Tutu believed that this would heal the divided and violence-stricken nation, and open it to an integrated and hopeful future (Tutu, 2000).

South Africa is a highly relevant example for this book because it can be seen as a kind of microcosm of the situation in the colonized world. The relation between blacks and whites during the apartheid regime is reminiscent of the global relation between former colonies and former colonial powers. So perhaps the South African way of overcoming its apartheid legacy can be applied on a global scale? Could forgiveness for past injustices be a way forward for global relations? Is forgiveness an instrument to overcome the past and open the future towards an integrated world?

In order to assess forgiveness as a way to overcome past injustices we have to raise a number of questions. First, what is the meaning of forgiveness? Is forgiveness unconditional, or should forgiveness only be given if the perpetrator fulfills some requirements? Is it possible to forgive on behalf of someone else – for example on behalf of one's forefathers, who were the victims of past wrongs – and is it viable for representatives of a harmed group to forgive on behalf of its members? Finally, how is forgiveness related to rectificatory justice?

The meaning of forgiveness

What does forgiveness imply? There are two parts to forgiveness: First, the victim is aware of a harm done, and second, in light of this awareness, he or she overcomes any responses to the offence that involve resentment towards the perpetrator or any attempts to take revenge (Garrard and McNaughton, 2010: 90). An unpaid debt is remitted. Thus, forgiving is a performativity; something happens when forgiveness is offered (Swinburne, 1989: 85). In this way, forgiveness could be unilateral; it is given to someone without his or her knowledge.

Bilateral forgiveness entails an apology from the perpetrator. The perpetrator apologizes for the harmful act and hopes for forgiveness. The victim can forgive if the resentment towards the perpetrator has been overcome, and the past wrongs are – if not forgotten – at least no longer influencing the future relations between the victim and the perpetrator. Margret Walker says that "forgiveness should restore... the conditions of moral relationship" (Walker, 2006: 162). If the victim, after proclaiming forgiveness, is nevertheless still full of hatred towards the perpetrator, forgiveness has not actually taken place.

Is forgiveness unconditional or does it presuppose some kind of penance from the perpetrator? In principle both options are possible and in the real world we find both unconditional and conditional forgiveness. We hear amazing stories of individuals who in spite of the grave injuries inflicted upon them are prepared to forgive without any conditions (Ibid.: 175–176). However, forgiveness normally requires that a perpetrator fulfills certain demands. The perpetrator should acknowledge the harm, apologize, and repent. Repentance entails that the perpetrator regrets what was done, is conscious of the harm and suffering caused, and assures the victim that the deed will not be repeated (Griswold, 2007: 63–64).

We have previously discussed the possibility that descendants will claim rectification for misdeeds against their forefathers. Is it also possible for descendants to forgive harms against their forefathers? Can, for example, a son or a daughter forgive on behalf of their dead parents? Forgiveness means that a victim overcomes resentment towards a perpetrator. Forgiveness is a victim's response to a harm and a perpetrator and in this way tied to the victim. Therefore, only the person who has herself suffered from maltreatment is in a position to forgive. Forgiveness cannot be offered on behalf of someone else. As a consequence, the possibility of being forgiven is definitely past when a wronged person has died.

Forgiveness for colonial wrongs

Is then forgiveness a viable alternative to rectification for colonial wrongs? Is it possible for a group, say the Herero tribe or a former colony, say Kenya – or rather their legitimate representatives today – to forgive the former colonists for what they did to their nations during colonialism? And, vice versa, can the former colonizers – in these cases Germany and Great Britain – offer apologies and nothing more, and be forgiven?

Official representatives of Germany and Great Britain could declare that they wish that their state had not done the deeds, express regret, and make a commitment that this kind of deed is foreign to them today. Is it then possible for legitimate representatives of a maltreated group to forgive? Could, for example, representatives of Herero or Mau Mau forgive Germany or Britain on behalf of their peoples? First, as was argued in the previous section, only now living persons can forgive. Hence, only individuals, like the survivors of the detention camps in Kenya are in a position to forgive. The Herero victims of the German genocide are all dead. Thus, we face an asymmetric situation; representatives of states can apologize but only individual members of the groups that were subject of the injustice can forgive.

Second, apologies from former perpetrators are superficial, meaningless, disrespectful, and annoying if they are not associated with supportive actions. The former colonial power must offer the victims something of value. So normally apologies are coupled with duties to compensate for past wrongs and to establish new relations based on equality and reciprocity. This, then, is the language of justice; perpetrators have some duties and the victims some rights.

Reconciliation

Let me now move on to a discussion of the relation between rectification and reconciliation. What does reconciliation entail? The South African reconciliation process – or at least the idea behind it developed by Bishop Desmond Tutu – can be seen as paradigmatic. Reconciliation is forward-looking. The aim of reconciliation is that former enemies should be able to coexist and cooperate in the future and the process can be described in the following way:

1. There is a conflict between A and B.
2. Both A and B have the intention to overcome the conflict and establish harmonious relations. Reconciliation is a forward-looking process.
3. By exploring the history behind the conflict, A and B will search for a mutual understanding of the past and the reasons behind the conflict. Reconciliation is a "process of mutual accommodation," as Thompson writes (Thompson, 2002: 52) or, to use Villa-Vicencio's words, the aim is "to discover, understand and acknowledge common ground" (Villa-Vicencio, 2009: 54).
4. In a situation where the relation between the parties is asymmetrical (A is dominant and B is subordinate), as in South Africa during apartheid, reconciliation also presupposes efforts to achieve symmetry, that is, equality.
5. Finally, to achieve reconciliation, if A has harmed B, A should make all possible efforts to compensate B for what A did to B in the past, even though in the present circumstances compensation might amount to symbolic gestures.

The symbolic character of compensation to the victims is stated by Desmond Tutu. According to Tutu, the message from the Truth and Reconciliation Commission to the victims of apartheid was:

> We acknowledge that you suffered a gross violation of your rights. Nothing can ever replace your loved ones. But as a nation we are saying, we are sorry, we have opened the wounds of your suffering and sought to cleanse them; this reparation is a balm, an ointment, being poured over the wounds to assist their healing. (Tutu, 2000: 61)

When is reconciliation achieved? According to Thompson, when

> the harm done by injustice to relations of respect and trust that ought to exist between individuals or nations has been repaired or compensated for by the perpetrator in such a way that this harm is no longer regarded as standing in the way of establishing or re-establishing these relations. (Thompson, 2002: 50)

In South Africa during the truth and reconciliation process, reconciliation presupposed that the perpetrators acknowledged what they had done but not necessarily that they also apologized. The perpetrators' acknowledgement of what they had done was sufficient for the Commission.

Rectificatory justice, forgiveness, and reconciliation

So, how is rectificatory justice related to forgiveness and reconciliation? First one can notice that the three concepts cover similar conceptual realm, that is, the question how to deal with harms done in the past. Rectificatory justice implies that the victims of harm and injustice have rights and, conversely, that the perpetrator have duties. As Rawls says, the concept of justice implies the assignment of rights and duties (Rawls, 1971: 5).

In contrast, forgiveness is a gift from the victim to the perpetrator, sometimes offered unconditionally and sometimes in response to an apology. Reconciliation entails elements of both forgiveness and justice – or perhaps more correct – is a result of forgiveness and/or rectification, but the emphasis is on the relations between the parties; how to achieve dialogue and mutual understanding between victim and perpetrator in order to establish peaceful future relations.

Acts of rectificatory justice and forgiveness can sometimes be complementary and sometimes alternatives. If we take South Africa as a case in point, it seems that attempts to achieve reconciliation are not fully successful, largely due to the lack of rectificatory justice. The victims of atrocities under apartheid were asked by the Truth and Reconciliation Commission to "forgive and forget" as an alternative to rectification, which, as Garrard and McNaughton point out, added to the wrongs done to the victims. Victims had the right to claim compensation and even demand punishment of the perpetrators by virtue of what they had gone through in the past, but they were told to forgive and forget (Garrard and McNaughton, 2010: 60). Furthermore, contempt for rectification among the white community and business circles has left open sores in the society. As Brandon Hamber argues, the unfulfilled demands for compensation for harms during apartheid have led to disappointment, increasing social conflicts and the lack of trust in the government among the mostly poor, black majority (Hamber, 2007: 267–270).

But there are also other issues. Can one really expect states to make apologies similar to those of individuals? Are states not basically motivated by self-interest, while apologies are acts motivated by moral concerns? And are apologies perhaps just an easy and cheap way for a state to free itself from historical burdens, asks Richard Vernon. He therefore suggests a "sincerity test" in order to check whether the political apology is sincere. Ways for a state to pass the sincerity test include making a constitutional amendment or supplementing an apology with compensation to the victims (Vernon, 2012: 81–83). The worry that political apologies could just be empty words should be taken seriously. If they are to be meaningful and lead to rectification and reconciliation, they must be part of a strategy involving other measures.

The duty to rectify for past wrongs is forward-looking: it aims at improving the moral quality of future relations (De Greiff, 2007). As Margaret Walker writes:

> The direct concern of restorative justice is the moral quality of future relations between those who have done, allowed, or benefited from wrong and those harmed, deprived, or insulted by it. (Walker, 2006: 385)

I have in this chapter discussed rectification, forgiveness, and reconciliation as ways to overcome colonial injustices in the past. They overlap in certain respects but, in relation to political conflicts, rectificatory justice has priority, and reconciliation will hopefully be a result.

12
Is a Generous Immigration Policy a Way to Rectify Colonial Injustices?

Introduction

Migration from former colonies to former colonial powers represents a large portion of 20th-century migration. This migration has been facilitated by generous laws regarding immigration and citizenship. For example, after World War II Britain granted citizenship to hundreds of millions of colonial subjects. Every person born in the British Empire was, according to common law, a British subject and Commonwealth citizen. As a consequence many Indians, Pakistanis, and people from the Caribbean migrated to the United Kingdom and the non-white population grew from around 30,000 in the 1940s to 3 million at the end of the century (Hansen, 2000).

Immigration to France followed a similar development. Like Great Britain, France provided citizens from its colonies privileged immigration status. The Evian Accords regulating the relations between France and Algeria after Algeria's independence instituted "freedom of movement" between the countries (Naylor, 2000; 83–84; Vasileva, 2011). In 2010, 5 million immigrants, that is, people born outside France, were residing in France. About one-third of them came from Algeria and Morocco and approximately 6% of the French population consists of people of Maghreb origin. Likewise, post-World War II immigration to the Netherlands consisted mainly of immigrants from former colonies, not least the Moluccas, who were given residence rights when Indonesia refused to grant independence to the islands (Focus Migration, 2011).

During colonialism different kinds of links between colonizer and colonized were established, and in general these links facilitated present-day immigration from former colony to former colonial power. Colonized peoples were often culturally influenced – or perhaps better, dominated – by the colonial power and they adopted its language and religion. In comparison with immigrants from nations who lack historical bonds, the cultural commonalities established during colonialism facilitate integration for immigrants from a former colony. This fact undermines a frequent communitarian argument against immigration. For example, David Miller argues that liberal democracies have reasons to limit immigration in order to preserve and defend their "public culture." According to Miller, immigration will endanger the preservation of the national language of the receiving nation and pose a threat to things people value like "its public and religious buildings, the way its towns and villages are laid out" (Miller, 2005: 39; see also Walzer, 1983: 39). However, immigrants from former colonies who share a language and culture with the receiving nation will not pose this alleged threat. Thus, Miller's argument is of less relevance to immigrants from former colonies who are familiar with the culture and master the language.

More recently, anti-immigration sentiments have grown in Europe, not least in former colonial powers like Britain, the Netherlands, Belgium, and France. A relatively open immigration policy, at least towards their former colonies, is being criticized. Should immigration laws be strict or generous? Should Europe opt for welcoming a substantial number of asylum seekers and other immigrants or close its borders? Today, immigration is a much discussed issue and there are many arguments raised in the debate for and against generous immigration laws. This chapter is limited to a single argument that is not often mentioned in the debate, namely that a generous immigration policy towards ex-colonies is a way for former colonial powers to rectify for colonial injustices.

Rectification for colonial wrongs entails some kind of compensation (see Chapter 9). There are many ways for former colonial powers to compensate and one possibility is for them to open their borders to migrants from their former colonies. Would a generous immigration policy be an appropriate way for former colonial powers to compensate for past wrongs? Are there reasons to be skeptical?

Symmetry

A generous immigration policy for migrants from former colonies would amount to a symmetrical procedure for rectification. While colonialism, at least in a number of cases, implied migration of Europeans to the colonies (of British citizens to Rhodesia, Kenya, and South Africa, of Germans to South West Africa, and of French to Algeria, for example), migration in the opposite direction could be seen as an appropriate way to rectify. Europeans who migrated to the colonies benefitted from the resources of the colonies in the first place and the present immigrants from former colonies to Europe can benefit from the welfare of the now affluent European nations. In fact, the Europeans claimed a right to migrate that their descendants want to deny their former subjects.

An obvious problem with this argument is that, if taken literally and imply a *pro rata* policy in favor of immigrants from former colonies, citizens from former colonies who did not receive many immigrants from Europe, like Uganda and Sudan, would be discriminated against. If the aim of generous immigration laws is to rectify for historical wrongs, the number of Europeans who migrated to a particular colony seems to be irrelevant. Instead, it is the harm of colonization that is the decisive reason for rectification.

Remittances

Another argument for seeing a generous immigration policy as an appropriate way to compensate for past wrongs is that emigration is valuable for the former colony. The migrants send money back to their families. Remittances from immigrants to their home countries are welcome financial contributions to people in the homeland who live in poverty. For example, according to different estimations, remittances from Algerian workers in France in the 1960s enabled between 1.25 and 2 million Algerians to subsist (Naylor, 2000). The volume of remittances is expanding. In 2004, the World Bank estimated that the annual value of transferred remittances was about US$150 billion, which was three times the value of the development assistance provided to low-income nations, and the UN Global Commission on International Migration reports that remittances "now play an essential role in sustaining national and local economies" (Global Commission on International Migration, 2005: 29f.).

However, even if remittances are welcome and much needed contributions to people living in developing countries, they have so far had only a minor long-term impact on the economic situation of those countries. In fact only about 10% of remittances go to savings or investments (Ibid.). It could be argued that remittances are an integral part of a global structure characterized by inequality and dependency. Hence, although remittances are alleviating poverty in the short term, the consequences for long-term economic development in a former colony may even be counterproductive. Therefore, to treat remittances from immigrants to their home countries as a way for colonial powers to compensate for colonial wrongs is unconvincing.

Brain drain

A flip side of a generous immigration policy and increased migration from a former colony to Europe is the exit of the best educated workers from the developing nations, the so-called "brain drain." The developing nation has typically invested in the education of these emigrants but does not gain from their work. Instead these highly educated persons move to a developed nation to practice their profession in order to enjoy better remuneration and standards of living, and so on. For example, nurses and doctors from developing nations who are much needed at home are often employed in developed nations. The Global Commission on International Migration provides some striking figures: from 2000 to 2004, 16,000 African nurses registered to work in the United Kingdom alone; only 50 out of the 600 doctors trained in Zambia since its independence are still working in their homeland; and of the 1,200 doctors trained in Zimbabwe since independence only 360 were still practicing there in 2001 (Benatar, 2007).

The fact that highly educated professionals as well as workers in the most active phase of their lives leave their poor home country to work in a developed nation is detrimental to development (Brock, 2009). Thus, generous immigration laws in Europe seem to be an impediment to the reparation of the former colonies. From their point of view, if a generous immigration policy means that they lose many educated citizens, it looks more like a continuation of the old colonial regime than a means of compensation for former exploitation.

A right to migrate

Do the ethics of migration in fact have anything to do with the relation between nations? In his critique of Michael Walzer's assertion that receiving nations have the right to refuse entry to immigrants, Joseph Carens argues that the real ethical issue at stake is the individual rights of migrants (Carens, 1987); the right to migrate is even stated in the Universal Declaration of Human Rights, Article 13: 2. However, this argument is flawed. It fails to recognize that there are instances when a nation's interest could take priority over individual rights. Besides the conflict can also be described as a conflict between individuals' rights: on the one hand, individuals' right to migrate, and on the other, individual's rights to health care and other vital benefits. Let me explain.

In exceptional situations the collective interest of a nation could take priority over individuals' rights. For example, if a nation is hit by a natural catastrophe or threatened by a military attack, the government may have to force people to help to relieve victims or enlist in the army even at the expense of their individual rights. In a similar way it is at least conceivable that politicians in a developing nation could consider imposing restrictions on the emigration of doctors and nurses if so doing would mean that citizens have access to life-saving health care that they otherwise would not have (Oberman, 2013).

A liberal immigration policy in Europe might lead to an increased brain drain and thus create further problems in already stricken poor nations. It is worth noting that in the discussion of whether national interests collide with migrants' rights, the issue is usually the interests of the receiving wealthy nations in Europe and North America (see, for example, the arguments for restricted immigration in Walzer, 1983; Miller, 2000). The interests of the developing nations are rarely discussed.

The conflict between the interests of the developing nation and those of individual migrants can also be seen as a conflict between different individuals' basic rights. On the one side are the rights of the migrants and on the other the rights of individuals in the developing countries who run the risk of being without necessary health care because of a drain of doctors and nurses. The argument that a generous immigration policy could be detrimental to the interests of the former colony entails that migration may violate the basic rights to health care and other primary goods of individuals living in the former colony.

Conclusion

Migration from former colonies to former colonial powers represents a large part of 20th-century migration. The issue discussed in this chapter is if a generous immigration policy towards people from former colonies is an appropriate means for the European nations and former colonial powers to compensate for colonial injustices.

Emigration from developing nations has both positive and negative economic consequences. Immigrants send large amounts of money back to their country of origin but migration also entails a brain drain from the poor nations to the wealthy. The majority of migrants are people with motivation and education, who are much needed in their home countries. Besides, remittances tend to preserve a relation of dependency between the former colonial power and the colony. Hence, although it is difficult to estimate, migration seems on the whole to be a negative phenomenon for developing nations. If this is the case, a generous migration policy is not an appropriate means for former colonial powers to compensate their former colonies for past injustices. Yet, this conclusion does not exclude that there might be other humanitarian and cosmopolitan reasons for a generous immigration policy (see, for example, Carens, 1987, 2013; Benhabib, 2005).

13
Changing the Global Order: The Case of TRIPS

In Chapter 2 I argued that the present global order to a large extent mirrors the colonial structure. However, the dominance of the former colonial powers – plus the United States, which from the 19th century developed into a leading neo-colonial power – is currently being challenged. There are new competitors on the global scene, primarily the former semi-colony China, South East Asian nations, and India. Even within some of the established global institutions, the power structure is gradually shifting.

As I have argued throughout this book, rectificatory justice after colonialism is both backward-looking and forward-looking. There are many cases of pending duties of apology and compensation, and there is a need to establish new and equal global relations substituting the traditional (i.e., colonial) relation of dominance–subjugation.

In this chapter I examine the negotiations within the World Trade Organization (WTO) concerning trade-related intellectual property rights (TRIPS), and in particular the Doha summit in 2001. My question is whether the Doha summit could work as a model for how more equal relations between the former colonial powers, the global rich, and the former colonies, the global poor, might be realized.

TRIPS and the Doha Declaration

The Agreement on trade-related aspects of intellectual property rights has been widely discussed and questioned. Economist Joseph Stiglitz argues that TRIPS is detrimental to the interests of both rich and poor nations because it leads to monopolies and higher prices (Stiglitz, 2006). According to Peter Singer, TRIPS illustrates the limitations of national sovereignty within the WTO that hits the weaker member states, that is, those with less bargaining power, particularly hard (Singer, 2004). Aidan Hollis and Thomas Pogge see TRIPS in the light of an international institutional order, which perpetuates inequalities. They argue for a Health Impact Fund that would finance innovation and the production of medicines for diseases that haunt the poorest people (Hollis and Pogge, 2008). Ebenezer Durojaye argues that in international law there is a major difference between intellectual property rights and human rights. The former are guaranteed by the state, while the latter "are inalienable and timeless" (Durojaye, 2008: 68); and Lisa Forman argues for "the primacy of human rights over trade obligations" (Forman, 2007: 347).

In particular, critics have accused TRIPS of favoring property rights over public health in the developing world. The implications for access to HIV medicines have especially been highlighted in the debate. Oxfam, for example, argues:

> Every year, millions of impoverished people around the world die of preventable diseases simply because they cannot afford to buy the medicines they need to survive. This is one of the most tragic outcomes of the international trade rules that govern intellectual property – they put the price of life-saving drugs out of the reach of patients in poor countries. (Oxfam, 2008)

TRIPS was signed in 1994. Members of the WTO have to comply with the agreement. TRIPS covers literary and artistic works as well as inventions and brands. New inventions, products, and processes "in all fields of technology" (Art. 27: 1) – contentiously including pharmaceuticals and agrochemicals – can be subject to patenting or trademarking. TRIPS stipulates that patents on inventions and new products, for example pharmaceuticals, give the patent holder a monopoly for a period of (normally) 20 years from the filing date (Gervais, 2003). However, TRIPS specifies a number of limitations and exceptions "aimed at fine-tuning the balance that has to be found between the legitimate interests of right holders and of users" (WTO, 2008).

The TRIPS-agreement is controversial. It globalized a property rights regime in the interest of multinational companies but as we shall see not necessarily in the interest of the global poor (see Chapter 2). As a consequence of patenting, the producer with the patent right can set the price without competition from others. Cheap medicines will no longer be available on the market. TRIPS is especially criticized for limiting access for poor people in developing countries to pharmaceutical such as medicines for the treatment of HIV/AIDS, TB, malaria, and so on. Two billion people, that is, one-third of the global population, lack access to essential medicines and a majority of HIV-infected people lack access to life-saving, antiretroviral therapies (WHO, 2004). The United Nations' Millennium Development Report task force reported in 2012:

> Data from a number of national and subnational surveys implemented in developing countries indicate that their access to affordable (generic) essential medicines has improved only slightly. Average availability of selected essential medicines was 51.8 per cent in public sector health facilities and 68.5 per cent in the private sector over the period 2007–2011, up by a few percentage points on both counts from the previous measurement.... Prices of available essential medicines continue to be relatively expensive in developing countries, that is, they are several times greater than the international reference prices (IRPs). New data show only minor improvement. The aforementioned surveys show that average prices were still 2.6 times higher in the public sector compared to IRPs. Patients pay five times more in the private sector of developing countries. (United Nations, 2012: 61–62)

For example, in Nigeria the price of a course of antiretroviral drugs ranges between US$100 and 200 per month, which obviously makes them inaccessible to the majority, who live on one dollar a day (Durojaye, 2008). Due to undeveloped health care systems, lack of infrastructure, and weak and corrupt governments, vital medicines are difficult to access in most poor countries. High prices as a consequence of patenting are then an additional barrier.

TRIPS covers other vital goods besides pharmaceuticals. One is seeds. The extent of the impact of TRIPS on access to seeds in poor countries is debated. A study by Danish Church Aid argues that TRIPS contributes to rising prices on commercial seeds, which makes them unaffordable for farmers in developing countries. Furthermore, plant varieties are being protected by plant-breeders' patent rights, which will limit access for non-patent holders. The report concludes: "It is apparent that the TRIPS agreement may pose severe problems for poor farmers in accessing seeds and agricultural technology, and this may lead to increased poverty and hunger" (Danish Church Aid, 2005).On the other hand, a recent report on intellectual property rights (IPR) and seeds (Quakers in the UK, 2009) argues that there is no immediate conflict of interests. The vast majority of the world's farmers cultivate their land with seeds they have saved from previous harvests in the traditional way. However, the report also notes that more and more farmers are becoming dependent on commercially produced seed. Hence, in the long run there is a risk that TRIPS will conflict with the poor's need for seed.

The wealthy, industrialized nations typically dominate research and development. The OECD countries accounted for 91% of the 347,000 new patents issued in 1998. And according to the United Nations' Human Development Report, only 0.6% of resources spent on health research were dedicated to vaccines for HIV/AIDS and malaria, epidemics that primarily threaten the global poor (UNDP, 2001). From this perspective, TRIPS seems to perpetuate a structural injustice by using legal means to restrict poor countries' access to vital means for development. The British Commission on Intellectual Property Rights writes:

> [I]t can safely be said that the effect of applying patent rights globally will be to benefit very considerably the holders of patent rights, mainly in developed countries, at the expense of the users of protected technologies and goods in developing countries. (Commission on Intellectual Property Rights, 2002: 21)

As was noticed above, TRIPS applied limitations to patent rights for reasons of emergency. Article 27: 2 declares:

> Members may exclude from patentability inventions, the prevention within their territory of the commercial exploitation of which is necessary to protect *ordre public* or morality, including to protect human, animal or plant life or health and Article 31 allows the waiving of patent rights "in the case of a national emergency or other circumstances of extreme urgency". (WTO, 1994)

However, in the 1990s pharmaceutical companies in the United States and Europe, supported by their governments, made efforts to extend the application of the agreement as much as they could. For example, they put pressure on South Africa and Brazil to abstain from producing generic HIV medicines in spite of the huge number of AIDS patients in these countries and in the developing countries where the cheap medicines could be marketed (t'Hoen, 2003).

The reactions from developing nations and NGOs like Oxfam and Médecins sans frontières were sharp. In the "Amsterdam Statement" they argued that public health should be the framework for interpreting the key features of the WTO agreement (WHO, 1999). Perhaps surprisingly, these reactions led to changes in policy by both the United States and European governments.

The African Group in the WTO took the initiative to put the emphasis on public health in the upcoming follow-up conference in Doha, Qatar, and Zimbabwe, the head of the African Group, declared:

> We propose that Members issue a special declaration on the TRIPS Agreement and access to medicines at the Ministerial Conference in Qatar, affirming that nothing in the TRIPS Agreement should prevent Members from taking measures to protect public health. (Quoted in t'Hoen, 2003)

In response to these criticisms and the need for clarification of how TRIPS should be interpreted, the WTO Doha Ministerial Conference in 2001 followed the African proposal. In situations of national emergency and extreme urgency, the compulsory licensing of necessary drugs is permissible, according to the so-called Doha Declaration. Paragraph 4 states:

> We agree that the TRIPS Agreement does not and should not prevent Members from taking measures to protect public health. Accordingly, while reiterating our commitment to the TRIPS Agreement, we affirm that the Agreement can and should be interpreted and implemented in a manner supportive of WTO Members' right to protect public health and, in particular, to promote access to medicines for all. (WTO, 2001)

A state may license a company to produce generics when faced with a public health problem. In addition, the exceptions to pharmaceutical patent protection were extended until 2016 for the least developed countries (WTO, 2001; Gervais, 2003; Correa, 2006). In 2003 the WTO General Council added that producers of generic medicines may export pharmaceutical products made under compulsory license. As a consequence, the UN special envoy on HIV/AIDS pleaded with the industrialized countries to manufacture generic drugs for Africa (Rimmer, 2008; 89).[1]

The Doha Declaration has been interpreted as a success for the least developed countries. The World Health Organization states:

> The Declaration responds to the concerns of developing countries about the obstacles they faced when seeking to implement

measures to promote access to affordable medicines in the interest of public health in general, without limitation to certain diseases. (WHO, 2014)

The WTO agreements thus allow compulsory licensing in cases of urgency. However, in opposition to the spirit of the Doha-declaration, some producer countries try to avoid this through bilateral agreements, so-called TRIPS-plus agreements. This means that the producer country enters into regional and bilateral trade agreements on condition that the partners limit the markets for generic pharmaceuticals. The United States in particular has raised the level of patent protection in a number of bilateral agreements with other nations (Rimmer, 2008: 90; Sridhar, 2008: 83; Correa and Matthew, 2011; Forman, 2012).

The possibility of bypassing patents in cases of emergency, already expressed in TRIPS but strongly emphasized in the Doha Declaration after controversies over the interpretations of TRIPS, challenges the property rights regime. Critics of TRIPS argue that it made life-saving pharmaceuticals unaffordable for poor people. They further argue that the right to health is more important than the protection of property rights, and that property rights should extend only to the point where they come into conflict with the right to health and other basic necessities.

When the Doha Declaration exempted pharmaceuticals, this was seen as an instance where a global institution, in this case the WTO, decided that poor countries should receive benefits at the expense of rich and powerful corporations and nations.

Limiting the global property rights regime as a way to rectify

As we noticed in Chapter 2, the global intellectual property rights regime institutionalized by the WTO mirrors the post-colonial system. However, the atrocious consequences for the poor of the patenting of life-saving drugs raised strong opposition from developing countries and NGOs. And, perhaps surprisingly, both the European Union and the United States changed their positions, which made the Doha Agreement possible.

The encouraging outcome of the Doha conference illustrates how rectification for colonial wrongs could be achieved. People living in the former colonies who are struck by diseases will get access to cheap medicines that are invented by researchers in the wealthy nations and marketed by their pharmaceutical companies. This is one way to rectify for past wrongs. However, if the Doha Declaration signified a paradigm shift in the relations between poor and rich nations, it has been followed by few similar initiatives.

Ten years after the Doha Declaration, Correa and Matthew summarize its implications in the following way:

> In sum, the Doha Declaration has had a clear impact on the international discourse relating to IPRs and access to medicines and some impact on the implementation of national laws and the use of TRIPS flexibilities, but has not been sufficient to prevent TRIPS-plus demands, concessions and commitments in FTAs [Free Trade Agreements] and other bilateral agreements that may negatively affect access to medicines. (Correa and Matthew, 2011)

Thus, it is too early to say whether the Doha Declaration was a paradigm shift. But it was perhaps an early sign of how rectification may be put into practice.

14
Conclusions and Implications

Introduction

The idea of rectificatory justice connects the past to the present and the future. States and peoples stand in continuing relations to each other, and what was done in the past has enduring implications for present and future relations. Historical injustices against peoples and individuals generate rights among the victims and duties among the former perpetrators. There is an unpaid debt as long as rectification is pending.

What then does rectification require? In Chapter 9 I proposed the following requirements for rectification.

Case P

X (the **agent**: person, group, state, etc.) did A (**harm**: stealing, wounding, oppressing, killing, etc.) to Y (the **victim**: a person, group, state, etc.) at t1 (**time**).

Given Case P, rectificatory justice requires at t2 that

i X acknowledges the harm (A) done to Y,
ii X apologizes for A,
iii X (or X's descendants) compensates Y (or Y's descendants) with B (something valuable: money, etc.) or returns what was taken at t1.

We noticed in Chapter 8 that it is rare for former colonial powers to acknowledge, and even more uncommon for them to apologize for, past injustices. It did in fact happen in 2004, when Germany apologized for the genocide of the Herero, but, for example, Belgium has so far not even acknowledged its guilt in relation to the Congo. However, according to a principle of rectificatory justice, both the Herero population and the Congolese have a right to apologies as well as to compensation.

What would rectification for colonial wrongs mean today? Surely, acknowledgment, apology, and compensation. But it is perhaps equally important to view present and future global relations through lenses informed by history. The present global structure was shaped by colonialism and it is time to change it. A constructive process of rectification is future-oriented. When relations between the formerly colonized and colonizing are on equal terms with regard to trade, political and economic influence, and so on, rectification is on its way. But rectification is pending as long as the relations remain unequal and the global structure mirrors colonial relations. Let me quote Rui Horvana, a former Frelimo adherent and minister of the state of Mozambique, whom I interviewed:

> Perhaps there is a case for reparation. The grandchildren of slave owners still benefit from slavery and the grandchildren of slaves are still suffering from that historical fact. Because of history we are not equal today. Now we have to look forward, but the partnership with the former colonial power needs to be equal. We have to create our own identity, not the one imposed on us.

In a comment on Thomas Pogge's theory of global justice, Erin Kelly and Lionel McPherson argue for a "cosmopolitan cooperationist" account of global justice. In discussing the content of Rawls's duty of assistance they argue that "societies that have helped to cause or have proximately benefited from the poverty of other societies may have a corrective duty ... to help to lift those burdened societies out of poverty" (Kelly and McPherson, 2010: 113). But why are the authors so modest? Why only "may have" a corrective duty?

Justification of rectification

What are the reasons for rectification for historical injustices? Why should we be reminded of what happened in the past? Is it not better to forget past harms and look forward? Perhaps rectification will open wounds that have been healed? Then, rectification would rather threaten than benefit present and future harmonious relations between nations.

There might be some truth in this objection to rectification. On the other hand, the purpose of rectificatory justice is not to dig into long-forgotten conflicts. It is only when wounds are *not* healed and when the victims have *not* forgotten the historical injustice that rectification is brought to the fore. In situations when rectification is justified but pending, peaceful coexistence is based on shaky grounds. There is not "stability for the right reasons," to borrow Rawls's expression (Rawls, 1999: 12f.). Stability for the right reasons is not based on power or compromises, but on mutual recognition and reciprocity. "Right reasons" would therefore in this situation mean that peoples and nations are reconciled. Rectification might thus be necessary for long-lasting harmonious relations between nations and peoples.

The foremost justification for rectification is that it is a way to realize justice. To quote Rawls again: "[J]ustice is the first virtue of social institutions, as truth is of systems of thought" (Rawls, 1971: 3). This applies also to rectificatory justice. A state that has treated a group of its citizens in an unfair way is obliged to recompense them. Similarly, a nation that has not recompensed another nation for earlier injustices owes a debt to it.

Rectification is also a requirement for a Society of Peoples, Samuel Freeman argues. When interpreting Rawls's view in *The Law of Peoples,* he writes:

> So just as Rawls might have supported as a provisional measure [the] preferential treatment of minorities ... so too he could have supported as a temporary measure a global distribution principle, to rectify the history of exploitation, expropriation and gross violations of human rights endured by burdened peoples around the world. (Freeman, 2006: 251)

Thus, according to Freeman's reading of Rawls, rectification for past wrongs could be a condition for the establishment of a Society of Peoples governed by the Law of Peoples. In this interpretation, rectification is a way to restore a moral equilibrium characterized by reciprocity, mutual respect, and peaceful relations between peoples. Exploitation, expropriation, and violations of human rights have upset the moral equilibrium, and rectification is a way to restore it.

The principle of rectificatory justice states that a former perpetrator has a moral duty to rectify the past wrongs. Some critics have argued that emphasizing rectification will lead to an attitude of "victimization" (Barkan, 2000: xvii). The former victim then adopts a role of wronged person that is detrimental to a future-looking, constructive approach. Instead of trying to improve his or her situation, the victim remains in helplessness and need of support. There might be instances of this psychological reaction. However, as a criticism of rectificatory justice it is beside the point. Rectification is not based on charity but on rights. A relevant parallel is if A has not paid back a debt to B. Then, B has a right to get his or her money back and the psychological attitudes involved – for example whether B feels neglected or cheated – are beside the point.

When a state fails to rectify past wrongs, or when others fail to demand rectification, it sends the message that norms for international relations, like the ones John Rawls proposes in his *Law of Peoples* (Rawls, 1999), are irrelevant and unimportant. Margaret Walker writes:

> To fail to reprove wrongdoers or to fail to hold responsible those to whom responsibility reasonable falls is to cast doubt on the authority of norms, to authoritatively if implicitly mark exceptions to them, or to indicate that wrongdoers are beyond the reach of the community or its norms. (Walker, 2006b: 32)

In our case, the wrongdoers are states and the community the Society of Peoples, to speak with Rawls. States that adhere to norms for international relations and who want to refer to them in their foreign policy are themselves obliged to rectify their own past violations of these norms.

The breaking of treaties and bi-lateral agreements is one kind of historical wrong. Janna Thompson takes the treaty of Waitangi between Maori chiefs and the British government in 1840 as a case in point. When states enter into a treaty, it is assumed that the treaty should be kept also by the descendants if there are no tenable excuses for not doing so. If the treaty is broken, the deceitful party has an obligation to rectify (Thompson, 2002: 27). Agreements and treaty obligations are "trans-generational," which means that the descendants of the parties to the treaties or agreements have obligations, regardless of the fact that they themselves did not act. They have commitments solely on the grounds of their ancestors' decisions. "Trans-generational commitments creates trans-generational obligations," as Thompson writes (Ibid.: 37). This justification of rectification is limited to the breaking of agreements and treaties.

Rectificatory justice is not only backward-looking but also forward-looking and rectification can be justified by its beneficial consequences. Former colonies that still suffer from historical injustices can be expected to have a resentment against the former colonial power. Rectificatory justice aims at restoring relations and will ideally lead to cooperation and harmonious relations. As Janna Thompson argues, nations want to coexist in the future and peaceful coexistence is dependent on the absence of animosity based on past wrongs (Thompson, 2002: 25; Walker, 2007).

Rectification has implications not only for the victim of past wrongs but also for the perpetrator. When discussing justice for black Americans, Alfred Brophy writes:

> But even beyond the power of apologies and truth commissions to shape the public's understanding of history and the current effects of that history, apologies and truth commissions shape our identity. They tell us how we view ourselves and how those left "outside history" – left outside the American dream – are included (or excluded). (Brophy, 2006: 145)

Brophy's discussion refers to rectification for black Americans and the identity of Americans, but his argument may have relevance to former colonial nations involved in rectificatory processes after colonialism. When rectification entails the acknowledgment of past injustices, apologies, and compensation, this will most likely have similar beneficial effects on the nation's self-image. Janna Thompson writes: "To be worthy of respect, a nation has to be prepared to fulfill its historical responsibilities" (Thompson, 2002: 68). A nation that wants to be a respected international actor must repay its historical debts.

Likewise, Spinner-Halev expresses a forward-looking view on rectificatory justice in the following words: "Justice does not mean that peoples or communities take responsibility for the past, but rather that political communities take responsibility for the present and future" (Spinner-Halev, 2012: 81). Spinner-Halev fails to see the reasons for rectification; the fact that an injustice done in the past needs to be rectified. Although he does not account for the importance of nations taking responsibility for their past, he has a point that the discussion of rectificatory justice, also is future-oriented. The future gain of rectification is not the main reason, but, as Miller says, "an incidental bonus" (Miller, 2007: 147).

Furthermore, as Richard Vernon underlines, there is a link from the past to the present. Past injustices are often reproduced in the present. Present holdings were perhaps unjustly acquired in the past, and present unjust international relations were established in the past (Vernon, 2012: 123–124). Hence, there is a continuation of complicity from the past to the present and future generations. To acknowledge and rectify for what happened in the past is one way to both better understand and take responsibility for the present and the future.

In this section I have questioned the relevance of the objection that rectificatory processes will reopen wounds and create conflicts. I have argued that in cases when rectification is appropriate, the wounds are not yet healed and peace is built on fragile grounds. Instead, rectificatory justice is a condition for lasting peace and stability. I have further argued that rectification is a way to realize justice, restore a moral equilibrium, and respect the rights of victims of past wrongs. There are other beneficial consequences of rectification. Former perpetrators will through rectification enhance their international reputation, and rectification will restore the self-respect of the citizens of a nation that is guilty of historical wrongs.

Global equality

> The wrong of colonialism can be shown in the departure from an associative ideal that fails to respect equality and reciprocity in the creation of norms and often also in the substantive principles governing the association. (Ypi, 2013: 186)

The colonized neither participated in the construction of the norms that should guide the political association nor influenced the political decision-making that led to their colonization. Neither did formal independence imply justice or "the ideal of political association" (Ibid.) characterized by equal relations and reciprocity.

In the aftermath of colonialism, global relations are characterized by inequality, dominance, and subjection. The high-income countries have a per capita income 60 times higher than that of low-income countries, and a few nations, with the United States in the forefront, have a dominant influence over global politics and economics (World Bank, 2014).

Further, colonialism seems to have left a sense of inferiority, illustrated by my Master's student's remark: "Everything Pakistani is today considered of less worth compared to the West" (Chapter 1). As Rajeev Bhargava argues, colonialism meant not only economic exploitation and political domination for hundreds of years, but also a changed mindset of the colonized subjects, implying a loss of cultural means for identity formation and self-respect (Bhargava, 2013).

In various ways we still live in a period of "post-colonialism," meaning a historical period characterized – politically, economically, and conceptually – by colonial relations. But perhaps we are finally leaving this historical period behind. Even if the West still dominates the global order, Western dominance is being gradually challenged. Both China and India are increasing their economic and political influence, as are Brazil and some other Latin American countries.

The legacy of colonialism will be overcome when global relations are characterized by equality and reciprocity. Global equality could be seen as a utopian goal and a discussion of the implications of this goal and of ways in which we might come closer to it is beyond the limits of this book. Let me just hint at some discussions and strategies for a transformation of the global power structure.

As we saw in Chapter 2, the power structure of the international organizations mirrors to a large extent colonial power relations. This even holds for the United Nations. No African or Latin American nation and only one Asian nation is a permanent member of the most powerful decision-making unit, the Security Council (one permanent member representing six-sevenths of the world population!). In their efforts to become permanent members of the Security Council, Japan, India, and Brazil – as well as Germany – have formed what is called the G4 group. From the perspective of global distributive justice, it is doubtful whether Germany and Japan should become permanent members. However, in order to increase international equality, both India and Brazil, and even some African nations, should be permanent members. The reform proposal presented by UN General Secretary Kofi Annan in 2005, to increase the number of seats in the Security Council by two African, two Asian, and one Latin American seats, was aimed at democratizing the United Nations (United Nations, 2005). This model would also help to distance it from the post-colonial era.

Even the structures of the Bretton Woods institutions, the IMF and the World Bank, are undemocratic and mirror colonial structures. Social scientists like Joseph Stiglitz, David Held, and Jan Art Scholte have proposed ways of reforming them so that they will be more democratic and accountable to the global poor (Stiglitz, 2006; Held, 1995; Scholte, 2000). In practice, the so-called BRICS countries, Brazil, Russia, India, China, and South Africa, are challenging the IMF and the World Bank by creating an alternative development bank (Daigle, 2012).

Political cosmopolitans argue for a democratic global government (Tännsjö, 2008). As Immanuel Kant argued more than 200 years ago, and many others have since, although there might be good reasons to favor such a political construction, it is neither politically feasible nor morally desirable (Kant, 1992; Tan, 2004). However, to come nearer the goal of global equality and to transcend the post-colonial era, global governance organizations like the WTO, IMF, and World Bank ought to be more responsive to the interests of poorer and weaker nations.

The following proposal of the United Nations' Open Working Group on Sustainable Development Goals for 2030 points in a similar direction:

> 10.6 Ensure enhanced representation and voice of developing countries in decision making in global international economic and financial institutions in order to deliver more effective, credible, accountable and legitimate institutions. (United Nations, 2014)[1]

Criteria for the legitimacy of global governance institutions are formulated by political theorists Allen Buchanan and Robert Keohane (Buchanan and Keohane, 2006). After discussing various proposals for legitimacy criteria, they propose the following: first, legitimacy requires that the institution must not commit serious injustices, like violating human rights; second, global governance institutions should provide benefits that could otherwise not be obtained; third, such institutions must live up to "institutional integrity," that is, realize their goals and not act contrary to their moral ideals; and finally, they must live up to reasonable standards of accountability and transparency.

What then should be expected of global governance institutions if they are to contribute to a change in the present unequal global structure? Buchanan and Keohane argue that they "should also accommodate and even encourage the possibility of developing more determinate and demanding requirements of justice" (Ibid.: 421). In the light of the present unjust global structure the global institutions should contribute to changes in the direction of global justice. This would be one way to get away from a post-colonial global structure.

Does rectificatory justice add anything to distributive justice?

I argued in Chapter 2 that there is a missing premise in the present discussion on global justice. The discussion has focused on issues of global distributive justice, cosmopolitanism vs nationalism, and the globalization of human rights, but the ethical implications of the colonial legacy for the present unjust world order have so far been largely neglected. To get a comprehensive view of global justice we should also include the idea of rectificatory justice in the discussion.

Authors who have contributed to the discussion on global justice, like Charles Beitz (1979), Thomas Pogge (1989), Kok-Chor Tan (2004), Simon

Caney (2005a), Darrel Moellendorf (2009), and Gillian Brock (2009), to mention just a few, argue for various notions of global distributive justice and they propose redistributions in favor of the global poor. Does not global rectificatory justice imply similar redistributions, and does this not imply that arguments for rectification are redundant?

In line with this objection Leif Wenar argues under the heading "The Primacy of Distributive Justice" that

> backward-looking considerations add no weight to claims for reparations... Only forward-looking factors give us reasons to repair historical injustice... Reparations, when they are due, are reparations not for the sake of the past, but for the sake of the future... [R]ectificatory justice has "no independent force" and adds nothing to distributive justice. (Wenar, 2006: 396, 402)

What then – if anything – are the ethical implications of a theory of global rectificatory justice? Does it add anything substantial to global distributive justice?

Global rectificatory justice and global distributive justice are not unrelated. Compensation motivated by rectificatory justice normally implies, like distributive justice, a redistribution of resources. But it would be odd if a former colony that prospers today could demand compensation for past wrongs from a former colonial power that is today poorer than itself. Hence, a demand for compensation for past wrongs can only be justified when the past wrongs leave traces in the present. In this way distributive justice influences the practical implications of rectificatory justice. This said, a former colony may with good reason demand other kinds of rectification than economic compensation. For example, its people might have been humiliated and suppressed during colonialism. For this the former colonial power should pay recompense, for example through "restorative justice" in order to repair the relationship. This view is shared by Wenar when he argues that reparations might lead to relations of respect and mutual trust that were hurt by previous injustices (Wenar, 2006).

As we noticed in Chapter 5, it is difficult to estimate the economic implications of colonialism for the former colonies. In line with Robert Nozick, one could argue that patterned principles for global distributive justice are the best way to realize global rectificatory justice. Nozick writes:

> Perhaps it is best to view some patterned principles of distributive justice as rough rules of thumb meant to approximate the general results of applying the principle of rectification of injustice. For example, lacking much historical information, and assuming (1) that

> victims of injustice generally do worse than they otherwise would and (2) that those from the least well-off group in the society have the highest probabilities of being the (descendants of) victims of the most serious injustice who are owed compensation by those who benefitted from the injustices ... then the *rough* rule of thumb for rectifying injustices might seem to be the following: organize society so as to maximize the position of whatever group ends up least well-off in the society. (Nozick, 1974: 230–231)

Similarly, global rectificatory justice would imply "patterned principles" of global justice so that the global basic structure maximizes the position of the globally least well-off, that is, the poorest nations.

According to theories of global distributive justice, there is a need for global redistributions in favor of the poor. A theory of global rectificatory justice after colonialism has similar implications. However, even though the social and economic implications are similar, the motives behind them are different. The motives behind a moral duty to redistribute resources in favor of the poor are not solely based on principles of fairness, rationality, or equality, as argued by different theories of global distributive justice. A theory of global rectificatory justice offers additional motives for redistribution. It assumes that the present injustices at least partly derive from colonialism. Surely, it strengthens the moral duty to redistribute if it was the former colonial nations that actively, or through negligence, contributed to the present underdevelopment in their former colonies. Generally speaking, it makes a great difference to an agent's motives to come to the rescue if she has caused a harm rather than just being aware of a harm being done. As a consequence, the former colonial nations have today a duty to rectify for past wrongs that adds to a general duty of fairness.

Thus, the rectificatory motives for redistribution are other than the motives following from theories of distributive justice. This implies that even those who contest arguments for global distributive justice might approve of the reasons for global rectificatory justice. Hence, a theory of global rectificatory justice is complementary to a theory of global distributive justice and it enables us to develop a more comprehensive understanding of the need and motivation for global justice.

The journey has started ...

Kenya

Kenya was a British colony until its independence in 1963. In Chapter 4 I referred to Kenya as an example of how a colonial power resisted the well motivated attempts of colonized people to achieve liberation. In the detention camps thousands of Kenyans were subjected to atrocities like torture and rape.

Historian Caroline Elkins, who has written *Imperial Reckoning, The History of British Colonial Policy Towards Kenya*, raises at the end of her book the following question:

> How is it possible to evaluate the impact that this war had on the hundreds of thousands of men and women who were detained in the camps and villages of British colonial Kenya? There is no record of how many people died as a result of torture, hard labor, sexual abuse, malnutrition, and starvation. If the British did keep records of these deaths, they were destroyed long ago. (Elking, 2005: 366)

And, as Elking points out, this war had a lasting impact on the surviving victims. She quotes a Kikuyu woman speaking out about the loyalist collaborators:

> "I hate them; I hate them for what they did to us", she said. "We all hate them and will not speak to them if we see them outside of church. We even refuse to go to their funerals, which is against the church, but they didn't go to the funerals of our husbands and children and parents when they killed them. Aye, I despise them." She paused before continuing. "You know," she finally said to me, "this will only change when everyone knows what happened to us. Maybe then there will be some peace once our people are able to mourn in public and our children and our grandchildren will know how hard we fought and how much we lost to make Kenya free for them." (Ibid.: 367)

In 2011 four surviving victims of the detention camps went to London to claim rectification. Their case was tried by a British court. This could have been another failed and soon forgotten effort to achieve justice but surprisingly it was not. Instead the British government, and in particular its Minister of Foreign Affairs William Hague, listened to the Kenyans' grievances and responded. In a speech, which has the potential to become memorable, Hague acknowledged the harms, apologized on behalf of Britain, and promised compensation to the 5,229 of the detained Kenyans who were still alive.

On June 6, 2013 William Hague said in the House of Commons:

> I would like to make it clear now and for the first time on behalf of Her Majesty's Government that we understand the pain and grievance

> felt by those who were involved in the events of the emergency in Kenya. British Government sincerely regrets that Kenyans were subject to torture and other forms of ill treatment at the hands of the colonial administration. The British Government sincerely regrets that these abuses took place and that they marred Kenya's progress towards independence. Torture and ill treatment are abhorrent violations of human dignity, which we unreservedly condemn. (House of Commons, 2013)

Hague denied any British judicial liability for the war in Kenya 50 years ago.

He said to the House:

> We continue to deny liability on behalf of the Government and British taxpayers today for the actions of the colonial administration in respect of the claims, and indeed the courts have made no finding of liability against the Government in this case. We do not believe that claims relating to events that occurred overseas outside direct British jurisdiction more than 50 years ago can be resolved satisfactorily through the courts without the testimony of key witnesses, which is no longer available. It is therefore right that the Government have defended the case to this point since 2009. (Ibid.)

One reason for the difficulty in finding evidence is that official documents relating to British policy in Kenya had been destroyed by the authorities (Daily Nation, 2013). Nevertheless, even if there are judicial obstacles to a court process, the outcome illustrates the possibility of a moral verdict. From a moral point of view, the British guilt is clear and rectificatory justice necessary. Hague accepted, as we saw, moral liability and, on this basis, reasons to apologize and rectify. He also emphasized that rectification would enable reconciliation and future cooperation between Kenya and Britain.

Hague promised the payment of around £20 million to the survivors and that the British government would finance a memorial in Nairobi to the victims of torture and ill-treatment.

The claims of the Kenyans and the response of the British government can be seen as evidence that not only legal but also moral claims for justice have a relevance in relations between states. The response of the British government to the claims of the Kenyans may be seen as an exemplar of rectificatory justice.

The Caribbean movement for rectification

Efforts for rectification after colonialism have been most energetic in the Caribbean. The initiative to demand rectification for slavery and the slave trade gained force on the bicentenary of the abolition of the British transatlantic slave trade in 2007. Representatives of Caribbean governments claimed rectification from Britain and other European nations that had benefitted from the slave trade (Beckles, 2013: 223–229).

In July 2013 the heads of governments of the Caribbean Community (CARICOM) issued a declaration demanding reparation for the genocide of indigenous populations and for slavery and the slave trade during colonialism. They set up the CARICOM Reparation Commission with representatives of the governments to prepare reparatory demands. The chair, Prime Minister Baldwin Spencer of Antigua, declared at the meeting:

> We know that our constant search and struggle for development resources is linked directly to the historical inability of our nations to accumulate wealth from the efforts of our peoples during slavery and colonialism. These nations that [were] the major producers of wealth for the European slave-owning economies during the enslavement and colonial periods entered Independence with dependency straddling their economic, cultural, social and even political lives. (CARICOM, 2013)

The Commission has addressed not only Britain but also France, for its colonial legacy in Haiti, the Netherlands, for its legacy in Surinam, and other European nations that were involved in the slave trade, like Spain, Portugal, Norway, Denmark, and Sweden (The Guardian, 2013).

In March 2014 the heads of state of 15 Caribbean nations approved a ten-point plan for rectification, including demands on European countries to apologize for their involvement in the slave trade and to pay compensation to the descendants of slaves who are still victims. The heads of state claimed that the European nations should "devise a development strategy to help improve the lives of poor communities in the Caribbean still devastated by the after-effects of slavery (Pilkington, 2014).

Is it really reasonable to demand rectification for trespasses that took place for such a long time ago? Are we today responsible for the acts of our ancestors? The questions are justified. But, as I have argued throughout this book, the answer is yes. As the Caribbean commission shows, there are still victims of the consequences of the slave trade and the fact that no nation so far has apologized or compensated is an added injustice.

Notes

2 The Discussion on Global Justice: A Missing Premise

1. The Gini coefficient measures equality 0 is complete income equality and 1 is maximum inequality (one person has all income).
2. By forced migrants I mean migrants that move from their country of residence not because of free will but due to severe political, social, or economic conditions.

3 Colonialism

1. Besides Ferguson and Boahen, I have used some general sources for my overview of the history of colonialism like Ferro (1987), Waites (1999) and Macqueen (2007) and literature on particular areas, periods, and countries.
2. Ferguson has been accused of trying to "rehabilitate the empire" (Drayton, 2010), and Boahen is said to "tell the story [of European colonialism in Africa] from the other side" (Boahen, 2011: cover blurb).

4 Five Cases of Colonialism

1. Democratic Republic of Congo ranks 186th among the world's nations in terms of development (UNDP, 2013).
2. On the situation in East Africa in 1955, the British Royal Commission reported that there was no way back for the colonies while their traditional social structure was destroyed. "Nor ... can they go forward, or even stand still, under their present customary, legal and economical organization of land, labor and capital." There could only be a stand still due to the fact that there was no "common level of education and wealth, irrespective of divisions of tribe or race ... so long, in other words, as the situation resulting from colonial rule was allowed to persist" (quoted in Davidson, 1991: 322). According to Davidson, the situation was similar in the greater part of colonized Africa.
3. One could certainly question the paternalism behind the example, but let us ignore that for the sake of the illustration.

8 Claims for Justice after Colonialism

1. See the home page Political Apologies and Rectifications (2014), http://political-apologies.wlu.ca/doclist.php?cp=2&rpp=5&sort=title.
2. Just before the British were forced to leave Kenya, they moved boxes with documents containing information on what had happened during the colonial war and in the detention camps to Britain. The same thing happened when the British left other colonies. The documents have been kept locked away in the Department of Foreign Relations. Now the documents are accessible and

they show that the British government was well aware of what methods were used against the opposition in Kenya and in other colonies.

9 The Meaning of Rectificatory Justice after Colonialism

1. Strangely enough, when giving the example of Britain in Victorian times, Miller treats Britain's benefits from industrialization separately from its assumed present non-benefits from imperialism.
2. What is less well known is that slavery was practiced in the Swedish colony Saint Barthélemy in the Caribbean. Slavery was not abolished there until 1847 (Mayer and Fick, 1993).
3. There are of course a few exceptions to this, for example Hong Kong, Macau, and the Maldives.
4. As the apology of Pope John Paul II for the sack of Constantinople in 1204 illustrates, even apologies delivered a long time – in this case 800 years – after the wrongs were committed could be meaningful, that is, if the historical act has reverberations today (Neumann, 2014).

10 Rectificatory Justice – Philosophical Challenges

1. I owe this argument to Maren Behrensen.

13 Changing the Global Order: The Case of TRIPS

1. As a matter of fact, HIV medicines are not patented in all countries in Africa. However, in South Africa, the only African country that can produce medicines, 13 out of 15 HIV medicines are patented (Peterson et al., 2010).

14 Conclusions and Implications

1. Interestingly, in an earlier draft of the proposal the aim was "equitable representation," of developing nations but this was changed to "enhanced representation" (Beyond 2015).

Bibliography

Acemoglu, D. & Robinson, J., 2012. *Why Nations Fail? The Origins of Power, Prosperity and Poverty*. London: Profile Books.

Acholi Times, 2014. *Lamogi Continues Pursuit for Compensation from Britain for Injuries Inflicted in 1911*. [Online] Available at: http://www.acholitimes.com/index.php/acholi-news/2241-lamogi-continues-pursuit-for-compensation-from-britain-for-injuries-inflicted-in-1911 [Accessed 24 04 2014].

Anderson, D., 2005. *Histories of the Hanged: The Dirty War in Kenya and the End of Empire*. New York, London: W. W. Norton.

Aristotle, 1980. *The Nichomachean Ethics, Book V:4*. Oxford: Oxford University Press.

Armitage, D., 2000. *Ideological Origins of the British Empire*. Port Chester, NY: Cambridge University Press.

Armstrong, C., 2012. *Global Distributive Justice*. Cambridge: Cambridge University Press.

Associated Press, 2010. *Apology to Tribes – US Apologizes to American Indians for Mistreatment*. [Online] Available at: http://www.nativetimes.com/news/tribal/3651-apology-to-tribes-us-apologizes-to-american-indians-for-mistreatment [Accessed 09 04 2013].

Beitz, Charles. 2000. Rawls' Law of Peoples, *Ethics*, 110(4), pp. 669–696.

Banerjee, A. V., Benabou, R. & Mookherjee, P., 2006. *Understanding Poverty*. Cary: Oxford University Press.

Barkan, E., 2000. *The Guilt of Nations*. New York: W. W. Norton.

Barratt-Brown, M., 1963. *After Imperialism*. London: Heinemann.

BBC News, 2004. *Germany Admits Namibia Genocide*. [Online] Available at: http://news.bbc.co.uk/2/hi/africa/3565938.stm [Accessed 12 01 2012].

BBC News, 2005. *Kenya Wants UK '"Atrocity" Apology*. [Online] Available at: http://news.bbc.co.uk/2/hi/africa/4318277.stm [Accessed 22 04 2014].

Beauchamp, T. & Childress, J., 2001. *Principles of Biomedical Ethics*. Oxford: Oxford University Press.

Beckles, H., 2013. *Britain's Black Debt*. Jamaica: University of West Indian Press.

Beitz, C., 1979. *Political Theory and International Relations*. Princeton: Princeton University Press.

Benatar, S. B., 2007. An Examination of Ethical Aspects of Migration and Recruitment of Health Care Professionals from Developing Countries, *Clinical Ethics*, 2(2).

Benhabib, S., 2005. *The Rights of Others, Aliens, Residents and Citizens*. Cambridge: Cambridge University Press.

Bethell, L., 1984. A Note on the Native American Population on the Eve of the European Invasions, in L. Bethell, ed. *The Cambridge History of Latin America*. Cambridge: Cambridge University Press.

Beyond 2015. Campaigning for a global development framework after the millenium development goals. Brussels 3 July 2014. http://www.beyond2015.org/sites/default/files/B2015JulyOWGreactionfullFINAL.pdf [Accessed 2014 09 29].

Bhargava, R., 2013. Overcoming the Epistemic Injustice of Colonialism. *Global Policy,* 4(4), pp. 413–417.

Boahen, A. A., 2011. *African Perspectives on European Colonialism.* New York: Diasporic African Press.

Borras Jr, S. & Franco, J., 2012. Global Land Grabbing and Trajectories of Agrarian Change: A Preliminary Analysis. *Journal of Agrarian Change,* 12(1), pp. 34–59.

Boxill, B., 2003. A Lockean Argument for Black Reparations. *The Journal of Ethics,* 7, pp. 63–91.

Brock, G., 2009. *Global Justice: A Cosmopolitan Account.* Oxford: Oxford University Press.

Brooks, R., 1999. *When Sorry Isn't Enough: The Controversy over Apologies & Reparations for Human Injustice.* New York: NYU Press.

Brooks, R., 2003. Reflections on Reparations, in J. Torpey, ed. *Politics and the Past.* Oxford: Rowman & Littlefield, pp. 103–116.

Brophy, A. L., 2006. *Reparations: Pro and Con.* Oxford: Oxford University Press.

Bräutigam, D. A. & Knack, S., 2004. Foreign Aid, Institutions, and Governance, *Economic Development and Cultural Change,* 52(2).

Buchanan, A., 2000. Rawls's Law of Peoples: Rules for a Vanished Westphalian World. *Ethics,* 110, pp. 697–721.

Buchanan, A. & Keohane, R., 2006. The Legitimacy of Global Governance Institutions. *Ethics and International Affairs,* 20(4), pp. 405–437.

Burns, E. B., 1982. *Latin America: A Concise Interpretive History.* 3rd edn. New Jersey: Prentice-Hall.

Butt, D., 2009. *Rectifying International Injustice: Principles of Compensation and Restitution between Nations.* Oxford: Oxford University Press.

Cabrera, L., 2010. *The Practice of Global Citizenship.* Birmingham: Birmingham University Press.

Caney, S., 2005a. *Justice beyond Borders.* Oxford: Oxford University Press.

Caney, S., 2005b. Cosmopolitan Justice, Responsibility, and Global Climate Change. *Leiden Journal of International Law,* 18 (2005), pp. 747–775

Carens, J. H., 1987. Aliens and Citizens: The Case for Open Borders. *The Review of Politics,* 49(2), pp. 251–273.

Carens, J. H., 2013. *The Ethics of Immigration.* Oxford: Oxford University Press.

CARICOM, 2013. *Heads Agree on Reparations Follow-Up Action.* [Online] Available at: http://www.caricom.org/jsp/pressreleases/press_releases_2013/pres147_13.jsp [Accessed 07 07 2013].

Chamberlain, M. E., 1998. *European Decolonization in the Twentieth Century.* London: Longman.

Chamberlain, M. E., 2010. *The Scramble for Africa.* 3rd edn. Harlow: Pearson.

Cobain, I., 2014. *The Guardian.* [Online] Available at: www.theguardian.com [Accessed 09 04 2014].

Cobain, I. & Hatcher, J., 2013. Kenyan Mau Mau Victims in Talks with UK Government over Legal Settlement. *The Guardian* [Online] Available at: http://www.theguardian.com/world/2013/may/05/mau-mau-victims-kenya-settlement [Accessed 06 05 2013].

Cobain, I. & Norton-Taylor, R., 2012. Sins of Colonialists Lay Concealed for Decades in Secret Archive. [Online] Available at: http://www.theguardian.com/uk/2012/apr/18/sins-colonialists-concealed-secret-archive [Accessed 15 04 2014].

Cohen, A., 2009. Compensation for Historic Injustices: Completing the Boxill and Sher Argument. *Philosophy and Public Affairs*, 37(1), pp. 81–102.

Cohen, G., 2008. *Rescuing Justice and Equality*. Cambridge, MA: Harvard University Press.

Commission on Intellectual Property Rights, 2002. *Integrating Intellectual Property Rights and Development Policy*. London: Commission on Intellectual Property Rights.

Correa, C. M., 2006. *Trade Related Aspects of Intellectual Property Rights: A Commentary on the TRIPS Agreement*. Oxford: Oxford University Press.

Correa, C. & Matthew, D., 2011. The Doha Declaration 10 Years on and Its Impact on Access to Medicines and the Right to Health, *UNDP Discussion Paper*. [Online] Available at: http://www.undp.org/content/dam/undp/library/hivaids/Discussion_Paper_Doha_Declaration_Public_Health.pdf

Daigle, K., 2012. Rising Powers Consider Alternative to World Bank, Others. *Washington Times*. [Online] Available at: http://www.washingtontimes.com/news/2012/mar/28/rising-powers-consider-alternative-to-world-bank-o/, [Accessed 01 10 2014].

Daily Nation, 2013. UK Officials Burned, Dumped 'Embarrassing' Kenya Colonial Documents. [Online] Available at: http://www.nation.co.ke/news/Britain-Kenya-colonial-documents/-/1056/2093736/-/x71x9x/-/index.html [Accessed 02 12 2013].

Danish Church Aid, 2005. You Reap What You Sow: A Call for a Declaration on the TRIPS Agreement and Food Security. [Online] Available at: www.danchurchaid.org/news_publications/publications [Accessed 30 04 2014].

Davidson, B., 1991. *Africa in History*. New York: Collier Books, Macmillan Publishing.

Davis, M., 2002. *Late Victorian Holocausts: El Niño Famines and the Making of the Third World*. London: Verso.

Daily Monitor, 2014. Govt Returns Bunyoro Kingdom Property. [Online] Available at: www.monitor.co.ug [Accessed 07 14 2014].

De Greiff, P., 2007. Justice and Reparations, in J. Miller & R. Kumar, eds. *Reparations: Interdisciplinary Inquiries*. Oxford: Oxford University Press, pp. 153–176.

De Greiff, P., 2008. *The Handbook of Reparations*. Oxford: Oxford University Press.

De Las Casas, B., 1992. *A Short Account of the Destruction of the Indies*. London: Penguin.

De Schutter, O., 2012. *Fisheries and the Right to Food*, New York: United Nations (A/67/268). Available at: http://www.srfood.org/images/stories/pdf/officialreports/20121030_fish_en.pdf. [Accessed 01 10 2014].

Deutsche Welle, 2012. Holland Recognizes France's 'Brutal' Colonization of Algeria. [Online] Available at: http://www.dw.de/hollande-recognizes-frances-brutal-colonization-of-algeria/a-16467606 [Accessed 22 04 2014].

Deutsche Welle, 2013. Netherlands Apologizes Formally to Indonesia for Colonial Killings. [Online] Available at: http://www.dw.de/netherlands-apologizes-formally-to-indonesia-for-colonial-killings/a-17084816 [Accessed 22 04 2014].

Digeser, P. E., 2001. *Political Forgiveness*. Ithaca and London: Cornell University Press.

Dillard, D., 1967. *Economic Development of the North Atlantic Community: Historical Introduction to Modern Economics*. New Jersey: Prentice-Hall.

Dower, N., 2009. *The Ethics of War and Peace.* Cambridge: Polity Press.

Drayton, R., 2010. The British Empire and Deaths in Kenya. [Online] Available at: http://www.theguardian.com/education/2010/jun/16/british-empire-kenya-deaths [Accessed 14 04 2014].

Duggan, C., 2007. *The Force of Destiny: A History of Italy Since 1796.* New York: Houghton Mifflin.

Duignan, P. & Gann, L. H., 1975. Economic Achievements of the Colonizers, in P. Duignan & L. H. Gann, eds. *Colonialism in Africa 1870–1960, Vol. 4, The Economics of Colonialism.* Cambridge: Cambridge University Press, pp. 673–697.

Durojaye, E., 2008. Compulsory Licensing and Access to Medicines in Post Doha Era: What Hope for Africa? *Netherlands International Law Review,* 55(1), pp. 33–71.

ECOS, 2010. *Unpaid Debt: The Legacy of Lundin, Petronas and OMV in Block 5A. Sudan 1997–2003.* Utrecht: European Coalition on Oil in Sudan.

Elkins, C., 2005. *Imperial Reckoning: The Untold Story of Britain's Gulag in Kenya.* New York: Henry Holt and Company.

Elliott, J. H., 1984. Spain and America in the Sixteenth and Seventeenth Centuries, in L. Bethell, ed. *The Cambridge History of Latin America, Vol I.* Cambridge: Cambridge University Press, pp. 287–340.

Elster, J., 1993. Ethical Individualism and Presentism. *Monist,* 76(3), pp. 333–349. (Online version pp 1–10).

Elster, J., 2004. *Closing the Books: Transitional Justice from a Historical Perspective.* Cambridge: Cambridge University Press.

Erskine, T., 2003. Assigning Responsibilities to Institutional Moral Agents: The Case of States and "Quasi-States," in T. Erskine, ed. *Can Institutions Have Responsibilities? Collective Moral Agency and International Relations.* Basingstoke: Palgrave Macmillan, pp. 19–30.

Fairbank, J. K., 1992. *China: A New History.* Cambridge and London: Belknap.

Fanon, F., 2004. *The Wretched of the Earth.* New York: Grove Press.

Ferguson, N., 2004. *Empire: How Britain Made the Modern World.* London: Penguin Books.

Ferro, M., 1997. *Colonization: A Global History.* London: Routledge.

Focus Migration, 2011. *The Netherlands.* [Online] Available at: http://focus-migration.hwwi.de/The-Netherlands.2644.0.html?&L=1, http://focus-migration.hwwi.de/France.1231.0.html?&L=1, retrieved 2012–10–29 [Accessed 29 10 2012].

Forman, L., 2007. Trade Rules, Intellectual Property, and the Right to Health. *Ethics and International Affairs,* 21(3).

Forman, L., 2012. From TRIPS-plus to Rights-plus? Exploring right to health impact assessment of trade-related intellectual property rights though the Thai experience. Social Science Research Network. Available at http://ssrn.com/abstract=2241172. [Accessed 07 14 2014].

Frank, A. G., 1967. *Capitalism and Underdevelopment in Latin America.* New York and London: Monthly Review Press.

Freeman, M., 2002. Past Wrongs and Liberal Justice. *Ethical Theory and Moral Practice,* 5.

Freeman, S., 2006. Distributive Justice and the Law of Peoples, in R. D. Martin, ed. *Rawls's Law of Peoples: A Realistic Utopia?* Oxford: Blackwell Publishing, pp. 243–260.

Friends of the Earth, 2010. Africa: Up for Grabs: The Scale and Impact of Land Grabbing, Ugbowo, Nigeria.
Friends of the Earth International, 2012. Land, Life and Justice. How Land Grabbing in Uganda Is Affecting the Environment., Livelihoods and Food Sovereignty of Communities. Amsterdam and Kampala: Friends of the Earth International.
Furtado, C., 1959. *The Economic Growth of Brazil : A Survey from Colonial to Modern Times*. Berkeley: University of California Press.
Galeano, E., 1971. *Las venas abiertas de América Latina*. Madrid: Siglo XXI.
Gann, L. H. & Duignan, P., 1967. *Burden of Empire: An Appraisal of Western Colonialism in Africa South of the Sahara*. Stanford: Hoover Institution Press.
Gann, L. H. & Duignan, P., 1978. *The Rulers of British Africa 1870–1914*. London: Croom Helm.
Garrard, E. & McNaughton, D., 2010. *Forgiveness*. Durham: Acumen.
Gervais, D., 2003. *The TRIPS Agreement: Drafting History and Analysis*. London: Sweet & Maxwell.
Gewald, J.-B., 1999. *Herero Heroes: A Socio-Political History of the Herero of Namibia, 1890–1923*. Oxford: James Currey and Ohio University Press.
Global Commission on International Migration, 2005. Port of the Global Commission on International Migration. [Online] Available at: Report of the Global Commission on International Migration 2005, http://www.unhcr.org/refworld/publisher/GCIM.html. [Accessed 29 10 2012].
Greiff, D., 2007. Justice and Reparations, in J. Miller & R. Kumar, eds. *Reparations: Interdisciplinary Inquiries*. Oxford: Oxford University Press, pp. 153–175.
Griswold, C., 2007. *Forgiveness: A Philosophical Exploration*. Cambridge: Cambridge University Press.
Grotius, H., 1712/2004. *The Free Sea*. Indianapolis: Liberty Fund.
Guardian, The, 2013. Slavery Compensation: Caribbean Nations Propose Mau Mau Model. [Online] Available at: http://www.theguardian.com/world/2013/jul/26/caribbean-countries-slavery-compensation-claim [Accessed 22 01 2014].
Guardian, The, 2013a. UK to Compensate Kenya's Mau Mau Torture Victims. [Online] Available at: http://www.theguardian.com/world/2013/jun/06/uk-compensate-kenya-mau-mau-torture [Accessed 07 06 2013].
Hamber, B., 2007. Reparations as Symbol: Narratives of Resistance, Reticence, and Possibility in South Africa, in J. Miller & R. Kumar, eds. *Reparations: Interdisciplinary Inquiries*. Oxford: Oxford University Press, pp. 252–279.
Hansen, R., 2000. *Citizenship and Immigration in Postwar Britain*. Oxford: Oxford University Press.
Hare, R., 1963. *Freedom and Reason*. Oxford: Oxford University Press.
Hart, J., 2003. *Comparing Empires: European Colonialism from Portuguese Expansion to the Spanish-American War*. Basingstoke: Palgrave Macmillan.
Held, D., 1995. *Democracy and the Global Order: From the Modern State to Cosmopolitan Governance*. Stanford: Stanford University Press.
Hill, R., 2002. Compensatory Justice: Over Time and between Groups. *The Journal of Political Philosophy*, 10, pp. 392–419.
Hochschild, A., 1999. *King Leopold's Ghost*. Boston: Mariner books.
Hollis, A. & Pogge, T., 2008. *The Health Impact Fund: Making Medicines Available for All*, New Haven, CT: Incentives for Global Health.

House of Commons, 2013. Official Report, Parliamentary Debate. [Online] Available at: http://www.publications.parliament.uk/pa/cm201314/cmhansrd/chan13.pdf [Accessed 09 04 2014].

Howard-Hassmann, R., 2003. Moral Integrity and Reparations for Africa, in J. Torpey, ed. *Politics of the Past.* Oxford: Rowman and Littlefield, pp. 193–216.

Howard-Hassmann, R., 2008. *Reparations to Africa.* Philadelphia: University of Pennsylvania Press.

IMF, 2014. International Monetary Fund. [Online] Available at: http://www.imf.org/external/about/histcoop.htm [Accessed 11 04 2014].

Inikori, J., 1982. Introduction, in J. E. Inikori, ed. *Forced Migration: The Impact of the Export Slave Trade on African Societies.* London: Hutchinson, pp. 13–60.

Inikori, J. & Engerman, S., 1992. *The Atlantic Slave Trade.* Durham: Duke University Press.

International Organization for Migration, 2013. International Organization for Migration. [Online] Available at: http://www.iom.int/cms/home [Accessed 19 08 2013].

Kant, I., 1992 (1795). *Perpetual Peace.* London: Thoemmes Press.

Kelly, E. & McPherson, L., 2010. Non-Egalitarian Global Fairness, in A. Jaggar, ed. *Thomas Pogge and His Critics.* Cambridge: Polity Press, pp. 103–122.

Kohn, M., 2014. Colonialism, in E. Zalta, ed. *The Stanford Encyclopedia of Philosophy.* Stanford: Stanford University Press. (Spring 2014 Edition, forthcoming), Available at http://plato.stanford.edu/archives/spr2014/entries/colonialism.

Kukathas, C., 2006. Who? Whom? Reparations and the Problem of Agency. *Journal of Social Philosophy,* 37, pp. 330–341.

Kulke, H. & Rothermund, D., 1996. *A History of India.* New York: Routledge.

Kurowska, B., 2008. Reparations Politics – A Case Study of the Reparations Demands of the Herero towards the Federal Republic of Germany. FEPS Working Papers, 1.

Kwarteng, K., 2011. *Ghosts of Empire: Britain's Legacies in the Modern World.* London: Bloomsbury.

Kymlicka, W., 2002. *Contemporary Political Philosophy: An Introduction.* Oxford: Oxford University Press.

Landes, D., 1998. *The Wealth and Poverty of Nations: Why Are Some So Rich and Other So Poor?* New York: W. W. Norton.

Laquer, W., 1969. *The Israel-Arab Reader: A Documentary History of the Middle East Conflict.* London: Weidenfeld and Nicolson.

Lean, S., 2003. Is Truth Enough? Reparations and Reconciliation in Latin America, in, J. Torpey, ed. *Politics of the Past on Repairing Historical Injustices.* Blue Ridge: Rowman & Littlefield.

Locke, J., 1977. *Two Treatises of Government.* London: Dent.

Lonsdale, J., 2011. Introduction, in *African Perspectives on European Colonialism.* New York: Diasporic Africa Press, pp. i–vi.

Loomba, A., 2005. *Colonialism/Postcolonialism.* 2nd edn. London: Routledge.

Lovejoy, P., 2000. *Transformations in Slavery: A History of Slavery in Africa.* 2nd edn. Cambridge: Cambridge University Press.

Lyons, D., 1982. Justice and Entitlement, in J. Paul, ed. *Reading Nozick: Essays on Anarchy, State and Utopia.* Oxford: Blackwell Publishing.

Macalister, T., 2011. BP "Has Gained Stranglehold Over Iraq" after Oilfield Deal Is Rewritten. *The Guardian* [Online] Available at: http://www.theguardian.

com/business/2011/jul/31/bp-stranglehold-iraq-oilfield-contract [Accessed 11 04 2014].
MacIntyre, A., 1981. *After Virtue*. London: Duckworth.
Macqueen, N., 2007. *Colonialism*. Harlow: Pearson.
Maddison, A., 2002. Asia in the World Economy 1500–2030 AD. *Asian Pacific Economic Literature*, 20, pp. 1–37.
Malaysiakini, 2007. Special Report: The Hindraf Protest. [Online] Available at: http://www.malaysiakini.com/news/75315 [Accessed 22 04 2014].
Maybury-Lewis, D., 2002. Genocide against Indigenous Peoples, in A. L. Hinton, ed. *Annihilating Difference: The Anthropology of Genocide*. Berkeley: University of California Press, pp. 43–57.
Mayer, F. & Fick, C., 1993. Before and after Emancipation: Slaves and Free Coloreds in Saint Barthélemy (French West Indies) in the 19th Century. *Scandinavian Journal of History*, 18(4), pp. 251–273.
Meredith, M., 2005. *The State of Africa: A History of Fifty Years of Independence*. Johannesburg: Jonathan Ball Publisher.
Milanovic, B., 2012. Global Income Inequality by the Numbers In History and Now: An Overview. *The World Bank*. [Online] Available at: http://elibrary.worldbank.org/docserver/download/6259.pdf?expires=1370942851&id=id&accname=guest&checksum=4D7514BC0B2BAF8A2DD927C818F1AAC6
Mill, J. S., 1962. *Considerations on Representative Government*. London: Gateway.
Miller, D., 2000. *Citizenship and National Identity*. Cambridge: Polity Press.
Miller, D., 2005. Immigration: The Case for Limits, in *Contemporary Debates in Applied Ethics*. Oxford: Blackwell Publishing, pp. 193–206.
Miller, D., 2006. Collective Responsibility and International Inequality, in *Rawls's Law of Peoples: A Realistic Utopia?* Oxford: Blackwell Publishing, pp. 191–205.
Miller, D., 2007. *National Responsibility and Global Justice*. New York: Oxford University Press.
Miller, J. & Kumar, R., 2007. *Reparations: Interdisciplinary Inquiries*. Oxford: Oxford University Press.
Minerals and Mining in Africa, 2005. *Africana: The Encyclopedia of the African and African American Experience*, 2nd edn. [Online] Available at: http://oxfordindex.oup.com/view/10.1093/aasc/9780195170559.e.2667 [Accessed 11 04 2014].
Moellendorf, D., 2009. *Global Inequality Matters*. Basingstoke: Palgrave Macmillan.
Morray, J.P. 1968. The United States and Latin America, in J. Petras & M. Zeitlin, eds. *Latin America, Reform or Revolution*. Greenwich: Fawcett.
Morris, D., 1963. Towards a Reinterpretation of 19th Century Indian Economic History. *Journal of Economic History*, December.
Moutafakis, G., 1966. The Colonial Heritage of East Africa, in S. A. B. Diamond, ed. *The Transformation of East Africa*. New York: Basic Books.
Mörner, M., 1969. *Rasblandningen i Latinamerikas historia*. Stockholm: NoK.
Naylor, P. C., 2000. *France and Algeria: A History of Decolonization and Transformation*. Gainesville: University Press of Florida.
Neumann, K., 2014. Introductory Essay: Historians and the Yearning for Historical Justice. *Rethinking History*, 18(2), pp. 145–164.
Nozick, R., 1974. *Anarchy, State and Utopia*. Oxford: Oxford University Press.
OAU, 1981. African [Banjul] Charter on Human and Peoples' Rights, adopted June 27, 1981, OAU Doc. CAB/LEG/67/3. [Online] Available at: http://www1.umn.edu/humanrts/instree/z1afchar.htm [Accessed 01 17 2013].

Oberman, K., 2013. Can Brain Drain Justify Immigration Restrictions? *Ethics*, 123(3), pp. 427–455.

Ortiz, I. & Cummins, M., 2011. *Global Inequality: Beyond the Bottom Billion*. New York: UNICEF.

Osimiri, P., 2010. Redistribution or Rectification for Global Justice? *Peace Review: A Journal of Social Justice*, 22(4), pp. 357–364.

Oxfam, 2008. Patients before Profits: TRIPS and Trade Rules on Intellectual Property. [Online] Available at: http://www.oxfamamerica.org/whatwedo/issues_we_work_on/trade/news_publications/trips/art4190.html, [Accessed 04 07 2008].

Oxford Business Group, 2012. Gaining Traction: The Rubber Industry Is on the Move. [Online] Available at: http://www.oxfordbusinessgroup.com/news/gaining-traction-rubber-industry-move [Accessed 11 03 2014].

Palmer, A., 2000. *Colonial Genocide*. Adelaide: Crawford House Publishing.

Palmer, R. R., 1966. *Nya Tidens Världshistoria, 1 and 2*. Stockholm: Svenska bokförlaget, Norstedts.

Parfit, D., 1984. *Reasons and Persons*. Oxford: Oxford University Press.

Peterson, M., Hollis, A. & Pogge, T., 2010. A Critique in Need of a Critique. *Public Health Ethics*, 3(2), pp. 178–185.

Pettit, P., 2006. Rawls' Peoples, in R. Martin & D. Reidy, eds. *Rawls's Law of Peoples: A Realistic Utopia*. Oxford: Blackwell Publishing, pp. 38–55.

Pilkington, E., 2014. *The Guardian*. [Online] Available at: www.theguardian.com [Accessed 11 03 2014].

Pogge, T., 1989. *Realizing Rawls*. Ithaca and London: Cornell University Press.

Pogge, T., 2002. *World Poverty and Human Rights*. Cambridge: Polity Press.

Pogge, T., 2005. Real World Justice. *The Journal of Ethics*, 9, pp. 29–53.

Political Apologies and Reparations, 2014. [Online] Available at: http://political-apologies.wlu.ca/doclist.php?cp=2&rpp=5&sort=title [Accessed 22 04 2014].

Porter, A., 1994. *European Imperialism 1860–1914*. Basingstoke: Palgrave Macmillan.

Pulford, C., 2007. *Casualty of Empire: Britain's unpaid Debt to an African Kingdom*. Woodford Halse, UK: Ituri Publications.

Quakers in the UK, 2009. Seeds of Hunger: Intellectual Property Rights on Seeds and the Human Rights Response, Backgrounder No 2, Thread Series. [Online] Available at: http://www.3dthree.org/pdf_3D/3D_THREAD2seeds.pdf [Accessed 31 08 2010].

Quarles, B., 1969. *The Negro in the Making of America*. New York: Collier Books.

Radio Netherlands Worldwide, 2011. *Netherlands Apologises 1947 Indonesia Massacre*. [Online] Available at: http://www.rnw.nl/international-justice/article/netherlands-apologises-1947-indonesia-massacre [Accessed 12 12 2011].

Rawls, J., 1971. *A Theory of Justice*. Cambridge, MA: Harvard University Press.

Rawls, J., 1999. *The Law of Peoples*. Cambridge, MA: Harvard University Press.

Rediker, M., 2007. *The Slave Ship: A Human History*. New York: Viking.

Returning Africa's Stolen Artifacts (I), 2011. Chikaforafrica. [Online] Available at: http://chikaforafrica.com/2011/11/14/returning-africas-stolen-artifacts-i/ [Accessed 08 10 2013].

Rimmer, M., 2008. Race against Time: The Export of Essential Medicines to Rwanda. *Public Health Ethics*, 1(2), pp. 89–103.

Risse, M., 2012. *On Global Justice*. New York: Princeton University Press.

Rodney, W., 1972. *How Europe Underdeveloped Africa.* London: Bogle-L'Ouverture Publications.

Royal Museum for Central Africa, 2011. History. [Online] Available at: http://www.africamuseum.be/museum/about-us/museum/history/Congomuseum [Accessed 10 07 2011].

Said, E., 2003. *Orientalism.* 3rd edn. London: Penguin.

Sarkin-Hughes, J., 2011. *Germany's Genocide of the Herero: Kaiser Wilhelm II, His General, His Settlers, His Soldiers.* Cape Town: University of Cape Town Press.

Satz, D., 2007. Reparations, Interdisciplinary Inquiries, in J. Miller & R. Kumar, eds. Oxford: Oxford University Press, pp. 153–176.

Schefczyk, M., 2009. Untangling Historical Injustice. *International Justice Review,* 9, pp. 4–9.

Scholte, J. A., 2000. *Globalization: A Critical Account.* Basingstoke: Palgrave Macmillan.

Sen, A., 2000. *Development as Freedom.* 2nd edn. New York: Anchor Books.

Sepinwall, A., 2006. Responsibility for Historical Injustices: Reconceiving the Case for Reparations. *Journal of Law and Politics,* 22(3).

Sher, G., 1980. Ancient Wrongs and Modern Rights. *Philosophy and Public Affairs,* 10(1), pp. 3–17.

Sher, G., 2005. Transgenerational Compensation. *Philosophy and Public Affairs,* 33(2), pp. 181–200.

Singer, P., 1972. Famine, Affluence, and Morality. *Philosophy and Public Affairs,* pp. 229–243.

Singer, P., 2004. *One World: The Ethics of Globalization.* 2nd edn. New Haven: Yale.

Spinner-Halev, J., 2012. *Enduring Injustice.* Cambridge: Cambridge University Press.

Sridhar, D., 2008. Improving Access to Essential Medicines: How Health Concerns Can Be Prioritised in the Global Governance System. *Public Health Ethics,* 1(2), pp. 83–88.

Stanton, K., 2011. Canada's Truth and Reconciliation Commission: Settling the Past. *The International Indigenous Policy Journal,* 2(3).

Stein, B., 2010. *A History of India.* 2nd edn. Chichester: Wiley-Blackwell.

Steward, N., 1951. Divide and Rule: British Policy in Indian History. *Science and Society,* 15(1), pp. 49–57.

Stiglitz, J., 2002. *Globalization and Its Discontents.* London: Penguin.

Stiglitz, J., 2006. *Making Globalization Work.* London: Allen Lane.

Swinburne, R., 1989. *Responsibility and Atonement.* Oxford: Clarendon Press.

Tahana, Y., 2013. Treaty Settlements: Long and Winding Road to Resolving the Past. *The New Zealand Herald,* 4 June.

Tan, K.-C., 2004. *Justice without Borders.* Cambridge: Cambridge University Press.

Tan, K.-C., 2007. Colonialism, Reparations, and Global Justice, in J. Miller & R. Kumar, eds. *Reparations: Interdisciplinary Inquiries.* Oxford: Oxford University Press, pp. 280–306.

Tännsjö, T., 2008. *Global Democracy: The Case for a World Government.* Edinburgh: Edinburgh University Press.

The Low Countries, 2011. An Awkward Anniversary. [Online] Available at: http://www.dbnl.org/tekst/_low001199601_01/_low001199601_01_0011.php [Accessed 22 04 2014].

The Telegraph, 2011. Namibia to Collect Herero Skulls from Germany. [Online] Available at: http://www.telegraph.co.uk/news/worldnews/africaandindianocean/namibia/8788072/Namibia-to-collect-Herero-skulls-from-Germany.htm [Accessed 10 04 2014].

The World Bank, 2014. How We Classify Countries. [Online] Available at: http://data.worldbank.org/about/country-classifications [Accessed 21 01 2014].

The World Bank, u.d. Gini Index. [Online] Available at: http://data.worldbank.org/indicator/SI.POV.GINI [Accessed 28 10 2013].

t'Hoen, E., 2003. *TRIPS, Pharmaceutical Patents*. [Online] Available at: http://www.who.int/intellectualproperty/topics/ip/tHoen.pdf [Accessed 08 01 2014].

Thompson, G., 2003. *Governing Uganda: British Colonial Rule and Its Legacy*. Kampala: Fountain Publishers.

Thompson, J., 2002. *Taking Responsibility for the Past, Reparation and Historical Justice*. Cambridge: Polity Press.

Torpey, J., 2003. *Politics and the Past: On Repairing Historical Injustices*. Lanham: Rowman and Littlefield.

Tutu, D., 2000. *No Future without Forgiveness*. New York: Image Books.

UNDP, 1992. *Human Development Report: Global Dimensions of Human Development*. New York and Oxford: UNDP.

UNDP, 2000. *Human Development Report*. New York: UNDP.

UNDP, 2001. *Making New Technologies Work for Human Development: Human Development Report 2001*. New York: UNDP.

UNDP, 2005. *United Nations Development Report*. New York: UNDP.

UNDP, 2013. United Nations Development Report. [Online] Available at: http://hdr.undp.org/en/content/human-development-report-2013 [Accessed 23 01 2014].

UNEP, 2011. Environmental Assessment of Ogoniland Report. [Online] [Accessed 11 04 2014].

UNHCR, 2012. Global Trends. [Online] Available at: www.unhcr.org/4c11f0be9.html [Accessed 05 05 2013].

United Nations, 1948. Convention on the Prevention and Punishment of the Crime of Genocide, Resolution 260 (III) A of the United Nations General Assembly. [Online] Available at: http://www.hrweb.org/legal/genocide.html [Accessed 21 08 2013].

United Nations, 1960. Declaration on the Granting of Independence to Colonial Countries and Peoples. Adopted by General Assembly Resolution 1514 (XV) of 14 December 1960. [Online] Available at: http://www.un.org/en/decolonization/declaration.shtml [Accessed 04 04 2013].

United Nations, 2001. World Conference against Racism, Racial Discrimination, Xenophobia and Related Intolerance. [Online] Available at: http://www.un.org/WCAR/coverage.htm [Accessed 01 02 2013].

United Nations, 2005. In Larger Freedom: Towards Development, Security and Human Rights for All. [Online] Available at: http://www.un.org/largerfreedom/contents.htm [Accessed 06 06 2012].

United Nations, 2012. The Global Partnership for Development: Making Rhetoric a Reality. [Online] Available at: http://www.who.int/medicines/mdg/mdg8report2012_en.pdf?ua=1 [Accessed 30 04 2014].

United Nations, 2009. Durban Review Conference, Geneva April 20–24, 2009. [Online] Available at: http://www.un.org/durbanreview2009/ [Accessed 09 05 2009].

United Nations Population Division, 2008. United Nations Population Division, International Migration Stock. [Online] Available at: http://esa.un.org/migration/ [Accessed 19 08 2013].

Wachtell, N., 1984. The Indian and the Spanish Conquest, in L. Bethell, ed. *The Cambridge History of Latin America*. Cambridge: Cambridge University Press.

Wade, R. H., 2001. The Rising Inequality of World Income Distribution. *Finance and Development, A Quarterly of the International Monetary Fund*, December.

Waites, B., 1999. *Europe and the Third World: From Colonisation to Decolonisation c. 1500–1998*. New York: St Martins Press.

Waldron, J., 1992. Superseding Historic Injustice. *Ethics*, 103.

Waldron, J., 2007. Why Is Indigeneity Important? in J. Miller & R. Kumar, eds. *Reparations: Interdisciplinary Inquiries*. Oxford: Oxford University Press, pp. 23–42.

Walker, M. U., 2006a. Restorative Justice and Reparations. *Journal of Social Philosophy*, 37, pp. 377–395.

Walker, M. U., 2006b. *Moral Repair: Reconstructing Moral Relations after Wrongdoing*. Cambridge: Cambridge University Press.

Wallerstein, I., 1970. The Colonial Era in Africa, in P. A. G. L. H. Duignan, ed. *Colonialism in Africa 1870–1960, Vol 2*. Cambridge: Cambridge University Press, pp. 399–421.

Wallerstein, I., 1989. *The Modern World-System 3, Vol. 3: The Second Era of Great Expansion of the Capitalist World-Economy 1730–1840s* (Studies in Social Discontinuity) Academic Press.

Valy, B., 2007. Mozambique Takes Ownership of Cahora Bassa Dam, Southern African News Features. [Online] Available at: http://www.sardc.net/editorial/newsfeature/07501107.htm [Accessed 11 10 2013].

Walzer, M., 1983. *Spheres of Justice: A Defense of Pluralism and Equality*. New York: Basic Books.

Wamala, E., 2008. Status to Contract Society: Africa's Integrity Crisis. *Journal of Global Ethics*, 4(3), pp. 195–205.

van den Beld, T., 2002. Can Collective Responsibility for Perpetrated Evil Persist Over Generations? *Ethical Theory and Moral practice*, 5.

Vasileva, K., 2011, Population and Social Conditions. *Eurostat*. Nr 34. [Online] Available at: http://epp.eurostat.ec.europa.eu/cache/ITY_OFFPUB/KS-SF-11-034/EN/KS-SF-11-034-EN.PDF [Accessed 17 12 2013].

Vernon, R., 2012. *Historical Redress, Must We Pay for the Past?* London and New York: Continuum.

Villa-Vicencio, C., 2009. *Walk with Us and Listen*. Georgetown: Georgetown University Press.

Voget-Kleschin, L. A. Ott K., 2013. Introduction to the Special Issue of the Journal of Agricultural and Environmental Ethics on Ethical Aspects of Large-Scale Land Acquisition in Developing Countries. *Journal of Agricultural and Environmental Ethics*, 26(6), pp. 1059–1064.

Wenar, L., 2006. Reparations for the Future. *Journal of Social Philosophy*, 37, pp. 396–405.

Wertheimer, A. & Zwolinski, M., 2013. Exploitation, in E. Zalta, ed. *The Stanford Encyclopedia of Philosophy*. Available at: http://plato.stanford.edu/entries/exploitation/ [Accessed 20 01 2014].

Who Controls Africa's Minerals? 1997. [Online] Available at: http://american_almanac.tripod.com/minerals.htm [Accessed 06 06 2013].

WHO, 1999. Amsterdam Statement on Access to Medicines. [Online] Available at: http://apps.who.int/medicinedocs/en/d/Jh1461e/1.4.html#Jh1461e.1.4[Accessed 15 08 2010].

WHO, 2004. *Medicines Strategy: Countries at the Core 2004–2007,* Geneva: WHO.

WHO, 2014. The Doha Declaration on the Trips Agreement and Public Health. [Online] Available at: http://www.who.int/medicines/areas/policy/doha_declaration/en/ [Accessed 03 01 2014].

Wikipedia, 2012. List of Wars by Death Toll. [Online] Available at: http://en.wikipedia.org/wiki/List_of_wars_by_death_toll [Accessed 17 January 2013].

Williams, C., 2003. Quixotic Haiti Seeks French Restitution. *Los Angeles Times,* June 14.

Winter, S., 2006. Uncertain Justice: History and Reparations. *Journal of Social Philosophy,* 37, pp. 377–395.

World Bank, 2013. Poverty. [Online] Available at: www.worldbank.org/en/topic/poverty [Accessed 11 04 2014].

World Bank, 2014. World Bank Group. [Online] Available at: http://wdi.worldbank.org/table/1.1 [Accessed 11 04 2014].

WTO, 1994. Agreement on Trade-Related Aspects of Intellectual Property Rights. [Online] Available at: http://www.wto.org/english/tratop_e/trips_e/t_agm0_e.htm [Accessed 10 03 2012].

WTO, 2001. Doha Declaration, Declaration on the TRIPS Agreement and Public Health. [Online] Available at: http://www.wto.org/english/thewto_e/minist_e/min01_e/mindecl_trips_e.htm [Accessed 30 09 2010].

WTO, 2008. What Are Intellectual Property Rights? [Online] Available at: http://www.wto.org/english/tratop_e/trips_e/intell_e.htm, [Accessed 12 02 2008].

WTO, 2014. World Trade Organization. [Online] Available at: http://www.wto.org/ [Accessed 11 04 2014].

Yale University, 2010. Genocide Studies Program. [Online] Available at: http://www.yale.edu/gsp/colonial/belgian_congo/

Young, A., 2008. Call for Apology to All Maori for "Past Atrocities." [Online] Available at: http://www.nzherald.co.nz/nz/news/article.cfm?c_id=1&objectid=10492348 [Accessed 09 04 2013].

Ypi, L., 2013. What's Wrong with Colonialism. *Philosophy and Public Affairs,* 41(2), pp. 158–191.

Ypi, L., Robert, G. & Christian, B., 2009. Associative Duties, Global Justice, and the Colonies. *Philosophy and Public Affairs,* 37(2), pp. 104–135.

Index

CPSIA information can be obtained at www.ICGtesting.com
Printed in the USA
LVOW04*0351180915

454717LV00008B/33/P

9 781137 466112